D0350469

INSPECTOR OLDFIELD

AND THE

BLACK HAND

SOCIETY

AMERICA'S ORIGINAL GANGSTERS
AND THE U.S. POSTAL DETECTIVE
WHO BROUGHT THEM TO JUSTICE

WILLIAM OLDFIELD AND VICTORIA BRUCE

TOUCHSTONE

New York   London   Toronto   Sydney   New Delhi

Touchstone
An Imprint of Simon & Schuster, Inc.
1230 Avenue of the Americas
New York, NY 10020

First Touchstone hardcover edition August 2018

TOUCHSTONE and colophon are registered trademarks of Simon & Schuster, Inc.

For information about special discounts for bulk purchases, please contact Simon & Schuster Special Sales at 1-866-506-1949 or business@simonandschuster.com.

The Simon & Schuster Speakers Bureau can bring authors to your live event. For more information, or to book an event, contact the Simon & Schuster Speakers Bureau at 866-248-3049 or visit our website at www.simonspeakers.com.

Interior design by Kyle Kabel

Manufactured in the United States of America

10 9 8 7 6 5 4 3 2 1

Library of Congress Cataloging-in-Publication Data is available.

ISBN 978-1-5011-7120-8
ISBN 978-1-5011-7122-2 (ebook)

To my sister, Allison; my father, Edward Fulton; and mother, Terry; great-grandfather John Frank and great-grandmother Margaret Galena Oldfield; everyone within the Oldfield and Iacone families who never gave up on our family secret, and especially to those within the United States Postal Inspection Service who risk their lives every day for all of us.

—William H. Oldfield

CONTENTS

PROLOGUE

On the night of April 18, 1908, in the railroad town of Bellefontaine, Ohio, eighteen-year-old Charles Demar walked into the fruit shop he owned with his uncle, Salvatore Cira, and put a bullet into his uncle's head. Salvatore's body was discovered later that night by his wife among crates of bananas and apples spattered with his blood. When the police arrived, Mrs. Cira appeared not to understand them, or at least she pretended she didn't speak English. This wasn't surprising, as the police commonly ran into this problem with Italian immigrants who wanted nothing to do with law enforcement on any level. The most preyed-upon victims were completely unwilling to give police any leads, even if they'd personally seen a suspect commit a crime against a loved one.

It's not that the Bellefontaine police lacked investigative skills. No law enforcement institution in the nation had been able to penetrate the crime-ridden neighborhoods across America that absorbed six million Italian immigrants in the last two decades of the 1800s. Increasingly in the papers, the gruesome crimes were credited to "Black Hand" criminals because of several recovered threat letters eerily penned by "La Mano Nera." Only after massive criminal activity in New York City's Lower East Side began to bleed into surrounding neighborhoods did the NYPD form a group of five Italian-American police detectives. The "Italian Squad," under renowned detective

Joe Petrosino, was having some luck by 1908 and making arrests for individual crimes, especially bombing incidents.

The Bellefontaine cops searched the premises of Demar's Fruit Importers and collected as much evidence as they could. There was no sign of forced entry, and they found cash in a drawer untouched. What they did find on Cira's body tipped them off to the idea that the murder was more sinister than a random killing. In the dead man's pants pocket, there were two letters written in Italian. Knowing they had no chance of getting anywhere by interviewing friends or relatives of Cira, the cops were hopeful that the letters would lead to a break in the case. They also knew that their work was done, because the letters put the murder squarely under the jurisdiction of the United States Post Office Department and its prominent inspectors.

The Bellefontaine Police brought the letters in a secure pouch to the U.S. Post Office in Columbus. The enormous four-story federal building on Third and State Streets was the closest post office to Bellefontaine where a Post Office inspector was domiciled. There they found Inspector no. 156, Frank Oldfield, a diminutive man in a well-fitting suit, chomping away on a cigar. Oldfield pushed some papers and files aside and opened the letters. He made a quick visual scan of the documents with his magnifying glass. A satisfied smile appeared on his face.

Since arriving in Columbus in 1901, the forty-one-year-old Oldfield had become one of the most aggressive and successful Post Office inspectors in the service. He'd run down safecrackers, exposed a corruption ring between a U.S. congressman and the New York City assistant district attorney, and busted crooks on the railroads for robbing the mail. But there was nothing Oldfield wanted more than to "run to earth" what he believed was an international organized crime ring spanning America all the way to

PROLOGUE

Palermo, Sicily: truly bad guys whose members called themselves The Black Hand Society.

Few people knew that U.S. Post Office inspectors were the country's most powerful federal law enforcers at the time. Long before the FBI came into being, U.S. Post Office inspectors had jurisdiction all over the world. The presidentially appointed position gave a Post Office inspector authority to take over an investigation from any law enforcement agency in the country if the United States mails were used in any fashion. He could bust a crime ring anywhere on earth if one of the suspects so much as licked a U.S. postage stamp and sent a letter or package through the mail. Inspectors moved about on the railways where every train had a postal car, hopping on anywhere at a moment's notice and flashing a silver badge in lieu of fare. They went with a vengeance after train robbers who grabbed pouches of cash and valuables in transit across the country, even on ships across the ocean. Inspectors had the legal authority to commandeer any vehicle they needed: a horse and buggy, a train—even a steamer ship—if it meant catching a crook. They dressed in plain clothes, carried concealed weapons, and worked mostly under the radar, using secret coded telegrams to update headquarters along the way. But with all their incredible crime busts, not one Post Office inspector had yet had a single break into the crimes of the Black Hand Society.

CHAPTER I

THE PRINTER

The Printer of this Paper, with great Pleasure, acquaints the Public, that his Proposal for Establishing an American Post Office, on constitutional Principle, hath been warmly and generously patronized by the Friends of Freedom in all the great Commercial Towns in the Eastern Colonies, where ample Funds are already secured, Postmasters and Riders engaged, and, indeed, every necessary Arrangement made for the Reception of the Southern mails, which, it is expected, will soon be extended thither.

As therefore the final success of the Undertaking now depends on the Public Spirit of the Inhabitants of Maryland and Virginia, it is not doubted, from the recent Evidence they have given of their Noble Zeal in the Cause of liberty and their Country, but they will cheerfully join the rescuing the Channel of public and private Intelligence from the horrid Fangs of Ministerial Dependents; a Measure indispensably necessary in the present alarming Crisis of American Main.[1]

—William Goddard,
publisher of the *Pennsylvania Chronicle*, 1775

At the turn of the twentieth century, during Frank Oldfield's tenure as a Post Office inspector, there was no more vital institution in America than the United States Post Office Department. Post offices were the country's brain centers; the postal routes its circulatory system. Radio was still in its infancy. Police stations had telephones, but few citizens had telephones in their homes. Vital correspondence, news of the day, and all manner of goods were delivered through a complicated but fluid network by thousands of postal workers. The job of a U.S. Post Office inspector was to make sure people and businesses received their mail without obstruction. Inspectors were also empowered to stop any crime that made use of the postal service. It was not just a law enforcement job, but an appointment to an elite force charged with the smooth and safe operation of the country.

The origins and importance of the United States Post Office date back to the American Revolution. The first mail system independent from England was called the Constitutional Post. It was specifically developed and designed to carry out treason against oppressive rulers across the Atlantic and suture together fiercely independent colonies into one cohesive nation. The postal network was something so vast and complicated that it would normally have taken years of toiling over by councils of subversive strategists to implement. But in the decade leading up to the Revolution, only one man was the driving force behind a post free from British control. That man was William Goddard, a printer, a newspaperman, and a revolutionary desperate to unhinge the new world from the old.

The seed for Goddard's ingenious plan took hold during the summer of 1755 when he was a fifteen-year-old teenager living with his family in New London, Connecticut.[2] Goddard's mother, an educated woman named Sarah Updike, got him a job at the print shop in nearby New Haven run by the famous printer James Parker, once an apprentice and now a close colleague of Ben Franklin. Sarah was hoping her son would learn a trade, because his father, Giles, was not going to be around for long. In his fifties, Giles, a physician, was already bedridden with gout, among other ailments of an excessive lifestyle common to wealthy New Englanders. Obese and in chronic pain, he was confined to bed as uric acid built up in his swelling feet.

The young Goddard arrived in New Haven, a somewhat odd, overeducated teenager for the seaport town. Parker, his new boss, was also New Haven's postmaster. Local printers commonly were chosen by the British government to be the postmasters of cities and towns. It made sense. The printers sold all kinds of official legal forms and papers. What apparently didn't concern the Crown was something that it would live to regret in spades: the town printers were often the newspapermen as well. And newspapermen were highly educated and often became very interested in freeing the colonies from oppressive taxation and British rule. Across the colonies, rumblings of revolution began to brew with the setting of type in darkened print shops.

The British had completely missed this, because ever since the Queen Anne Act of 1710, they had been desperately trying to get a functioning post in the colonies that would earn them some revenue. By 1737, when Benjamin Franklin took over the Philadelphia Post Office, the entire system was a mess. The British service operated with heavy losses due to theft and mismanagement. As he did with most challenges, Franklin looked pragmatically at how to fix it. He hired better post riders. He added mile markers, or mile stones, for postage calculating (rather than just having riders mark trees with an axe).[3] He was so successful that sixteen years later, on August 10, 1753, the British gave Franklin the job of joint postmaster general of the colonies along with William Hunter, the postmaster of Williamsburg, Virginia. Franklin was in charge of the northern post, and Hunter, everything south of Annapolis, Maryland.

In his new position, Franklin was now responsible for making certain that revenue didn't slip into the pockets of wayward employees or thieves. Franklin set up a way to audit accounts and improve account-ing methods. He established new post offices all the way to Quebec, Canada. He also went around investigating the very service he was appointed to preside over by "regulating the several post offices and bringing the postmasters to account."[4] Under Franklin the British Post in the American colonies thrived and turned a profit for the Crown the very first year he was in charge. He continued to hold the position, even as he left for England in 1757 to represent the Pennsylvania colonists against the Penn family's unfair royal exemption from paying taxes to the colony or following laws enacted by the colonial legislature.[5]

Franklin was two years into his appointment as postmaster general when William Goddard arrived in the New Haven print shop. The work Goddard was charged with at Parker's press was definitely not intellectual, and probably boring for the kid with big aspirations. But the press was clean, efficient, and state-of-the-art, thanks to the new equipment Ben Franklin leased to James Parker in a sort of franchise arrangement that Franklin had with several colonial printers. Parker was a trusted businessman in New Haven and especially appreciated by the townspeople for producing the *Connecticut Gazette*.

The *Gazette* was Connecticut's first newspaper, a daily flyer that mostly printed ads, letters to the editor, and short news items on the back page. Parker also had a contract for all the printing for Yale University, mostly mysterious Latin texts that were probably less exciting to Goddard than what the newspaper held. The *Gazette* went out to everyone in town who paid a small subscription fee, and it entertained citizens for hours every day. Even those who were likely illiterate enjoyed listening to others read the long columns from top to bottom. Goddard instantly saw the power of the *Gazette*. It was communicating to the masses. It also gave James Parker power and prestige.

The front of Parker's shop was configured to be the town post office. Mail clerks worked the front desk, and postal carriers took the mail to destinations where receivers had the responsibility to pay for the postage. Goddard cleaned up the print shop and the post office, inked the printing forms with ink balls, and sometimes delivered the *Gazette*. Occasionally, Parker sent Goddard out on postal errands. "At just 15," Goddard wrote, "I was sent with a Rider from New-Haven to Middletown & Hartford, thence to N. London, and round by Seaboard to N. H. to estimate the Expense [to calculate postage for the mail]. Later on, in 1758, I went to N. York & Woodbridge to assist in the [post] offices there."[6] The routes traveled and the post offices visited on those trips were master classes to Goddard. He made a mental note to remember it all for future endeavors.

William's mother was an excellent keeper of the family's significant finances. When her husband, Giles Goddard, died, and William finished his apprenticeship in the New Haven shop, Sarah Goddard financed her son's own printing business in Providence, Rhode Island. It was 1762. The twenty-three-year-old Goddard rented a storefront on Benefit Street. He put up signs in the two windows facing the street advertising "All sorts of Blanks used in this Colony, neatly printed," and such commercial documents as "Policies of Insurance, Portage Bills, Bills of Lading and Sale, Letters of Attorney, Administration Bonds, Common Bonds, Deeds, Writs, and Executions."[7]

It was still exceedingly boring work for Goddard, who was not a lover of details or repetition. And while he had absorbed a lot about printing and the newspaper business, he didn't have Franklin's or Parker's business sense or charm with customers. He was, however, much appreciated by the locals as the first print shop in Providence. At the annual meeting of the Providence Library Company in September 1763, the board voted "that Mr. William Goddard Printer in

Consideration of his eminent usefulness to this Part of the Colony by introducing and carrying on amongst us the ingenious and noble Business of Printing shall have free Liberty to use the Books belonging to the Library."[8]

Out of a desire to liven his work and without putting much thought into the enormity of the idea, Goddard decided to follow the lead of many printers before him (most notably Ben Franklin, who published the *Pennsylvania Gazette* from 1729 to 1748) and publish a newspaper. On October 20, 1762, the first *Providence Gazette and County Journal* rolled off the presses in Goddard's small print shop.[9] It was an instant hit. The people of Providence enjoyed hearing about events in the other twelve colonies and particularly liked getting a taste of culture and political goings-on in Europe. They especially loved the advertisements.

It was as if the classifieds gave them a glimpse into their neighbors' secrets. *Arthur Fenner is selling his 53-ton sloop; Nicholas Brown & Co. wants freight and passengers for the Four Brothers, to set sail in six days' time for Philadelphia. John Cole is selling cordage and ship riggings; Mr. Lodowick Updike in Narragansett looks to recover a black gelding that ran off; Bennet & Nightingale want their debtors "to make speedy Payment" of their bills; John Jenks and Joseph Olney are concerned with a land development scheme in Nova Scotia.*

Since the ads were the main revenue generator, Goddard published eighteen pages of advertisements and saved just two pages at the back for news and commentary. There were no editorials. Instead, for political rants, there were letters to the editor, "expression of the views of citizens on questions which concerned the state," Goddard wrote.[10] In many cases, letters to the editor were signed with pseudonyms, and often these pseudonyms were those of the paper's publisher. Goddard, like many colonial businessmen, was becoming more and more politically inclined. Being a newspaper publisher allowed him to publicly rant (under an alias) against his favorite topic: the unbending tyranny of the British and King George III's oppressive taxation. While it was treasonous to stand up to the Crown, the law at the time didn't try too hard to figure out who was behind the scathing editorials, so Goddard and other early revolutionaries were mostly free to rail against British rule.

Being a printer and newspaper publisher was stable, but not very lucrative work, and Goddard had the added concern of supporting his mother and sister. Things began to look up around 1765, when the twenty-six-year-old Goddard decided to publish an almanac, something that many colonial printers were doing at the time, following Ben Franklin's famous *Poor Richard's Almanack*, which premiered in 1732 and had a twenty-five-year run. The annual publications detailing facts and statistical information about various localities had become incredibly important to the colonists. The almanac out of Goddard's shop, *New England Almanack for 1765*, was the work of thirty-three-year-old mathematician and astronomer Benjamin West.[11]

New England Almanack was a best seller in the small town, as almost everyone saw something in it that they needed. Narragansett Bay fishermen found the times the tide would roll in and out. Sunset and sunrise were accurately listed to the latitude and were important to pretty much everyone who worked a job of any kind. To the farmers in the fields, there was the precise day spring would come, and they would no longer be subject to freezing temperatures that would kill their seedlings. For homemakers and businessmen, there were practical issues such as the post rider schedule and when circuit court judges would come to preside over local courts.

Things got even better for Goddard when he received the postmastership appointment for Providence. It was Goddard's first position in the British postal system for the colonies. His new appointment linked him economically and logistically to New York City, Boston, and throughout the Northeast. It connected Goddard to colonial printers and newspapermen in cities along the Post Road, the artery traveled by postal riders and stagecoaches to deliver correspondence. Goddard now had undeniable influence in the community and in the larger world. This certainly appealed to Goddard's not-so-hidden elitist tendencies.

By 1765, Britain had become more dedicated than ever to shaking down the colonies for revenue. The British Parliament passed a law called the Stamp Act that forced American printers to use special, expensive paper stamped with a royal imprint for newspapers and all other public forms and documents.[12] Opposition to paying for the stamped paper erupted in the colonies with rallying cries and vehement opinion pieces in publications across the Northeast. Mail riders, who were all employees of the Crown, carried the newspapers that held the treasonous words.

Goddard, especially, went to work with a vengeance against the Stamp Act. In 1765 he wrote a *Gazette* column about what he felt was a killer of small businesses. The Stamp Act "renders it utterly impossible for us to pay for the large Quantities of Goods that are annually imported from Great-Britain, without reducing ourselves to the State of Slaves and Beggars."[13] The backlash from England was immediate. The British Post overcharged Goddard for postage, failed to deliver his *Providence Gazette*, and threatened to imprison him if he didn't use the stamped paper.

Goddard wouldn't be bullied. His words grew ever more venomous and erupted from him in long columns of smoky black type. While Goddard lacked business skills, he excelled at writing propaganda and rallying the troops. He was done being a subject of a corrupt and greedy king. He joined the "Sons of Liberty," a clandestine group subversively working on plans for independence from England by communicating through coded messages from Boston to New York. Along with Goddard, Paul Revere, and other newspapermen, printers and businessmen joined the secret society.[14]

For the British-appointed stamp agents, things got dicey. Those riding the route between Manhattan and Boston received death threats and resigned. New York's stamp master, James McEvers, quit after some of Goddard's acerbic letters were reprinted in Manhattan's *New York Gazette*. Britain seemed unable to control the printers and newspapermen who, like Goddard, were instigating the rebellion and meeting in secret to figure out how best to fuel it.

In October 1765, a *New York Gazette* reporter got wind that England was shipping its hated stamped paper to New York City under a private shipping contractor. In lower Manhattan on November 1, an angry mob burned an effigy of Cadwallader Colden, New York's royal governor.[15] Terrified, Colden refused to unpack the stamped paper. The British threw him out of office and commenced an all-out assault to shut down the dissident newspapers and stop correspondence among the rebels.

Ben Franklin, still in London, was fired in 1774 from his post as deputy postmaster general of the colonies when the Crown got wind of his growing sympathy for the rebels. Franklin rescinded his loyalty to the British and became staunchly on the side of the Revolution. Now he feared that the rebels' lines of communication would be broken. In a letter to Boston leaders of the Sons of Liberty, he expressed his concern that their "secrets are in the hand of Government" and "our News Papers in a time of public danger may be stopped."[16]

William Goddard was more furious than any of them. He believed that more than any other American printer, he was badly mistreated by the ministerial Post Office. Other Sons of Liberty were ignoring the thing he thought most important—free lines of communication for the rebels. So the fiercely independent Goddard began a one-man crusade to free the colonial mail from Britain's grip.

Goddard knew the Post Road well; he had ridden it many times as a teenager for James Parker, and later as the Providence postmaster. That road was owned by the king and controlled by British postal riders. But Goddard had a brilliant idea. He would start a "Constitutional" mail system hiring only post riders who had no political ties or loyalty to the British. First, he needed a more strategic location and a big-city newspaper from which to print his treasonous propaganda against the British. In what would become a pattern, Goddard left his Providence shop in the very capable hands of his sister, Mary Katherine.

On January 26, 1767, Philadelphia heavy hitters Joseph Galloway and Thomas Wharton joined Goddard to launch the *Pennsylvania Chronicle and Universal Advertiser Journal.* Goddard announced his aim was to make the *Pennsylvania Chronicle* "useful, instructive and entertaining." But that's not all he wanted. Goddard was a rebel, and he planned to use the *Chronicle,* editorially, as a political mouthpiece. Still, he was a staunch believer in a free press. He opened up the "letters to the editor" section to all parties and schools of thought. He wanted the paper itself to remain neutral. The unease between Joseph Galloway and his allies, who were still supporting the Crown, and Goddard and his allies, who wrote caustic columns against parliamentary taxation, soon reached a breaking point. Goddard was, in his own words, "in the disagreeable situation of standing, as it were, a victim between two fires."[17] Soon each side was hurling allegations against the other in the pages of Goddard's paper, and both factions were furious that Goddard wouldn't ban one side or the other. It was not a well-liked idea, having a paper's publisher remain neutral. On April 4, three months into publication, an agitated and indignant

Goddard defended his paper's position in a Philadelphia coffeehouse. When things got so heated by those demanding he take a stand for one side, he was forcibly thrown out. A rival publisher literally dragged him out by his hair.[18]

There were already six other newspapers in Pennsylvania, and the *Chronicle* was having a hard time getting a foothold. Goddard did not get along well with either of his partners, especially Galloway. Nevertheless, Galloway somehow managed to convince Goddard to sell the *Providence Gazette* and invest more of his own money in the *Pennsylvania Chronicle*. Goddard sent for his mother and sister to help run the day-to-day business as he went about the miserable job of trying to collect overdue subscription fees. With his mother's and Mary Katherine's help, business quickly began to pick up, and so did the reputation of the newspaper. In a short time, Goddard employed a team of twenty-two subscription agents working in Pennsylvania, Delaware, New Jersey, Maryland, and Virginia.[19] Over the next year, Goddard, even with the continued infighting among his partners, earned a stellar reputation for having the best newspaper in the Middle Colonies.[20]

The success of the paper didn't improve Goddard's temperament, though. At heart he was prickly, agitated, and untrusting. His attitude often had a way of undoing his considerable successes and likely contributed to his one great failing to come. Only his sister, Mary Katherine, and his mother had his confidence. His suspicions bled over into his personal life as well. Goddard was thirty years old and still unmarried when in 1770, his mother, Sarah Updike Goddard, died. Once again, his finances were a mess. He found it hard to have partners or friends. He thrived on squabbles and went after his adversaries with a vengeance. He attacked Galloway with brutal character assassinations published in various colonial newspapers. He called his partner "hot tempered and of choleric disposition." He tried to keep abreast of his business affairs, but his complete obsession for planning a revolution against England took most of his time.

In September 1771, after lengthy lawsuits against him by Galloway and his second partner, Thomas Wharton, Goddard landed in debtor's prison in the Philadelphia jail. If Galloway was hoping that would put an end to Goddard's revolutionary rhetoric and constant public attacks on his reputation, he was wrong. Signing himself "A Friend to Liberty," on September 23, 1771, Goddard had someone in the shop, likely his sister, publish a column attacking Galloway. "Even the worst of men have some pangs of conscience over their misdeeds. What then must be the feelings of one who has tried to destroy the liberty of his country . . . then a GALLOWAY, asserting the cause of slavery, reviling American honor, treacherously undermining the capital pillars of the Constitution of his NATIVE COUNTRY, and slandering one of her ablest Advocates?"

Goddard received a lot of support from those who believed he was unfairly targeted by the Pennsylvania Assembly, where Galloway held a high position. Emboldened by this public encouragement, Goddard busied himself in the Philadelphia jail, writing copy for the weekly *Chronicle* and railing against his enemies on two continents. With Mary Katherine in charge of the shop (even while creditors were trying to liquidate Goddard's assets), he did not need to worry about the *Chronicle* meeting its printing schedule. Finally, with the help of friends, Goddard partially paid off his debts to Galloway and Wharton. On October 14, 1771, Goddard announced his own release from jail in the *Chronicle*:

> *The Printer of this Paper, impressed by the most lively Sentiments of Gratitude, takes a sincere Pleasure, on this Occasion, of returning*

his warmest Acknowledgments to a Number of respectable Citizens, who, on the first Notice of the relentless Severity of Messrs. Galloway and Wharton, his former Partners in the Printing Business, generously united and made him a Loan of Money sufficient to extricate him from the Iron Hand of Oppression. He now enjoys the Sweets of Liberty, and is enabled, by the Generosity of some Friends, to continue in Business, in which his utmost Endeavors shall ever be exerted to give all possible Satisfaction to the Public, and show himself not altogether unworthy of the Favours he has received.

He signed the column "A Friend to Liberty not confined in the Common Jail, under Executions for Debts."

Being locked up in the Philadelphia jail and battling business partners did nothing to quash Goddard's appetite for rebellion against the Crown. He penned prolific anti-British propaganda under a variety of pseudonyms in the *Pennsylvania Chronicle*. He had a fair amount of success but was desperate to expand his influence further into the colonies. To do so, Goddard started the *Maryland Journal & Baltimore Advertiser* in the summer of 1773.[21] The *Journal* was the only newspaper in Maryland at the time, and to make sure that it ran like clockwork, Goddard put his highly competent sister, Mary Katherine, at the helm. "The MARYLAND JOURNAL will, positively be published, regularly, every Thursday Morning," the first edition proclaimed on Friday, August 20. "Then our Customers will have the earliest Intelligence from the Northward, before they could possibly obtain it by any other Mode of Conveyance."

After three months and twelve *Journal* editions, subscribers had signed on from all over the mid-Atlantic colonies and south to Virginia. Still, Goddard was exceedingly anxious and irritable. The British postal service was sabotaging both his new paper and his well-established *Pennsylvania Chronicle.* His papers were late to their destinations and sometimes didn't arrive at all. Subscribers who didn't get their copies didn't pay subscription fees, and the British Post was charging Goddard double the rate for normal postage. Most anything that came to his shop through the mail had clearly been opened and rifled through. Another problem was that news and correspondence from north and south didn't make it to his print shops on time or at all, so other papers scooped him. For Goddard, making sure his newspaper was delivered was vital to the independence of the colonies, so the determined printer came up with an idea.

In fall 1773, Goddard added a line item to his newspaper's budget: "a full-time post rider, solely dedicated to carrying the post to and from his Baltimore and Philadelphia shops." On November 27, Mary Katherine set the type for a help-wanted ad to run in both papers. "The PENNSYLVANIA CHRONICLE . . . will, by the Establishment of a new Northern Post, be able to visit its old Friends in this Province, from whom it hath, for some Time, been cut off by an arbitrary Decree of a malicious Postrider, late a Hostler in the Service of one of the Postmasters General."

Goddard suspected that it was Deputy Postmaster General Benjamin Franklin who was causing him such consternation by ordering the British Post to overcharge him and slow the delivery of Goddard's newspapers. Franklin was a close friend of Goddard's former business partner Joseph Galloway. At the start, Franklin loaned the *Pennsylvania Chronicle* money and a printing press, making him a sort of silent partner. Within its pages, Franklin penned many letters for the *Chronicle* railing against the unfair taxes on the colonies.[22] Franklin, though, soured on Goddard after Goddard repeatedly attacked Galloway in the letters to the editors of the *Chronicle.*[23] Always the pragmatist, Franklin did not like Goddard's modus operandi in business or politics. The feeling was mutual. Although Franklin had gained a stellar reputation among most members of the Sons of Liberty, Goddard felt that anyone who wasn't 100 percent on the side of the patriots from the beginning was a traitor to the cause of liberty and justice.

With Goddard's own post riders, the *Maryland Journal* took off. He became obsessed with the newfound power of having his own logistics force. Goddard knew that Committees of Correspondence, which began in the mid-1700s, worked exceedingly well to bypass the British during the tumult brought about by the Stamp Act. Riders would meet along the Post Road and pass along secret messages. Why not expand that clandestine system to all colonial correspondence?

To free himself from the daily grind of printing and newspaper publishing to pursue his goal, Goddard shut down the *Pennsylvania Chronicle* and left Mary Katherine in charge of the *Maryland Journal*. Goddard knew that his sister, although a talented and exceptional businesswoman, could not run both papers and the affairs of two print shops by herself. Goddard set the type on the last issue of the *Pennsylvania Chronicle* on February 8, 1774, with a teaser:

> . . . *a Matter I have engaged in, of a very interesting Nature to the common Liberties of all America, as well as to myself, as the Printer of a Public Paper, is brought nearer to a Conclusion.*

Mary Katherine announced that she would conduct the newspaper and printing business during her brother's coming absence. Goddard set up an office for his post in the London Coffee House, a meeting space built by Philadelphia merchants on the corner of Front and Market Streets.[24] Then, with great optimism and excitement, he set off along the Post Road. He had a well-formulated plan, and he practiced his sales pitch along the way. His strategy already worked on a small scale, not only delivering his newspapers with his own post riders, but subsidizing his costs by contracting out his employees to others blockaded and overcharged by the Crown. His ultimate plan would go far beyond newspaper deliveries. He was setting out to create what he called the Constitutional Post, a completely new postal system free from British control.[25]

What Goddard lacked in charm and business skills, he made up for in logistical genius and tireless lobbying efforts. He first stopped in Manhattan, where he met with the New York Sons of Liberty, among them Alexander McDougal, a merchant seaman who knew Goddard's history of strong resistance to the Crown. McDougal and the other New York Sons of Liberty were supportive of the idea, but not yet ready to commit. The act in itself was treasonous, punishable by hanging. And while this was the group to sign on if anyone would, they also had their own ideas on how best to free themselves from the British.

Goddard traveled along to Providence, the hometown of his first newspaper, where he met John Brown, a revolutionary who led the burning of a British Customs boat in 1772. Brown's hatred for the Crown matched Goddard's, and he knew and trusted Goddard from the days of the *Providence Gazette*. He was quick to give Goddard's plan his stamp of approval.

Goddard drummed up support in New Haven, New London, and Newport, where businessmen, printers especially, were anxious to have a safe means of distribution for their correspondence, newspapers, and pamphlets, especially those subversive and treasonous messages and propaganda. Goddard was invigorated, and he was not alone. Printers all around the colonies were beginning to feel very powerful. Words on paper were a formidable tonic. Rows of black type got people's attention, gave people courage against oppression, and deepened their belief that they were being unfairly treated by King George. And because all of the seventy-two colonial printers felt attacked by the Stamp Act, they began to ban together in their darkened print shops, not only printing but plotting a revolution. In 1941, historian Lawrence Wroth wrote eloquently of the "harassed individual with ink-stained fingers, half craftsman, half man of letters, who in dim and cluttered shops in all the considerable towns of the continent was fighting the battles of the Nation long before most of his fellow citizens realized that a war was in progress or that a Nation was being born."[26]

On Monday, March 14, 1774, an exhausted William Goddard arrived on horseback in Boston. He met with Samuel Adams, Paul Revere, and Benjamin Edes, the printer and publisher of the *Boston Gazette*, who, like Goddard, riled up the colonists against the British in his newspaper's columns. All three were excited about Goddard's plan. When Revere wrote to the New York Sons of Liberty on Goddard's behalf, he called the Constitutional Post "one of the greatest strokes our Enemies have met with (except the late affairs of the Tea)."[27]

It seemed like a go, but there was one hitch. In the back of his mind, Goddard knew that most of his treasonous contemporaries had some concern about his Constitutional Post, and all of them for the same reason. By then, the Sons of Liberty knew Ben Franklin was leaning toward alliance with the rebels. From London, Franklin had secretly forwarded communications between Massachusetts governor Thomas Hutchinson and the British Parliament—to the Sons of Liberty in Massachusetts.[28] In the letters, Hutchinson asked the Crown to send troops to crush the rising rebellion. Unknown to Goddard and others anxious to implement Goddard's colossal scheme, the British had found out and fired Franklin on January 31, six weeks earlier, for the "Pernicious Activity" of passing the Hutchinson letters to the colonists.[29] But none of this was yet known to Goddard and his contemporaries. Creating a new post to bypass the British system would definitely hurt Franklin's standing with the British Parliament. No one wanted to jeopardize the powerful Franklin's position or make an enemy out of someone they desperately needed to be on their side.

Revere's letter to the Sons of Liberty in New York on Goddard's behalf finished with the caveat "We are informed the Patriotic Doctor Franklin is severely threatened with the loss of that Place [deputy post-master general] under the British Minister. Many of the Patrons of this new Scheme were much concerned lest it should appear ungrateful to Doctor Franklin, especially at a Period when he has given such signal Proof of faithfulness to his Trust, in obtaining and sending over the treasonable Letters of Hutchinson. But perhaps the new Post-Office may be beneficial and more agreeable to the Doctor than ever was the old one."

Goddard was full of confidence and completely sure that his plan would be successful, regardless of Franklin's fate. He wrote to John Lamb, a leader of the Sons of Liberty in New York, about his meetings with Revere, Adams, and others in Boston. "I have not Terms to convey to you the Sentiments I entertain of their Magnanimity, Wisdom, Patriotism & Urbanity." Goddard knew that Lamb, the son of a convicted thief, was especially fearless. He was a successful wine merchant and optician and was one of the most aggressive of the New York revolutionaries. Goddard tried to hook Lamb by his ego and encourage the New York rebels to get the ball rolling before their Boston counterparts. If New York would sign on, Goddard offered, the city would have "the Glory of originating one of the greatest Plans that, as they say, was ever engaged in since the Settlement of this Country." If it seemed a little overblown, it wasn't. Goddard was absolutely certain that an independent post would be the most important lifeline in the coming revolution.

On March 17, an editorial by Goddard's Boston supporters appeared in colonial newspapers:

Boston, March 17. Last Monday arrived here Mr. William Goddard, Printer in Philadelphia, and Baltimore. The Cause of that Gentleman's Tour is interesting to all the Colonies, and we are happy to find that all of them through which he has come are thoroughly engaged in it. Mr. Goddard has long been noted as the Proprietor and Employer of a very FREE PRESS, and some four or five Years ago he began to feel himself distinguished on that Account, till at length the Exactions of the King's Post Rider became so enormous that they amounted to an entire Prohibition of the Continuance of his Business in the City of Philadelphia. Maryland, a great Part of Virginia, Pennsylvania and the Jersies, through which his Paper had circulated, became inflamed at the Insult; especially when it was known that Mr. Goddard had complained to the Postmaster, that sole Arbiter in this Case, and could not obtain the Shadow of a Redress. Nearly the whole Town of Baltimore, the first Merchants and Gentlemen in Philadelphia, assisted Mr. Goddard in establishing a Rider between those two Capitals, and have recommended the Plan to all the Colonies. Mr. Goddard has received the greatest Encouragement from every Colony through which he has passed, and all declare their Readiness to come into the Measure, provided it is adopted here.[30]

News finally arrived in the colonies that Franklin had been fired as joint postmaster general by the British secretary of the Post Office. The position in the colonies was now solely held by Franklin's joint postmaster general, John Foxcroft, a fierce loyalist. Foxcroft was a relative of Franklin's wife, and now had the mission to single-handedly keep the British postal system afloat in the colonies. Without Franklin, it was a daunting task. Foxcroft despised William Goddard, and when he got wind of Goddard's plan for a Constitutional Post, he went after him with a vengeance.

On April 5, 1774, John Foxcroft wrote to his superior in London, Anthony Todd, secretary of the British Post Office. He pointed out that Goddard's undertaking was illegal under British law, and that he had already consulted New York Colony's attorney general. "It will be best to commence a prosecution against Goddard as soon as sufficient proof can be had against him . . . he is only supported by a Set of licentious people of desperate Fortunes whose sole Consequence, nay even Dependence, is on their fishing in troubled Waters; Men of property both in and out of Trade hold him and his Scheme in the greatest Contempt and Abhorrence, as tending to disturb the public peace and Tranquility of America."[31]

Goddard knew Foxcroft was after him, but he was undeterred. Brimming with excitement and confidence, having more friends and supporters than he'd ever had in his life, the thirty-four-year-old printer wrote an article for the *Maryland Journal* on July 16, 1774. He cited Ben Franklin's firing by the British Parliament, now a well-known scandal in the colonies, as a rallying point for his Constitutional Post. The American people, "since the infamous Dismission of the worthy Dr. Franklin, and the hostile attack on the Town and Port of Boston, are unalterably determined to support a new constitutional Post Office on the ruins of one that hath for its Basis the slavery of America."[32]

Just over a week later in late July, Goddard mounted his trusted horse and rode down to Williamsburg, Virginia, to gain support for his plan from the South. Again, he found an easy sell to those who were already on the side of rebellion against England. The Williamsburg Committee of Correspondence members even recommended that the Continental Congress take over the Constitutional Post Office.[33] To Goddard, it seemed like the perfect way to take his upstart idea colonywide.

Goddard went back home to Baltimore to continue publicizing his plan with the general public. Many average citizens were now aware of it, thanks to a concerted effort by the rebel printers and others who wrote pamphlets on the wicked ways of England. Goddard kept up the assault on the Crown and called for a new postal system that would work far better than the corrupt, slow, and tyrannical British Colonial Post. His plan, he wrote, would save colonists from the "present American Post Office, ministerial in its creation, direction and dependence, which not only was tampering with private correspondence, but as well, was interfering with the circulation of our News-Papers, those necessary and important alarms in Times of public Danger." [34]

Although Goddard had solid written and oral support from his fellow revolutionaries, the majority of the work landed on his shoulders and was financed out of his own pocket. He likely engaged his sister, Mary Katherine, who shared his goal of American independence and was earning money at the Baltimore print shop to fund her brother's mission.

Those who doubted that Goddard could succeed in coordinating such a scheme were quite impressed when they learned that on December 31, 1773, the *Maryland Journal* published news of the Boston Tea Party, just two weeks after the riot in the Boston Harbor. The news had come straight from New York carried by Goddard's own post rider, one Mr. Butler. It was an impressive journalistic and logistical coup that New York and Baltimore were nearly on the same page in learning news of the insurrection.

In January 1775, Goddard traveled through the colonies again in efforts to expand and strengthen his system. He was spending money as fast as Mary Katherine made it and borrowing from friends to pay the riders and other logistical expenses. Still, he had no intention of slowing down. Then one night after meetings in Philadelphia, Goddard's past caught up with him. He was thrown in the city jail for debts he still owed Galloway.[35] He spent his days in a freezing cell writing caustic demands to the Pennsylvania Assembly to release him. He had no money to pay off Galloway, so he was forced into a kind of bankruptcy by the Assembly. On March 18, 1775, a legislator passed a bill for his release.

A month later, on April 19, 1775, the desperate need for secure lines of communication became clear to the Sons of Liberty and all rebel leaders in the American colonies. That morning, British forces arrived in Concord, Massachusetts, to disarm rebel militias outside Boston. Instead, they encountered an armed force in Lexington, and the first shots of the Revolution were fired. A rebel express rider left Watertown, Massachusetts, the same day and traveled the Post Road toward New York with word of the fighting. In each town along the way, Committees of Correspondence signed off after receiving the news. Secure communication was now an absolute necessity.

On May 29, 1775, the Continental Congress appointed a committee of delegates to organize an independent post. There were six members chosen, including the committee chair, Benjamin Franklin, who was now fully aligned with the patriots. "The present critical situation of the colonies renders it highly necessary that ways and means should be devised for the speedy and secure conveyance of Intelligence from one end of the Continent to the other," the Congress ordered the committee.[36]

Goddard was thrilled. There was no other scheme so well thought out as his. There could be no way for the committee to deny him the realization of his perfectly laid-out plan. He was nearly certain he would soon preside over an institution he'd poured his life and livelihood into for the past two years. The choice of committee members, however, left Goddard with some trepidation. Only Sam Adams and Ben Franklin knew the great logistical feat that he'd pulled off. Thomas Lynch from South Carolina was an unknown to him. It's unclear whether Goddard had a relationship with the other three delegates, Richard Henry Lee, from Virginia, or Thomas Willing and Philip Livingston from New York.

Led by the ultra-pragmatic Ben Franklin, the six members deliberated. A week went by, then two. Goddard heard nothing. He knew that Franklin knew the ins and outs of the British postal system better than anyone. Would Franklin come up with some sort of replacement based on the British system? Goddard nearly crawled out of his skin in anticipation. To better his chances, Goddard lobbied hard to the committee members, delineating his successes in transmitting secure and subversive correspondence across colonies. He told of his successful efforts from Rhode Island to Virginia. He reminded the members of his tremendous outlay of time and money.[37]

Finally, on July 25, the committee was ready to deliver its report to the Congress. Goddard's Constitutional Post would be adopted as the post of the colonies. Goddard, sitting in the Philadelphia State House, must have been ecstatic. All that was needed now was for Congress to vote to ratify the committee's recommendation. The next morning, Goddard went to Independence Hall and watched the deliberations of the Continental Congress, anticipating that if they adopted his plan they would surely name him as the top boss.

"Agreeable to the order of yesterday," the speaker began, "the Congress resumed the consideration of the report of the Committee on the post office; which being debated by paragraphs, was agreed to as follows: That a postmaster General be appointed for the United Colonies, who shall hold his office at Philadelphia, and shall be allowed a salary of 1000 dollars per year for himself, and 340 dollars per year for a secretary and Comptroller, with power to appoint such, and so many deputies as to him may seem proper and necessary.

That a line of posts be appointed under the direction of the Postmaster general, from Falmouth in New England to Savannah in Georgia, with as many cross posts as he shall think fit. That the allowance to the deputies in lieu of salary and all contingent expences [*sic*], shall be 20 per cent on the sums they collect and pay into the General post office annually, when the whole is under or not exceeding 1000 Dollars, and ten per cent for all sums above 1000 dollars a year.

That the rates of postage shall be 20 percent less than those appointed by act of Parliament. . . . That it be left to the postmaster general to appoint a secretary and comptroller."[38]

It was almost entirely Goddard's plan, with a few minor tweaks that he probably would have made anyway. The job of postmaster would pay him well. He could make back the money he had spent, pay off those he'd borrowed from, and finally live well. The miles and long days and sleepless nights, the tired horses, the lobbying, the articles and letters and out-of-pocket financing—it was all worth it. It must have felt too good to be true.

And it was.

A moment after the Speaker read the new Post Office guidelines, the entire Congress proceeded to elect the first postmaster general: Benjamin Franklin.

The sixty-nine-year-old Benjamin Franklin, new to join the Sons of Liberty against the evil English empire, was unanimously elected as the first postmaster general of the new American Post Office. Goddard was beyond furious. His heart and soul had gone into building the institution. It was snatched away in a single heartbeat. To add insult to injury, Franklin immediately appointed Richard Bache, his thirty-eight-year-old son-in-law, to the second-in-command position: secretary and comptroller. Finally, Franklin offered a stunned William Goddard the job of surveyor general.[39] It was an insult of the most egregious nature. The job was a consolation prize at best. The position meant that he would have to continue nonstop travel year-round setting up post offices around the colonies and investigating corruption in the service rather than run the whole show from its Philadelphia headquarters as he had expected to do. He'd make a paltry income rather than the generous salary of the postmaster general. On top of that, there was no stipulation in the statute to reimburse Goddard for his considerable expenses setting up the Constitutional Post. For a moment, Goddard thought of declining the offer, but he had no job, was in debt, and was desperately hopeful that he would be Franklin's successor when the old man retired. He swallowed his pride and agreed. At least he would be working on the plan he had created, even if he was subservient to Franklin, whom he tried his best not to outwardly despise.

Franklin drew up a pass that allowed Goddard to travel through the colonies and establish post offices and appoint postmasters and post riders. Under different circumstances, Goddard might have loved the work, but he struggled to find fulfillment as he rode endless miles through big cities and tiny hamlets. There was little pushback by the colonists. By now the British Post was falling apart and nearly everyone wanted a post office near their home. Anyway, there would soon be no choice but to use the new Constitutional Post to send and receive packages and correspondence. In December 1775, the Maryland Assembly forbade the Parliamentary Post to go through the colony, effectively ending the British postal system on Christmas Day.

Over the following months as surveyor general, Goddard added post office after post office and expanded the network beyond anything the British had ever done. He investigated fraud within the Post Office ranks and fired those abusing the new American mail system. He went after crooks who stole money and property from the mail carriers and post offices and had the criminals arrested by local sheriffs and constables.

All the while, a revolution began. General George Washington commanded the Continental Army, and battles erupted from Virginia to Canada. Goddard did not encounter fighting in his travels, and he was very good at his work. But he was not happy. He was still reeling from the pain of being passed over as postmaster, and he was still in debt.

After fulfilling his year-long contract, on June 30, 1776, just four days before the signing of the Declaration of Independence, William Goddard went to Congress and, with a long and blustery oration, petitioned the Board of War for a new appointment:

> To the Honourable Commissioners or Delegates from the several AMERICAN States, now sitting in General Congress in the City of PHILADELPHIA:
>
> The Memorial of WILLIAM GODDARD most respectfully showeth:
>   That the intolerable severity of Ministerial oppression having exposed to innumerable hardships your Memorialist, and other

Printers who manifested their zeal in defence of the invaded rights of *America*, and the iron hand of tyranny, having, by means of the Parliamentary Post-Office, pressed upon him more heavily, perhaps, than upon any other—his own sufferings and an ardent desire of serving his country prompted him to devise a plan for the total abolition of that engine of Ministerial extortion, fraud and revenge, by substituting for it a Post-Office on constitutional principles.

His undertaking was countenanced by all the friends of American freedom, several of whom contributed largely towards raising a fund sufficient to prosecute his plan, which the artificers used by the tools of despotism to discourage it rendered more expensive than it might otherwise have been. He was, however, very near reaping the fruits of his labour, and reimbursing his friends, when your most honourable House appointed one of your colleagues to superintend that important department under your direction; but the worthy officer intrusted with it not having been authorized to indemnify your Memorialist or his friends for the expense incurred by establishing Postmasters, hiring riders, and bringing the temporary establishment, in all its parts, to that state where your officer found it when it was resigned with all those advantages, a great loss is sustained by your Memorialist, as well as the persons who were more intimately connected with him in that voluntary service of the publick.

He then asked for the Assembly "to favour him with an opportunity to serve his country in the Army, where-ever the scene of action may be, if he be permitted to share in the glorious struggle in which his country is now engaged, and be rendered as serviceable as may be reasonably presumed from his known principles and character."[40]

The Board of War referred the matter to General Washington. Unfortunately for Goddard, Washington was trying to accept as few political appointees as he could to high ranks in the Continental Army. On July 29, 1776, in a letter to Congress, Washington argued that "the induction of Mr. Goddard into the Army as Lieutenant. Colo. would be attended with endless confusion."[41] One of Washington's aides assured Goddard that there were too many experienced officers who deserved promotions before such a political appointment could be made.

While Washington's take on political patronage put the brakes on Goddard's military aspirations, Ben Franklin's proclivity to nepotistic appointments ended Goddard's career with the Constitutional Post Office. After a year as postmaster general, Franklin turned over the powerful position to Richard Bache, his son-in-law. Deeply disappointed at being passed over again, a dejected thirty-seven-year-old Goddard, his brow furrowed and his hairline receding prematurely, took up residence once more in Baltimore with his sister. For a while, Mary Katherine Goddard's name still appeared as the publisher of the *Maryland Journal.* Mary Katherine had become a serious patriot in her own right. The well-respected printer, who was also the first female postmaster in the colonies, produced the original typeset copy of the Declaration of Independence, a daring and treasonous act in itself.

William Goddard officially took back control of the *Maryland Journal* from his sister in 1784 and her name fell off the masthead.[42] While history books have been kind to Mary Katherine, her brother's legacy as the creator of the Constitutional Post, an essential element of the American Revolution, was forever eclipsed by the good Dr. Franklin. However, William Goddard's role in protecting the Post from theft and corruption as the first surveyor general gave rise to the Post Office Inspection Service, which would soon become the most robust law enforcement service of the United States government.

Portrait of William Goddard around the time of the American Revolution and the adoption of the Constitutional Post by the Continental Congress in 1775.

CHAPTER 2

POLITICS

In 1883, more than a century after William Goddard retired as Post Office surveyor general, sixteen-year-old John Frank Oldfield seemed like an unlikely candidate for a future in the country's top law enforcement agency. Frank, as he was called by his family, was one of the most notorious troublemakers in the picturesque mill town of Ellicott City, Maryland. Born on January 2 in 1867, Frank was the smallest of five boys and only slightly bigger than his five sisters. His puny size gave him a big attitude and a desperate drive to get where he wanted to be. Like his mother, Wilhelmina, a first-generation German-American, he switched easily between stern and witty. He had a soft spot in his heart like his father, Hamilton, and he was 100 percent loyal to those close to him.

Young Frank engaged in diplomacy when necessary, but he truly loved a battle of wits. He solved conflicts with charm, coercion, and force. From primary school on, he was a smooth operator, working the system with finesse and fists. Perhaps because he had to defend himself from serious whippings by his older brother, William, Frank grew to love a good fight. To many, he appeared to be completely fearless and never backed down from a challenge.

The Oldfield family lived on Main Street in an economic boom-town that was the first stop out of Baltimore on the B&O Railroad. The town was established as Ellicott's Mills—the name of the biggest employer—in the mid-seventeenth century by two Mennonite brothers, who built the first merchant flour mill in the American colonies. The mill sat atop a 300-million-year-old granite outcrop in the northern Allegheny Mountains, above the fast-flowing Patapsco River that drove numerous company mills. Ellicott's Mills boasted the biggest production volume in the country and advertised the purest and most pristine flour in the world. The Patapsco River converged with the Tiber River, creating the perfect setting for running machines to mill timber, wheat, and cotton. Downtown Ellicott City thrived with bars, expensive restaurants, and a theater.

Frank's father, Hamilton Oldfield, was a fervent Republican, a devotee of Abraham Lincoln, and active in the early development of Maryland's Republican Party. During the war, Hamilton rode a desk as a volunteer quartermaster for the Patapsco Guard, a Union regiment deployed to defend the railroad. Hamilton saw no combat, barely left home, and was back at work in his two mills the day the war ended. In Ellicott City, there was no physical destruction from the war, but the fight that almost divided the nation continued to linger in the hearts and minds of Marylanders. Proslavery Southern Democrats were about half the population and still seething over their colossal defeat.

The Oldfields were wealthy and active in the community, but many kids at Frank Oldfield's private school lived like royalty. Some schoolmates' families inherited thousands of acres of rich Maryland soil from their successful colonial families of the 1600s. Frank studied with the likes of Charles Carroll VI, who lived on seven thousand acres of the most profitable tobacco and wheat plantations in Maryland, and whose great-grandfather signed the Declaration of Independence. Frank knew there was no possibility of ever rising to the level of the Carroll family. But he convinced himself it didn't matter. There was something more valuable than money: *power.*

All five Oldfield sons worked at the Hamilton Oldfield Iron and Pump Works or the nearby sawmill in which Hamilton was a partner. It was soon clear that Frank and his closest brother, Clarence, had no desire for the hard labor or the boring paperwork it took to become a successful business owner. Much more fun than working at the mill was delving into the political scene in Ellicott City and Howard County. Frank and Clarence fit perfectly with the new Republican Party. The platform was antislavery and probusiness and pushed for high tariffs to stimulate industry and protect workers.

Frank was twenty-one years old in 1888, when, as a political favor for supporting Republican candidates, his father was appointed postmaster of Ellicott City. This pleased Frank immensely. He could escape the hard labor in the family businesses and be hired by his father as a clerk at the post office instead. He would be paid well. And he would stay *clean*. He was obsessive about his hygiene, and he took great care in his appearance. He brushed his teeth zealously, went to the barber weekly, and dressed as if he worked on Wall Street, with the finest handmade suits from a Baltimore haberdashery.

As the postmaster was allowed to rent his own real estate to the federal government to use as the post office, Hamilton set up shop on the first floor of the Oldfield family home on Main Street. For a social climber and political animal like Frank, it was the perfect place to make connections. He knew everyone's business, chatted up the occasional tourists from Ohio mailing postcards, wrangled the day's issues with his Republican adversaries and Democrats alike, and flirted with Margaret Galena Fisher, the daughter of the baker next door. And he dreamed of bigger things.

There were two dueling Republican factions in Maryland, and when the political tide flipped four years later in 1892, Hamilton was ousted as postmaster. Though Frank didn't lose his recent promotion to "Secure Clerk," a bonded level job above a general clerk, he was not happy. Without his father running things, any additional promotions for the twenty-five-year-old were out of the question, and remaining a small-town postal clerk was definitely not what Frank Oldfield envisioned for his future.

After two years spending all his free time working political angles, in 1894 he ran for Howard County Republican Central Committee chair. Howard County encompassed several wealthy mill towns and massive wheat and tobacco plantations between Washington and Baltimore. Frank loved connecting with business owners and promising all the things a powerful Republican government could do in Democrat-heavy Maryland. He won easily. The position gave him his first taste of partisan power. He still clerked at the post office to support himself, but after he clocked out, he immediately switched over to being a party politician. He spent his afternoons walking Main Street, ducking into cafés for a bite to eat and chatting with everyone he met, or riding around town on one of his family's elegant horses.

At first, Hamilton Oldfield was delighted that Frank and Clarence were officially in the county's powerful political sphere. But it didn't take him long to realize they were going to give him the same headaches they always had. No sooner had Frank and Clarence arrived in Baltimore for the 1895 Republican convention than the brothers were in a brawl with Frank Higginbotham, their father's longtime rival from the competing Republican faction. As usual, the Oldfield family's stature got the boys out of trouble, but only after Hamilton shelled out forty-three hundred dollars for his sons' bail and then got the charges dropped.[1]

While the Republican Party dominated Howard County, Democrats were still a big part of the social fabric. And many of those Democrats were very much tied to southern proslavery sympathies. Frank, who was born two years after the Civil War ended, didn't think much about Democratic ideology or concern himself with the opposition's politics. That changed when Frank found himself forced to choose sides after a horrific murder just down the street from his home.

One frigid morning in February 1895, Daniel Shea, the well-loved owner of Shea's General Store on Main Street, was found by neighbors bludgeoned to death. A man named Jacob Henson was tracked down at his home outside the city. He was still covered in blood, and immediately confessed. Cloudy details emerged from the crime scene and Henson's constantly changing confessions. Henson, the son of a former slave, claimed he had gone over to talk to Shea, who was his boss, after drinking at O'Leary's bar across the street. He said the discussion turned into an argument and he was attacked by the much older storekeeper. He claimed he fought back in self-defense.

However it began, Shea was no match for Henson's alcohol-fueled brute strength, and Henson repeatedly cracked the old man's skull with a metal object. Before Henson left, he rifled through Shea's pockets, emptied the cash register, and left a cracked pocket watch that stopped the moment it crashed to the floor: *9:00 p.m.*

The entire city was horrified. Shea was a beloved member of the community, a kind old German immigrant who never married and had no kin, but was like family to many in the town. His store was a weekly stop for most everyone. None of it made sense to Frank Oldfield. Henson and his father had performed odd jobs for the Oldfields, and Frank felt affection for both father and son.

On March 27, 1895, the courtroom, which also happened to be the home of John O'Brian, saloon owner, was standing room only. Most everyone there wanted to see Henson hang. They also wanted to hear the salacious details of Henson's confession. Henson's father sat in the back. Henson's counsel made a powerful appeal before the twelve jury members: Henson was stupid, a halfwit, he didn't know what he was doing or the difference between right and wrong. His life should be spared.

The prosecutor read Henson's gruesome confession describing the scene of the crime and Shea's horrific injuries. At the defense table, Henson wept. A detective named Herman Pohler from Baltimore testified. He heard Henson's confessions while the prisoner was in custody in Ellicott City. Although he agreed that Henson was slow, and "stupid" at times, he felt he was still competent enough to realize the nature of his actions.[2] A number of psychiatrists who interviewed Jacob Henson while he was in jail came to the same conclusion.

Henson was found guilty of first-degree murder and sentenced to death. The judge declared his hanging would take place on June 7, 1895. Henson's attorney immediately asked for a suspended sentence. He wanted to file an appeal on the grounds that the convicted man was of questionable mind and did not know the difference between right and wrong.[3]

Frank Oldfield had mixed emotions while watching the proceedings. No one in the world believed that Henson shouldn't be found guilty, but Oldfield was not a supporter of capital punishment. While capital punishment was abolished in America in 1863, the practice resumed after the Civil War. Many, like Frank, were part of a growing movement working to end mandatory death sentences. He knew that Maryland governor Frank Brown, a northern Democrat, was not a supporter of the death penalty either. Frank was relieved when Brown agreed to have Henson evaluated one last time before making a final decision whether to commute the sentence to life imprisonment or let Henson hang.

Hearing mumblings in the crowd about lynching the convicted man, the state's attorney warned the gallery against trying anything stupid and promised that justice would prevail. One man yelled that if Henson wasn't put to death, there would most certainly be vigilante justice. Not sure that the Ellicott City police could or would protect the prisoner, Baltimore officers hurried Henson out a back door and secretly carted him to the jail.

Many Ellicott City southern Democrats despised free blacks and had no moral qualms about taking matters into their own hands and lynching Henson, whether he was guilty or not. It was a fact about his fellow citizens that Oldfield despised. It made him feel as if the South had not really accepted its loss. He knew organized cowards were out to recruit gang members from sympathetic white neighborhoods. They called themselves the "White Caps," and they loathed Republicans and northern Democrats supportive of free blacks like Governor Brown, who won his election with nearly 100 percent of the black vote. The Ellicott City Democrats were sure the governor would grant Henson clemency.

Oldfield knew precisely who was leading the call to lynch Henson. In a later hearing, Oldfield described how James Melvin, publisher of the *Ellicott City Democrat*, came to him after the trial. Melvin asked Oldfield to join a gang that planned to break Henson out of jail and hang him. Oldfield was disgusted. He told Melvin in no uncertain terms that he would have nothing to do with murdering a man who was about to be condemned to life imprisonment or worse, death. Oldfield believed in the rule of law, and though he did not believe in killing a convicted man, he would respect the court's decision. In what may have been the spark that led Frank to seek a career in law enforcement, he sought to find a way to stop Melvin and his friends from carrying out mob justice. If Melvin and his cronies went to lynch Henson, he would be there to stop them. As usual, Frank went to his brothers Clarence and William for help with his plan.

Oldfield Collection

Frank Oldfield circa mid 1890s, about the time he
was sheriff of Howard County, Maryland.

The night of March 28, 1895, after the jury handed Henson the
guilty verdict,[4] Frank convinced Clarence and William to come with
him to the jail. Pistols ready, they stood guard around the imposing
granite structure in the freezing cold until sunrise. Night after night
for more than a week they did this. Finally, with no sign of Melvin
and his colleagues, and the anger in town dying down, Frank decided
that Melvin would not be true to his word. Weeks went by, and Henson remained unmolested in his cell. Frank thought perhaps Melvin
wasn't able to drum up enough support, as Henson was soon to hang.

He was wrong. While Oldfield slept soundly on the night of May
27, a group of men, some wearing hoods, others in long robes that

hung over their heads down to their waists, and others with nothing more than a pocket handkerchief tied around their faces, silently climbed the steep road to the jail. It was just before midnight. Half of the men took positions as guards around the prison's perimeter. The warden was away on vacation, and his adult daughter and her husband were acting as caretakers. The couple was awakened by a loud bang as the locked jail door was battered down with a stout piece of iron. Coming to the head of the stairs with her husband, the warden's daughter saw a pistol pointed directly at her. She testified afterward that she couldn't identify the man because his face was covered, but she heard others go back through the corridor to Henson's cell. The man with the gun told the couple not to move.

Henson was asleep, locked behind the iron bars of the corridor as well as the door of his cell. The mob broke through the first door with a metal rod, snapping the lock. Henson heard nothing until the men used a sledgehammer to break the iron lock off his cell door. The terrified prisoner screamed for the men to take mercy on him. The warden's daughter pleaded desperately with the intruders not to kill Henson inside the jail.

A masked man tied a rope around Henson's neck. Others bound his hands behind his back and gagged him with a cloth. Then they shoved him out of the jail, violently pushing him up Merrick's Lane beyond the Patapsco Heights area, a short walk up Institute Hill. Several yelled at Henson to admit what he did with the victim's money. Henson, who was very weak, was at first able to walk under his own power. He fainted from fear when they came upon a large dogwood tree on the private property of A. B. Johnson. A few minutes after midnight, one man placed a noose around Henson's neck, tied the other end to a tree branch, and let Henson's body fall several feet under his own weight. Henson withered and convulsed, then went still. One of the

43

men pinned a card to the hanging corpse that said "*We respect our court and judges. Governor Brown forced the law-abiding citizens to carry out the verdict of the jury.—White Caps.*"[5]

When Frank heard the news the next morning, he was furious. He knew there would be no arrests, much less a conviction. The next day, the Ellicott City justice of the peace summoned a jury of inquest to look into the matter. But as in most lynching inquiries in Maryland, the jury concluded that "no evidence has been obtained to justify any criminal indictments or prosecution."[6]

Few in the town even called the lynching a crime. More than half of the community consented to the act and were quietly congratulating the lynch mob. Governor Brown, however, was livid. From the governor's mansion in Annapolis, he condemned the lawless proceedings. "Under these circumstances, in advance of their report and without the slightest reason for apprehension that the sentence of the law would be interfered with, the action of the lawless mob in breaking into the jail and hanging the prisoner cannot be excused," he said publicly.[7] "Indeed, no excuse whatever can be given for it, and no doubt it will be made the subject of inquiry by the grand jury at their next session. This deplorable incident, so injurious to the fair name of the State, strongly emphasizes the recommendation made by me to the last General Assembly to protect prisoners at all costs."

Oldfield stayed far away from southern Democrats after that. He was still chairing the Howard County Republicans and strategizing how to obtain the power he needed to make things happen in Ellicott City when an unfortunate stroke of luck came a year after Henson's murder. On July 2, 1896, Greenbury Johnson, the Howard County sheriff, fell off a trolley car on the way back from a Baltimore Orioles ballgame. He fractured his skull and died in the hospital.[8] When Frank heard of the forty-year-old sheriff's demise, he immediately went to his father, who put his political connections to work. At the time, Hamilton was again the postmaster, as he had campaigned for Governor Lowndes, a rare Republican governor in Maryland after forty years of Democrats.[9]

There were a number of candidates for sheriff, but even with zero experience in law enforcement, Frank got the job and was appointed directly by Lowndes. He was just twenty-nine years old. The sheriff position paid a whopping two thousand dollars a year, when the average annual salary was about three hundred dollars. It was a dream come true, even if Howard County didn't have nearly enough crime to keep Oldfield occupied. He went after a few thieves, arrested some drunks in a barroom brawl, and chased off a couple of vagabonds. He loved every part of it, especially when things got dicey. A month after he was sworn in, on September 18, 1896, he was attacked by a perpetrator resisting arrest.[10] Frank was left with a black eye he wore around town like a badge of honor.

There was no training for the sheriff position, so Oldfield used his well-tuned thinking cap and political schmoozing skills. He also wasn't beneath playing dirty. Frank soon gained a reputation for being a hothead as sheriff, and for using underhanded ways to deal with the low-level crime in Ellicott City. With Clarence, whom Oldfield deputized as a bailiff so he could work alongside his favorite brother, Frank went after a local couple for failing to pay their debts. When they wouldn't come up with the money, Frank and Clarence broke into the house and started selling off the couple's belongings to settle the debt. The couple, a Mr. and Mrs. Gordon, turned around and sued Oldfield. Frank backed off, and the case was dropped. While being a hard-ass came easily, Frank also had a compassionate side that came in handy. After a disoriented teen wandered from Baltimore along the B&O tracks and wound up lost, tired, and hungry in Ellicott

City, Frank took him in, cleaned him up, and kept him safe until his family was found.[11]

After he'd been in office a year, on July 29, 1897, Frank had his first major test as a law enforcement officer. "Early this morning, before seven o'clock, Sheriff Oldfield was informed that a strange Negro man was trying to sell a set of harnesses up the road," the *News* reported.[12] "From the description of the man which the sheriff was able to get he thought perhaps he was a man who had stolen a horse and buggy in Frederick County, and the officer hastened to overtake him. A short distance up the pike he saw the man near the road, just over among the trees. He went toward him, at the same time questioning him about a set of harnesses the man had with him in a bag. The sheriff informed the man who he was and told him to come along to Ellicott City."

Frank testified afterward that the suspect refused to come with him, picked up a piece of fence rail, and attempted to strike him. Then he jumped over a low fence and ran in a semicircle in a field. "The man sprang away from me," Oldfield said, "at the same time grabbing his hip pocket and bringing out a pistol, which he leveled at me. I then pulled my pistol and fired at him."

Oldfield hurried the man to his carriage with the assistance of George Neal, his driver, and took the suspect to the jail. The prisoner, identified by his family as George Thomas, was evaluated by Dr. William E. Hodges at the University of Maryland hospital. The bullet hit Thomas's groin and passed through the intestine, puncturing it in six places.[13] He could not be saved and died of his wounds two days later.[14] Oldfield was in shock. On August 2, the *Baltimore Sun* reported that "Oldfield stated that while he felt confident that the coroner's jury would exonerate him for all blame for the man's death, he yet was much depressed at the fateful determination of the pistol shot."[15] At a coroner's hearing, the statement by the sheriff was

46

corroborated by the buggy driver, and the jury promptly rendered a verdict. *Thomas was shot by Sheriff Oldfield while Oldfield was in the discharge of his duty*. Sheriff Oldfield was exonerated of any blame in the matter.[16] What was not mentioned in the hearing: In the hospital, Thomas testified that he was shot running away from the sheriff. The bullet pulled from Thomas by the coroner entered the deceased from the back of his torso.[17]

It was the first police killing in Ellicott City history. Oldfield never spoke about it after the day he was cleared, and the story never made it into the family lore. Whether the shooting death weighed heavily on his conscience is unknown. For the rest of his career, Oldfield would confront many armed criminals and take down dozens of pistol-wielding suspects. But he would never again fire his gun into the body of another man.

It's also unknown if Thomas's shooting cast a pall over Frank's law enforcement career, but things did not go well for some time afterward. When his appointed term was over, Oldfield ran for the office of sheriff, an elected position, and lost. Next, Frank ran for circuit court clerk for Howard County and quickly found himself in legal trouble. The *Baltimore Sun* reported on September 27, 1897, "The sheriff has recently been . . . accused of giving alcohol and buying votes. The cases disposed of were as follows: J. Frank Oldfield, attempt to bribe a voter and dispensing liquor on election day; three indictments; acquitted. Clarence H. Oldfield, electioneering; on indictment; demurrer to indictment sustained. The offences [*sic*], it was alleged, were committed at the Ellicott City municipal election held April 6, 1897."

Frank Oldfield was gaining a reputation across the state. Not a good one.

At a meeting with Governor Lowndes and state officials, Frank got a public call-out on his notorious behavior by Maryland's top executive.[18]

"Well, Sheriff," said the governor, "I am glad you escaped the penitentiary."

"Actually, Governor, I was arraigned on trumped-up charges which emanated from political enemies." Oldfield likely smiled his most convincing and charming smile. "I am a candidate for the Office of Clerk of the Circuit Court of Howard, and it was for the purpose of killing my prospects that I was indicted. But, Governor, I will be the Clerk all the same."

"That is the way to talk," said Lowndes, laughing.

Frank did not win the election. His political enemies did him in, painting him as a miscreant. Frustrated with his diminishing political prospects, he went back to the Post Office and did something he'd avoided as long as was humanly possible. The *Baltimore Sun* reported:

Ellicott City, MD, Dec. 16, 1897. The marriage of Ex-Sheriff J. Frank Oldfield and Miss Margaret Galena Fisher, second daughter of Mr. and Mrs. J. C. Fisher, of Ellicott City, was celebrated at half after 4 o'clock this afternoon at the Presbyterian Church in this city, by the Rev. Dr. Henry Branch, pastor of the church, performing the ceremony.

An immensely pleased and greatly relieved Margaret Galena finally captured the second Oldfield brother. To keep Frank from making a run for it, she kept the ceremony bare-bones. Even though there was nothing Margaret Galena loved more than a lavish affair, Frank bristled at pomp and circumstance. The bride had no attendants. She walked to the altar with the groom, probably with a death grip on his biceps. Still, there was no mistaking that Margaret Galena was going to make this day her own. The full-figured, self-confident woman ditched the typical white wedding dress. Instead, she appeared as a regal countess in an imperial purple gown with black tassels and velvet trim. On top of elaborate chestnut curls, she wore a black velvet Gainsborough hat with a plume of black feathers. The only hint of white appeared on her gloves and in her bouquet of roses. The church was filled with their friends to witness the ceremony.

No sooner were Mr. and Mrs. Oldfield back from a long honeymoon and settling into their new home in Ellicott City than Frank became engaged in a battle to save the life of one of his most cherished workers, a man who had become a close friend. Two weeks before his wedding to Margaret Galena, the first week of December 1897, Oldfield received word that his hostler, Joseph America, the man who took care of the Oldfields' horses, was in jail.

America was a giant of a man, muscled like a gladiator, with light brown skin, and taller than anyone in town. He was at a church cakewalk near Ellicott City.[19] Witnesses said that the forty-five-year-old America got in the middle of a fight between Isaiah Nelson and another man. Then he followed Nelson as he left the building. He pulled out his pistol and shot Nelson. Nelson died the next day. Locals knew there was bad blood between the two. It was a poorly kept secret that Isaiah Nelson was the reason that America's wife was no longer America's wife.

America was arrested trying to skip town on the road to Frederick. For four months, he was kept in the same freezing cell where Jacob Henson had languished years earlier. Frank went several times a week to see his good friend. He brought America blankets and home-cooked meals and coached him for the upcoming trial. Frank was a good listener, and when it came to someone close to him, he had undying compassion. Frank sat for hours with America while the giant lamented the killing, spoke of his love for his wife and hope not to receive a death sentence. His hopes were dashed on April 12, 1898. The *Baltimore Sentinel* reported:

> Joseph America was convicted this evening by a Howard County jury of murder in the first degree for shooting and killing Isaiah Nelson. Members of the jury say, from America's previous good character they were reluctant to find a verdict; that if it be carried out it will cause him to be hanged, and they further state that they will [be] united in a petition to the Governor to commute the sentence if the death penalty be imposed. Persons who know America well say he was always inoffensive and industrious, and his reputation was excellent before this trouble came upon him.

The next day, America rose, gripping a Bible in his enormous hands as Judge Thomas Jones entered the courtroom.

"Joseph America is sentenced to death. He will be hanged on a day designated by the governor," the judge declared. America showed no emotion.[20] Warden W. S. Hinmoun read a statement calling America a model prisoner who showed penitence and humility. America read the Bible and prayed daily.

Frank Oldfield immediately went into action to save his friend's life. He began a nonstop campaign to get as many high-level officials as he could to sign a petition asking for clemency for America. On June 17, he got a meeting with Governor Lowndes at the Maryland State House and presented the document. To Frank's immense relief, on July 10, a directive came from Annapolis. "The Governor directs that instead of being hanged that America be confined in the Maryland penitentiary for the full term of his natural life." America was moved to the great walled fortress in Baltimore, where he became known as Prisoner No. 14,782. He was sentenced to hard labor in the stone yard. Although heartbroken about his friend's plight, Frank felt better knowing that he could visit America often and bring his friend some news from home. Still, Oldfield and other supporters of America continued to fight for the convicted man, and twelve years after his incarceration, America was pardoned by Maryland governor Phillips Lee Goldsborough and released from prison. He was fifty-seven years old.[21]

Frank Oldfield was thirty-one years old when America went to prison and still had no substantial career path, which annoyed his father very much. To remedy the situation, in 1899, Hamilton Oldfield came up with an idea. The Oldfields were big supporters of James Albert Gary, a textile millionaire who ran for governor of Maryland but lost. After his loss, Gary was appointed to the top job at the United States Post Office, and favors were raining down on his supporters. Hamilton reached out to Postmaster General Gary, accentuating the very best of his second son's disjointed resume. Within weeks, John Frank Oldfield was appointed to one of the most important and powerful law enforcement positions in the country—the job of U.S. Post Office inspector.

The job would take him away from his beloved mill town, but it was an offer he couldn't refuse. A Post Office inspector had great influence and a comfortable salary. Additionally, the position offered immediate power. An inspector could bust a crime ring anywhere on earth if one of the suspects sent a letter or package through the mail. An inspector could take over a case from any law enforcement agency in the country if the United States mails were used in any fashion. Growing up with four brothers all constantly vying for the attention of their father, Frank had something to prove. He was about to do just that. On March 7, 1899, John Frank Oldfield was sworn in as the 156th Post Office inspector since William Goddard first rode across the colonies for the new American Post.

CHAPTER 3

THE RAVEN

In November 1890, a decade before John Frank Oldfield scored the coveted position of Post Office inspector, twenty-six-year-old Francis Dimaio was being fitted for a new suit in Manhattan. Afterward he picked out a derby hat in a brushed black felt. The most important detail Dimaio looked for in both the suit and the hat was that each item had a prominent label inside the lining with the name of the shop and the location where it was made: *New York City*. Dimaio checked himself out in the tall cheval mirror. It was a far cry from what he usually wore on assignment. But this was not Dimaio's usual assignment.

After acquiring the new suit, Dimaio's orders were to report to the home of Robert Pinkerton of the world-renowned Pinkerton National Detective Agency the following Monday. It was Saturday, so Dimaio spent Saturday and Sunday nights in a Brooklyn hotel, spending his days tooling around the borough. On Monday morning, he walked a bit, had lunch, and headed over to 71 Eighth Avenue, near Prospect Park.[1] The four-story stone townhome was massive by city standards, but still understated for the CEO of one of the country's largest firms.

The Pinkerton brothers, William and Robert, were co-owners of the agency. They'd taken charge of the company when their father, the famous Scottish-American detective Allan Pinkerton, died six years earlier.[2] Rather than buy into the concept of America's nouveau riche sons who lived in gilded mansions, the brothers were quite conservative with their money and their business, a fact much appreciated by their clients, who thanked them endlessly for very reasonable rates for services.[3]

The Pinkerton Detective Agency was an international power-house. At that time, the company contracted innumerable services to government and industry. Both William and Robert, born in 1846 and 1848 respectively, grew up knowing they would be in charge of their father's agency one day, and they transitioned into the roles well. Under their leadership the company had contracts with the largest banks, railroads, shipping companies, and mining operations in the country. They employed a force of security guards and undercover agents who worked with federal, state, and local police, and the U.S. Treasury. They employed expert number crunchers to investigate missing funds from company ledgers, and they had a tough group of agents/enforcers. Agents were firmly on the side of those paying their salaries, and they were not allowed to step into politics. If the Pinkerton brothers required them to bust up unions and rough up union organizers, they did just that with brutal efficiency.

A big portion of Pinkerton business was defending big business against unions. Pinkerton detectives were sent to spy on workers or act as toughs and strikebreakers. Pinkertons were in many ways a militia for hire. Under the Pinkerton brothers, the company grew to two thousand detectives and thirty thousand reserves. It was a force bigger than the standing army of the United States, causing the state of Ohio to outlaw the Pinkertons due to the possibility of their troops being hired out as a private army.[4]

The agency also had a Special Crimes Unit that tracked criminals across the globe. The operatives who made up the unit were Pinkerton's undercover experts, both men and women, who had amazing skill at penetrating the most subversive criminal gangs.[5] The Pinkertons' actions were often extralegal, but effective. Like a vast spiderweb, the Pinkertons' reach extended far and wide across America but remained almost invisible to the naked eye. That same web made the Pinkerton brothers two of the most politically connected and influential men in America.

Two years before Dimaio met William Pinkerton in person, he heard the Pinkerton Agency was looking for an Italian-American detective for its Philadelphia office. Mafia criminals were infiltrating steel and mining operations in Pennsylvania. When companies reached out to the Pinkertons, the brothers realized they had a severe deficit in their detective roster. The Pinkertons did not have a single Italian detective. They desperately needed someone to go undercover in the criminal underground. Dimaio, at twenty-four years old, knew immediately this would be the perfect job for him. Growing up in Italy, Dimaio learned English, French, Spanish, Portuguese, and many Italian dialects.[6] As a teen, he hired himself out as an interpreter. He soon realized opportunities were better in America. Like tens of thousands of others, in 1891 he set sail for New York City. He was twenty-one years old. Dimaio spent his first three years in the United States as a broker for a tugboat company—a fairly uninteresting job, but it acquainted Dimaio with characters who worked around the waterfront.

With the Pinkertons, Dimaio became an expert uncover agent. His exploits included running down criminals extorting money from mining companies in Pennsylvania, exposing Italian hit men, and infiltrating bands that robbed big manufacturers. Dimaio was a master of disguise. He could appear to be from the north of Italy or the islands of Sicily or Corsica or the coastal towns of Spain and Portugal. He could put on baggy wool trousers and swing a pickaxe like a coal miner. He could dock a ship coming into port with fellow sailors. He could put on an ill-fitting suit and go door-to-door selling housewares. He impersonated a Portuguese seaman, a Latin dance instructor, and an organ-grinder.[7] He was also tough as nails, and when he was undercover in a secret Mafia ring, he learned all the ways to (theoretically) carve up a victim. He was as stealthy as any detective could be and brilliant at getting people to talk to him. He refused to be photographed so no one could positively identify him later on, and he managed to never have his cover blown. He was fairly average looking, and no one could give a good description of him after he disappeared from the scene. The only thing that stood out about his appearance was Dimaio's hair, black like obsidian, which earned him the nickname *the Raven*.

Having heard of his Italian employee's extraordinary reputation in their Philly office, on October 23, 1890, Robert Pinkerton wrote to one of his directors in Pennsylvania. He wanted to know the director's thoughts about Dimaio's potential usefulness in investigating an unsolved murder in New Orleans. The director responded immediately, praising Dimaio's talents and work ethic, while clearly surprised that a person of Dimaio's ethnicity could rise to such a level. "I consider him one of the smartest Italians that I have ever seen," he wrote. "He can sing a good Irish song, and is very versatile, is also witty and quick of comprehension. I do not know of another man in the agency who is his equal in regard to work among Italians."

The director followed up after speaking with Dimaio with a second letter:

"I have just had a talk with [Dimaio] in regard to getting into the Mafia. He said he did not know whether he could join it, but thinks he could. . . . Dimaio tells me that the Mafia is quite strong in this city [Philadelphia] also in New York, but the Sicilians go to New Orleans, as it is the headquarters, and is better than Philadelphia or New York (maybe warmer). I have instructed him to let his beard grow, and when it has grown a little he makes about as complete a picture of an Italian brigand in this country as one could imagine."

And with that letter, the Pinkerton brothers decided that Dimaio would be perfect for this particular job.

Dimaio arrived at Robert Pinkerton's Brooklyn home near Prospect Park precisely on time at 2:00 p.m. The assistant superintendent of the Pinkerton Philadelphia office, Henry W. Minster, greeted him at the door. Robert Pinkerton was not home, but Minster ushered Dimaio into a bright front parlor, where he met Robert's older brother, William. The stern-looking forty-four-year-old Pinkerton had a reputation as a deep-thinking strategist; at sixteen years old, he had enlisted with the Union army in the Civil War, and he was a veteran of the Secret Service. William actually lived in Chicago but came to New York for this meeting, since his brother had another commitment. With a large oil painting of William's father, the late Allan Pinkerton, peering down upon the three men, William Pinkerton began to unravel the story for the young Italian operative.

The Pinkertons had solved many murders over the years, he told Dimaio, but none were so personal to the brothers as the murder of New Orleans police chief David Hennessy. Dimaio knew some details of the story he'd read in the Philadelphia newspapers. The murder had taken place two weeks earlier, on October 13, 1890. Apparently, as Hennessy walked to his house from work and was nearly home, a teenage boy stepped out of the darkness and began to walk alongside the chief, whistling. Out of nowhere, shotgun fire erupted, hitting Hennessy in multiple parts of his body. Hennessy was able to fire his pistol as he chased after the attackers, but he collapsed in the street after several blocks. He died three days later in the New Orleans hospital. He was able to speak a little bit during those three days, but he was unable to positively identify his attackers. He did tell the officers in charge of the investigation that "the Dagos" shot him.[8]

The crime was the most blatant attack against a top law enforcement officer by Sicilian criminals ever reported. Hennessy was a tough and fearless lawman, hell-bent on prosecuting the bosses of several Mafia bands now emboldened in the Crescent City and responsible for dozens of cold-blooded murders. Chief Hennessy was a Civil War veteran with the Union cavalry and had a long history of being incredibly tough on criminals. In 1881, Hennessy was a sergeant in the police department when he arrested Giuseppe Esposito, the first known Mafia kingpin in the city. Esposito's capture and deportation made Hennessy a lifelong enemy of Sicilian Mafiosi.[9]

New Orleans's mayor, Joseph Shakespeare, was a personal friend of Robert and William, and he came to them directly for help. The brothers didn't hesitate. Not only did they want to help bring Hennessy's assassins to justice, but the brazenness of the Mafia groups made the Pinkertons furious.[10] They wanted to do anything they could to put an end to the Sicilians' reign of terror.

Immediately upon learning of Hennessy's murder, William Pinkerton wrote to Mayor Shakespeare's secretary:

The murder dazed me. I could not collect my thoughts. Why anybody as courteous and brave and gentlemanly as Hennessy should be assassinated in the brutal manner in which he was, is a mystery to me. . . . I have known him since he was a boy in Chief Badger's office and watched him through the years develop into a fine man and wonderful police officer. Again all I can say is I am stunned, my heart goes out to his mother who I know he adored. Please give her my condolences. . . . I am in touch with Chief of

Detectives Gastner to offer the full facilities of our organization to help track down, arrest and convict these criminals.[11]

Dimaio knew some details of the story he'd read in the Philadelphia newspapers. Pinkerton updated Dimaio on what hadn't been reported. After the shooting, Mayor Shakespeare demanded raids on the Italian ghettos. The police rounded up more than a dozen Italian-Americans and locked them up in the Parish Prison at Conte and Orleans Streets. Joseph Macheca, a successful fruit merchant and enemy of Hennessy, was believed to be the leader of a large Mafia gang. He was in the Parish Prison along with the other suspects, but there were no eyewitnesses, and the government's evidence was weak. Pinkerton was very serious with Dimaio. "The disturbing information I have received indicates the state's case will fail," he told the young Italian. "Witnesses are being threatened and bribed. The gang is boasting openly to the prison guards that they'll be back in business before long, and there will be more killings, including those of police officers."

Engrossed in the story, Dimaio asked what he could do to help. It was an elaborate and intricate plan, Pinkerton said, and if Dimaio declined the job, there was no other detective in their ranks who could do it. "[Pinkerton] told me the assignment facing me would be very dangerous, and that when I learned the details . . . I could refuse it and it would not be held against me in the agency," Dimaio said in an interview decades later. "I had the confidence of ten men in those days, and I just told Mr. Pinkerton there wasn't any assignment I wouldn't accept."[13]

The details of the plan would have to wait. Pinkerton and Minster said that they had to connect with the Secret Service in Washington, D.C., to solidify the federal agency's support and get an agent in place in New Orleans. Dimaio was to come to Chicago a week later to meet again.[14]

Dimaio reconnected with William Pinkerton and Henry Minster in Chicago, and Pinkerton laid out the details of his plan. Dimaio would pose as Antonio Ruggiero, an Italian counterfeiter from New York. Ruggiero was a real person, a counterfeiter with an international reputation who they knew from sources was under arrest in a small town in northern Italy. In order for Dimaio to take on Ruggiero's persona, Pinkerton handed him a complete dossier on the counterfeiter.[15] In character, Dimaio would travel south on the train wearing the suit and hat he'd bought in New York. Sewn inside the lining of his vest and hat would be stacks of counterfeit bills. In a small town just north of New Orleans, Dimaio would stop for the night and pay for his hotel and meals with counterfeit money. The Secret Service would arrive and arrest him. From there, he would be taken to the prison in New Orleans where the suspects in Hennessy's murder were incarcerated. During his prison stay, Dimaio's job was to gain the trust of at least one of the suspected assassins and coax out a confession.

Dimaio listened intently as Pinkerton stressed the dangers of the assignment he was offering. "Certain people in New Orleans will not hesitate to order you killed if they find out who you are," Pinkerton said gravely. "I must warn you, you will be treated as a criminal from the first moment you are arrested. Only six people will know your real identity: myself, my brother, your boss here"—Pinkerton pointing at Henry Minster from the Philadelphia headquarters—"New Orleans district attorney Charles Luzenberg, the head of the Secret Service in Washington, and the New Orleans Secret Service superintendent." No one at the jail, none of the local police, or anyone near him would know who Dimaio really was. There would be no access to immediate help if he needed it.

Years later, Dimaio recalled his reaction. "With my heart in my throat, I said, 'Well, sir, when do I start?'"

Dimaio had another reason for his heart being in his throat. He was just six months married and about to depart on a honeymoon when he was called to Brooklyn.[16] He was likely afraid of breaking the news to his wife that he'd be on a secret mission in January rather than on a vacation at a fancy resort.

Dimaio spent a few weeks preparing for his mission with Minster's coaching. He role-played his character. "It was like playacting," Dimaio said in an interview with author James D. Horan in the early 1960s. "I would act out a scene and Minster would try and punch holes in it. Hour after hour I stressed habits, special Italian swearwords, the walk and manner of this man I had never met, until they were part of me."[17] Dimaio stitched the counterfeit money into the lining of his suit vest and derby hat. Then he dug deep into the history of New Orleans's criminal Mafia.

It was a Sicilian named Giuseppe Esposito whom many blamed for bringing the Mafia to New Orleans in the late 1870s.[18] Back in Sicily, Esposito was a well-known Mafioso and international criminal. After kidnapping an English clergyman named John Forester Rose, who was traveling in Sicily in 1876, Esposito made the clergyman write a ransom note to his brother in England with a demand to send an emissary with money. The British Parliament protested to the Italian government. But Esposito was unconcerned with the government in Rome and cut off the clergyman's ears and sent them to Rose's brother. This time the British government leaders were furious. To appease them, Rome ordered troops into Sicily to track down Esposito, but the kidnapper escaped to the mountains. From the inland hills above Palermo, Esposito ran a thriving Mafia business. Things heated up and several of his colleagues were arrested, so Esposito turned himself in to friendly authorities. Before the Palermo courts could put him on trial for murder and extortion, he escaped, first to Marseilles, France, then to New York. He ended up in New Orleans around 1877.

Esposito's reputation preceded him, and he was immediately leading crime factions with his right-hand man, Giuseppe Provenzano. Post–Civil War Reconstruction was not good to New Orleans. City appointees amassed fortunes by appropriating public funds. Police, teachers, and city workers went unpaid, and the city went deep into debt. A yellow fever epidemic hit the city in 1878, killing five thousand, mostly children. New Orleans was the perfect location for entrepreneurial mobsters. Criminal Italian immigrants took advantage of the city's wayward politicians and corruptible police, judges, and jailers. There was no fear of the law. Atrocious murders were common, with victims left bleeding in the streets as perpetrators walked away unpunished. If there ever was an arrest, the law was easily corruptible and usually powerless to convict. Open efforts to bribe or intimidate juries and judges alike were common as well.

Esposito and Provenzano were masters at Mafia business logistics and quickly ruled the docks and the South America fruit import business.[19] Esposito operated a small trawler in the harbor. On the masthead, its flag spelled out "Leone," the name of his idol, a top Mafioso and politician named Leone Marchesano from Palermo. In a few years, Esposito's thugs controlled the New Orleans fruit piers and the employment of longshoremen. Over the course of just one year, Esposito's henchmen murdered eighty-nine people. Esposito boldly and successfully formed the first Mafia in the American South.

As the most southerly of American ports and with a lawless reputation, over the years, New Orleans became a destination city for fugitives from Palermo's courts and prisons. The Italian quarter in New Orleans grew to resemble the most squalid neighborhoods of Palermo and Naples: dingy buildings with filth dumped into the streets creating an awful stench. Yelling, screaming, and constant chatter filled the air.

In addition to Esposito's and Provenzano's successes, after a few years, industrious members of the Italian neighborhood began to excel in businesses of the more legal sort. They were from the Italian mainland—fruit importers, those who traded wine, spirits, and textiles from South America, and those who imported treasures from their home country. Some opened shops and restaurants, and others operated warehouses to sell wholesale goods. However, success came with a price. Once any Italian began to show signs of prosperity, he had a whole new set of worries. The Mafia was not far behind, and it wanted a cut of the action. Their method was simple. A prominent, successful Italian received a letter demanding money to be delivered to a certain place at a certain time. Some of the victims feared for their lives or their families' lives so much that they paid the extortionists. Some ignored the letters and wound up dead. Esposito's reign of terror ended when he was arrested and deported by Chief Hennessy in 1881.[20] Afterward, in the power vacuum, new players emerged, vying for control of the thriving criminal enterprises. Esposito's New Orleans crime organization split into two factions: one group led by the Matranga family and another by the Provenzano clan.[21]

The relatively new government of Italy, sutured together in the 1860s into one country, tried to upgrade its depraved international reputation. The Italian consul at New Orleans, a Signor Corte, denounced the Mafia and warned new immigrants to keep their distance. Italian priests condemned the criminals during mass. But in the Italian ghetto, warnings and advice went unheeded as the killers accosted newcomers with offers they felt they couldn't refuse: *Join our ranks or pay with your life*. A decade passed, and the Sicilian Mafia became more and more emboldened in the Mississippi Delta.

In 1890 the number of assassinations credited to the sons of Palermo reached ninety-five souls.

To Francis Dimaio, the more he studied, the more intriguing the Hennessy story became. He stayed home in Philadelphia through the Christmas holiday, which probably made his new bride happy. Then on January 3, Dimaio and Superintendent Minster boarded a sleeper car on the Illinois Central Railroad to head south to Louisiana. Dimaio wore six thousand dollars' worth of faux currency in his suit and hat. The fake cash was the work of an expert Dutch counterfeiter named Charles Becker.[22] Over two nights, the men traveled until they reached Hammond, Louisiana. Hammond was a busy commercial center and important rail stop directly across Lake Pontchartrain from New Orleans. Minster wanted to be close to New Orleans if Dimaio needed help, but he knew his presence in the Crescent City would set off alarms, so he stayed in Hammond and kept a low profile.

Dimaio caught the next train north and rode twenty miles to Amite City, a small town surrounded by cotton plantations. With local residents who constantly concerned themselves with one another's business, it was the perfect place to begin the Pinkertons' elaborate plan. Dimaio found Mrs. Rogers's boardinghouse, signed in as Antonio Ruggiero, and paid for the room with his counterfeit bills. He then went off to find a meal and some things to buy. Dimaio lurked around town the next two days, making sure he was noticed, but not becoming too friendly with anyone.

Back in his Hammond hotel, Henry Minster called Secret Service agent Azariald Wilde at his office in the New Orleans Custom House.

"It's time," Minster told Wilde.

Agent Wilde was one of the five people briefed on the Pinkertons' plan. He knew exactly what to do next. He boarded the train to Amite City, marched into the boardinghouse, and arrested Dimaio at gunpoint. In front of a terrified Mrs. Rogers, Wilde ripped open Ruggiero's jacket and hundreds of counterfeit bills fell to the floor.[23]

"Wilde certainly put on a fine show," Dimaio told Horan. "He marched me inside the dining room, and someone brought down my valise with the queer money, which also had a six shooter. By this time the boardinghouse was in an uproar. Mrs. Rogers had fainted, and two of the guests ran to get their shotguns. After he handcuffed me, Wilde then went on to list all the crimes I was wanted for. It certainly sounded impressive." The news spread like wildfire through the tiny town, and by the time Wilde had a handcuffed Ruggiero at the train depot, a crowd mobbed the scene. One man, a local farmer, pushed his way toward the suspect.

"You gave me a fake twenty-dollar bill at the St. Louis Fair! You need to pay me, you thief!" he yelled.

Ruggiero yanked his arm free from Wilde's grasp, cupped his bound hands together, and swung at the man's face, knocking him senseless. The crowd surged toward Ruggiero with fists, chains, and ropes flying. Wilde shoved Dimaio onto the train's caboose, then jumped in after him just as the train took off.

On January 5, 1891, guards tossed Dimaio into a dank cellblock in the Orleans Parish Prison with a wooden bucket for a toilet that the guards called "The ice cream freezer."[24] It was the Italian section of the prison, and with Dimaio was a group of surly Sicilians accused of killing David Hennessy. Dimaio was instantly sized up by one of the mobsters. Frank Romero, a massive man who was a boss in the Matranga family mob, got his face within inches of Dimaio.

"Who the hell are you?" the suspicious Romero asked.

The counterfeiter Ruggiero was not interested in chatting or making friends, and without so much as a word, he punched the giant Romero in the chin from below, knocking him to the floor. In case the others thought about approaching him, Ruggiero spat at the retreating crowd, "Leave me the hell alone."

From a dark corner, Dimaio glowered and pretended to be completely disengaged, all the while clandestinely surveying the group. The mangy bunch had been locked up for months with little access to lawyers or visits with family, clean clothes, or showers. Within hours, Dimaio quickly identified the one person he would target. There was a younger man whom the others constantly harassed. He was small, nervous, and looked like the perfect stool pigeon. His name was Manuel Polizzi.

The introduction of Antonio Ruggiero to the cellblock, with his fancy suit and weird dialect, had the prisoners on edge. It seemed highly unlikely that he was a legitimate out-of-town criminal. "The government brought in a smart-looking fella on a counterfeit charge," Dimaio heard one of the prisoners warning the others. "Be careful. He may be a detective."

His first night in the prison, Dimaio lay awake on his cot and listened as one of the guards whispered a warning to a Sicilian prisoner he called Joe. "At least one detective is planning to infiltrate your gang," the guard said. "Watch out for that guy Ruggiero, no one from around here has ever heard of him." Dimaio spent a sleepless night, afraid that his cover would soon be blown, and that they'd be after him to kill him.

The next morning, Dimaio was sullen and indifferent to the others when a guard entered the cellblock, carrying a local newspaper. The paper was open to an article on the arrest of the international counterfeiter Antonio Ruggiero, who was caught red-handed by Secret Service in Amite City. The guard tossed the paper at Dimaio.

"There you are, Ruggiero; read all about yourself," he said.

Dimaio threw the newspaper to the floor.[25]

It was not a surprise to Dimaio when one of the other prisoners quickly picked it up, and the newspaper and its story made the rounds throughout the block. According to the paper, Ruggiero was an infamous Italian counterfeiter, connected to a gang with headquarters in New York, Philadelphia, and Chicago. In December, part of the gang was busted in Philadelphia, and federal agents seized more than one thousand dollars in counterfeit coins and bills and arrested seventeen Italian men and two women. Ruggiero was tailed from Chicago for several days, and was believed to be on his way to New Orleans to pass counterfeit two-dollar bills to local merchants during Mardi Gras.

That newspaper account helped build Ruggiero's credibility. In fact, he became something of a celebrity among the criminals. He also continued to be openly hostile toward the Hennessy suspects and didn't seem to care at all about anything the others spoke of regarding local gossip. As days passed, the gang members, who already had plenty of enemies within the institution, reached out frequently to the accused counterfeiter. Some offered him a share of food and wine delivered from their friends and family. Ruggiero was slow to come around, but eventually warmed up to the others.

In order for Dimaio to get word to the outside, the Pinkertons hired an attorney whose job was to visit Dimaio each day and sneak written messages back in balled-up paper to Secret Service agent Wilde. "Who you writing to?" the gang members would ask, suspiciously. "A blonde on Basin Street," Ruggiero told them.[26]

The attorney was not privy to Dimaio's actual undercover mission and was instructed not to read Dimaio's notes. He brought out bleak reports. Not only was Dimaio in constant threat of his life, the horrid food and contaminated water gave the operative a severe case of dysentery. Dimaio, with little weight to lose when he entered the prison, dropped thirty pounds in a month. At the same time, he had little to show for his efforts. None of the men ever discussed the Hennessy murder. Still, when he received a message that he could end the assignment, he refused to leave, promising that he would have a break soon.

Finally, there seemed to be an in. The immature Manuel Polizzi gradually began to warm up to Dimaio. "I made sure I was friendly but not overfriendly," Dimaio said in an interview. "This was an acquaintanceship that had to be carefully nurtured. One abrupt, false move, and it could end. He was eager to be nice but it was clear the boy was in fear of his life from the others." Dimaio played on Polizzi's real fears and his paranoia. Polizzi's family and friends delivered wine and food for him to the prison, but Dimaio convinced Polizzi that they'd been laced with poison. Dimaio described horrible prison deaths when suspects were fed lethal chemicals. One evening, when the prison guards came with spaghetti for dinner, a very hungry Polizzi sprinkled grated cheese over his dish. Dimaio knocked the fork out of his hand.

"Fool, can't you tell there's arsenic in that cheese," Dimaio whispered. "Someone's out to get you."[27]

Another evening, Polizzi offered to share a bottle of wine with his new friend Ruggiero. Dimaio put his nose to the bottle and took one sniff. "This is laced with cyanide," he said with complete conviction, and poured it out, to Polizzi's thankfulness and dismay.

In his fear and isolation, believing he was targeted for murder by his Mafia brothers, Polizzi attached himself to Ruggiero. In whispers in dark corners or out in the yard with his new friend, the neurotic Mafioso unraveled the story of Hennessy's murder.[28] Dimaio learned the locations and dates of the planning sessions and the names of the criminals involved. Polizzi told him of the random method used to select who would kill Hennessy, and the different roles of established Mafiosi and "greenhorn" associates. Polizzi even told Dimaio the name of the tune whistled by the young Mafioso upon Hennessy's approach:

the "Marcia Real" or "Italian Royal March." Dimaio took great pains to commit Polizzi's incredible story to his highly effective memory.

Dimaio wrote a short outline of Polizzi's confession and rolled the paper into a small pellet he handed off to his lawyer when he came to visit the next day. Perhaps the lawyer read the note before delivering it to Secret Service agent Wilde, because the attorney abruptly disappeared. The following day, Dimaio waited anxiously. When he was ready to leave the prison, the plan was to deliver a message to the attorney that would be a signal to Agent Wilde and Henry Minster on the outside. But the lawyer never showed. It took a few days for Minster to hire a new attorney and get word back from Dimaio that his assignment was a wrap.

Minster met Dimaio outside the prison and took him to a nearby hotel. William Pinkerton, District Attorney Charles Luzenberg, and Agent Wilde were waiting for him. All three were shocked by Dimaio's emaciated frame.[29] Pinkerton thought they should wait to debrief Dimaio until he had a chance to rest, but Dimaio would have none of it. He devoured plates of food while unloading the details of Polizzi's confession from memory to a stenographer. The next day, Luzenberg called a grand jury hearing. Dimaio testified for four hours, fell asleep in the witness chair, then came back the next day to finish.

On February 16, District Attorney Luzenberg levied indictments against nine members of the Mafia gang suspected of murdering Chief Hennessy and determined to hold them in jail until the trial. Dimaio offered to stay and testify, but Luzenberg feared that if he went public, Dimaio would be targeted for murder.

The trial made international news. The entire city of New Orleans was on pins and needles, waiting for the outcome. Would justice prevail, or would the gangsters threaten and coerce their way out of a conviction? The trial became especially dramatic when Manuel

Polizzi, wild with fear of being killed by his fellow prisoners, threw a fit, screamed in Italian, and begged for a private conference with the judge. Polizzi then offered his full confession to the judge through an interpreter. It didn't matter. Two private detectives paid by the mob had already infiltrated the jury. Even with Polizzi as an eyewitness naming names in the courtroom, on Wednesday night, October 15, 1891, the jurors found six of the men not guilty. On charges for the other three, the jury deadlocked.

Thousands in the city were in an uproar over the acquittals and mistrial. How could these murderers not be convicted with an eyewitness from their own gang? Two nights after the trial, the Sicilians had yet to be released. A group of lawyers, doctors, businessmen, and political leaders met in the city, determined not to let this travesty of justice go unpunished. The next day, an influential attorney named William Parkerson led a mob of about four hundred to the prison in the Tremé neighborhood. The crowd overtook the guards and busted down the doors with axes. It was the middle of the day, but there were no police anywhere on the streets to stop them.[30] The attackers dragged all nine men screaming from the cellblock into the streets. They had ropes ready and hung all nine men by their necks from lampposts or trees. Then they riddled the bodies with shotgun fire. Manuel Polizzi, having been terrified that he would be murdered by his own men, now hung with the other eight, killed by outsiders. Newspapers around the country congratulated the lynch mob and reported that the criminals were "Given Their Just Dues by an Enraged Mob."[31]

Afterward, the New Orleans police turned up the heat for anyone who looked suspicious. Any man who looked Mediterranean could get picked up just for walking down the street. Sicilians and Italians were rounded up indiscriminately and jailed whenever there was a crime against an Anglo. In fact, as Dimaio tried to leave the Crescent

City, he was arrested near the corner of Canal and Burgundy Streets on charges of vagrancy. He was released after a harsh warning, but as soon as he was out, he was arrested again before he could make it to the train station.[32] This time, the judge, annoyed at seeing a repeat offender so soon, was going to lock him up and keep him for a trial as a habitual criminal. Fortunately, Luzenberg and Pinkerton were still in town. They explained to the judge that the prisoner was wanted for serious crimes in another jurisdiction. Could they please have the miscreant placed in Pinkerton's custody? Pinkerton escorted Dimaio to the train station to make sure he got safely on the train. An exhausted and emaciated Dimaio returned to Philadelphia, received medical care, and then reportedly took a long vacation with his new bride in Atlantic City.

Wanting to get away from the constant police crackdowns, many Sicilians tied to the New Orleans Mafia groups left the South and headed north up the Mississippi to Pittsburgh, Chicago, New York, Indianapolis, Cincinnati, and Cleveland as the nineteenth century came to a close. They landed in cities all over the East and Midwest— everywhere Italian immigrant populations had prosperous economies. One Sicilian, named Antonio Lima, having beaten a murder conviction on appeal, left New Orleans around that time and landed in Ohio.[33] There he could operate under the radar of hapless police who had no idea how to infiltrate the Italian criminal community. And like many of his contemporaries from the hills above Palermo and the streets of Louisiana, Lima set up shop. With a small fruit business in Cincinnati as a front, Lima set his sights on the prosperous Italians in Columbus, Cleveland, and Cincinnati. It became a family affair when he was joined by his son, Salvatore. Their business grew over the next decade. So did their insatiable greed.

CHAPTER 4

SOCIETY OF THE BANANA

The view of the average Blackhander is so morally perverted that
he not only collects tribute from his victims (who pay in fear and
trembling), but he smiles on them benignly, as though to extort, in
addition to their cash, exclamations of sincere gratitude that he
permits them to live.[1]

—Robert Watchcorn

In 1905, Salvatore "Sam" Lima was, to all outward appearances,
living the American dream. The thirty-two-year-old father of four
had his own business in the small industrial town of Marion, forty
miles north of Columbus. Like most of America's industrial belt,
the area was growing quickly. Marion's population doubled from
seventy-five hundred to fifteen thousand between 1898 and 1908
as waves of workers were hired on with the Marion Steam Shovel
Company, a massive corporation that made construction equipment
for America's building boom.[2] For S. Lima's Fruit Commissioners
on 235 North Main Street, there was no shortage of hungry and
well-paid workers who came by daily for fruits and vegetables. In the
storefront of Lima's shop, bunches of bananas hung from the eaves,
and wooden crates offered the day's fresh produce to passersby. Lima
was able to supply fresh produce year-round by purchasing wholesale

from Italian importers who controlled the fruit business from South America and California.

Original stakeout photo shot by Oldfield's team during the Black Hand investigation. Salvatore "Sam" Lima (left) stands in front of his Marion, Ohio, fruit shop along with his family and brother-in-law Sebastian Lima (right). Sam was the leader of the Society of the Banana.

Like many immigrant businesses, S. Lima's was a family affair. Lima's wife, Mary, and his sister, Catarina, paid the fruit suppliers and invoiced the restaurants and shops that bought wholesale. The Lima women likely busied themselves with cleaning, cooking, and organizing the shop's inventory. Sam's brother-in-law, Sebastian, who was married to his sister, Caterina, also had the last name of Lima and was his right-hand man. Sebastian had come to America just a few years before. He looked after the horses and deliveries and was an all-around handyman who sometimes even helped watch Sam Lima's children, the oldest a girl about seven, the youngest a baby boy.

The front of the shop was everything the picture of an American Main Street business was supposed to be. The back of the shop was something else entirely.

In the wall of the rear room, Sam Lima's hidden safe held thousands of dollars in cash. Also in the safe were bundles of letters with coded words and threats, stacks of receipts for post office money orders to Sicily, and a leather-bound ledger listing names and payment amounts. In another book, there was a roster of members of what was called *The Society of the Banana*. At the top of the list was written: "The Directorate: Salvatore Lima, Sebastian Lima, Antonio Lima [Salvatore's father], and Giuseppe Ignoffo." Below the floorboards in the back of the house was more cash; in the walls, even more. And for easy access to the tools of Sam Lima's secret trade, a giant trunk of pistols, shotguns, cartridges, knives, and shiny stilettos with diamond-sharp points.

It was Sunday, a day of rest for most of the businessmen in Marion, Ohio, but not for Lima. He never missed a chance to make money. A few days earlier, he had sent messages to his colleagues to meet in Columbus for the day's mission. He never did business in his hometown. Locals in Marion probably had some idea of Sam Lima's side job, but he steered clear of making victims out of his friends, his customers, and his neighbors in Marion's Italian quarter.

Sam met his brother-in-law, Sebastian, and the two boarded the Toledo & Ohio Central Railroad south to Ohio's capital city. Sam Lima did not look like a criminal. He looked every part the Italian laborer. Even though he was flush with cash hidden in his store, and had huge reserves with his family back in Sicily, he still wore baggy trousers held up by suspenders over a rumpled work shirt. His face didn't reveal his sinister plots either. He actually looked quite harmless. His big round eyes were framed with long lashes. He had chubby cheeks and a sweep of a curl on the top of his head. He clearly loved to eat well, evidenced by a growing middle section mostly hidden by baggy work shirts. Sebastian, a few years younger than Sam, looked far more intimidating. He was actually somewhat shy, but he terrified victims as he stared them down, beady-eyed, his mustache neatly trimmed over a mouth that appeared cemented shut.

After arriving in Columbus, Sam and Sebastian took a streetcar to Italian Village, an area of the city settled by Italian immigrants that was now a thriving suburb. Sam Lima's target today was Mrs. Mary Fasone at 286 East Naghten Street. The fifty-eight-year-old woman lived less than a mile from the great Olentangy River that runs through Columbus. Fasone and her husband, Ignazio, owned the I.O. Fasone and Sons Grocery, a business that sold produce, tobacco, and dry goods.[3] Their home, like Lima's, also doubled as their store. Lima, in his search for new "friends" whom he could coerce into sharing their wealth with him and his business partners, had done his homework. The Fasones were doing quite well.

Near the Fasone store, the Lima brothers-in-law met up with Cologero "Charlie" Vicario, a twenty-nine-year-old baby-faced murderer from Bellefontaine. Vicario and his eighteen-year-old brother Antonio "Tony," also part of the gang, stood out among the other Sicilian mobsters because of their clean-shaven appearance. Rarely at the time did you find a Sicilian without a gigantic mustache. Salvatore Rizzo was also outside the Fasone store for the meet-up. Rizzo, in his early thirties and single, had a full-time job on a section gang on the B&O Railroad line. The railroad job was backbreaking, and Rizzo, who had unsuccessfully dabbled in criminal endeavors his entire young life, found working as one of Lima's henchmen much more to his liking.

The Fasone family business on Naghten Street in Columbus, Ohio, was a target of the Society of the Banana, receiving both Black Hand letters and in-person threatening visits by gang members. The Fasones were deposed and served as witnesses during the trial. Used as a trial exhibit.

Sam Lima knew from his sources that the husband, Ignazio Fasone, would not be around today. As it was Sunday, the store would be closed. Mary Fasone would not know who they were, but she would instantly know what the visit was about. Still, Lima and his colleagues would play it cool. This visit was not just to scare the Fasones into paying extortion demands. This was a reconnaissance mission. Lima's plan was to branch out into the entire Columbus Italian community.

For her part, Mary Fasone had been expecting and dreading this day.

Three weeks earlier, she and her husband had received the first extortion letter.[4] The couple had been lucky up until then. They knew countless Italian immigrants who had been harassed by threatening letters for years, many of them close friends. Many of them paid "tribute" in exchange for their lives. Some paid monthly, some every few months. No one spoke openly of it, but everyone knew. They were doctors, lawyers, shoemakers. There were rich business owners who gave thousands and barely surviving railroad workers forced to forfeit five dollars a week of their pay. Everyone knew of someone who had been killed for refusing. Others walked around with scars on their faces for declining to pay or refusing an invitation to join the criminal rings. Some, like Dr. Vincenzo Purpura, a wealthy Italian physician in Cincinnati, secretly paid off the extortionists. At the same time, he publicly campaigned to shut down immigration from Sicily and supported the death penalty for extortionists.

The letter to the Fasones was postmarked from Dunbar, Pennsylvania, on September 29, 1908, and demanded two thousand dollars.[5] That it was from another state was typical. The letters were never from nearby. The criminals commonly sent a letter "under cover" of another envelope to a colleague or even another victim. The recipient opened the first envelope, which contained instructions to send the enclosed letter from their local post office to the intended victim. The letter might arrive from far away, but the criminal who wrote it could be your next-door neighbor. The Fasones were directed to send a "trustworthy" individual with the money to a specific place by a Pittsburgh bridge. The note was written in flowing cursive signed ominously *The Black Hand*. Ignazio was a strong and stubborn man. He and Mary discussed the letter and what it meant for their future.

They'd worked very hard. Their entire savings would be gone if they paid what was demanded.

They decided to ignore the letter, but they couldn't ignore the threat. They now had to continually look over their shoulders, double lock their doors, and change their daily routines so as not to be targets going to and coming from the store. What they did not do was go to the police. Almost no Italian immigrant ever did. Going to the police was as good as signing your own death warrant. Besides, the police were unable to speak Italian and couldn't even talk to the majority of Italian immigrants. The local cops really had no idea what to do with crime in the Italian neighborhoods.

The Fasones likely hoped they'd have a bit of time to figure out what to do now that they had become targets of the extortionists. But ten days later, on October 9, 1908, another note came from Pittsburgh. *You have not done what you were asked, friend. You must pay us $2,000 or we will come for you. We will cut your heart out and you will die like a dog.*[6]

Mary Fasone was so terrified that she would have paid the money if she could. That kind of cash was almost impossible for any small Italian business to raise on such short notice. It was the equivalent of fifty thousand in 2018 dollars. Even if they were able to borrow money from relatives and pay it, the criminals would just send another demand. The continued extortion game would eventually ruin them. Once again, she and Ignazio ignored the extortionists' demands. Mary lived in fear every day. She desperately wished she wouldn't be home alone when the terrorists finally revealed themselves. Yet there she was.

The four men approached the Fasones' grocery store. They did not try to sneak into the building, but went straight to the door and pulled on the handle. It was locked, of course, because it was Sunday, and the store was closed. The young Charlie Vicario went to the side of the house and pushed on the door of the wagon shed. An iron bar kept him from being able to open the door, so he put his arm through, removed the bolt, and pushed it open. To the delight of the criminals, they found Mary Fasone, very much alone.

Even though she had anticipated this meeting, nothing prepared her for it. Her heart exploded in her chest. Her thoughts raced. She desperately hoped her husband or their son would somehow save her, but she also feared they'd all be killed if they tried. Still, she tried not to appear afraid.[7]

"What do you want?" she demanded of the intruders, as forcefully as she could.

"We came for tobacco," said Lima, toying with her.

"It's Sunday," Fasone replied, icily. "The shop is not open. I can't sell you tobacco, and I can't open the store."

Salvatore Rizzo moved close to Fasone, and just inches from her face he said, "Open the store. We want to come in."

Seeing no way out, Fasone opened up the side door to the shop. Sam Lima, Rizzo, and Vicario pushed their way in.

Fasone knew the visit was not about tobacco, but her instinct told her to play along. She grabbed a package of tobacco from a shelf, and with her hand shaking shoved it toward Lima.

"Here, take this and go."

Lima ignored her. The others stood in a semicircle around her. It was Rizzo who did most of the talking.

"Tell us about your neighbors," Rizzo demanded. "Who lives around here? Which Italians are making money? What are their names? Addresses?"

Fasone tried her best to give as little detail as she could, but she was terribly afraid that if she didn't give them any information, they would have no problem killing her. The three men stared her down. Sam Lima took notes. From behind her interrogators, Mary Fasone saw Sebastian Lima close the gate. The threatening move triggered Fasone's survival instinct. In a fraction of a second, without even thinking, she flew out the store door and startled Sebastian enough that she was able to escape through the gate into the street.[8] With Fasone screaming for help, the four men darted past her and ran in separate directions.

Fasone's getaway didn't rattle the group at all. It was all part of the game of cat and mouse. They had no fear that anyone would call the police, so once they reconvened, they decided to enjoy the scenery. What that meant was they wanted to see how their visit reverberated in the quiet suburb. Sam Lima stood in an alley, the others stood on street corners. And they watched. The neighbors came and went. Within hours, nearly everyone in the neighborhood knew what happened to Mary Fasone. All the passersby noticed the strangers loitering on street corners. All tried to pretend they didn't. And no one called the police.

The terror raining down on the Fasone household was far from over after the visit by Lima and crew. On November 2, 1908, another letter came from Pittsburgh. It said, in essence, pay or die. On December 14, 1908, there was a fourth letter, and again another on January 13, 1909. Each one demanded two thousand dollars payment and threatened the Fasones with death. Finally, after four months of living in constant fear of being murdered, like thousands of other victims, they began to pay.

The same horror the Fasones experienced was happening in Italian communities all across America—a wave of extortion, coercion, and murder, all pointing to the criminal sons of Sicily. And even though it was happening in the new world, the land of opportunity for millions of refugees, this was not a new business model at all. The strategies and methods of the Mafia, Camorra, and what was now known in America as The Black Hand were decades in development. These activities dated back to at least 1861 when Sicily was left to self-govern by a new government in Rome.

The Kingdom of Two Sicilies, consisting of the southern peninsula of modern Italy and the island of Sicily, was ruled by the House of Bourbon from 1815 until 1860. King Victor Emmanuel II of Sardinia united the entire peninsula and surrounding islands into the Kingdom of Italy in 1861. Populations in the northern territories slowly began to feel a sense of combined nationality and pride. A growing middle class took hold, and industry and commerce grew.

Sicily, as well as the area including Naples and its surroundings, was an afterthought in the new country. There was no strong political link to the central government in Rome. In Sicily, the power vacuum left citizens at the mercy of criminal rule by what became known as the Mafia, a term some attribute to a Sicilian playwright.[9] The Mafia infiltrated every aspect and institution on the island. Its members were protected by enabling church leaders and corrupt police. Judges and jailers were bought and paid for. Every type of crime was committed with impunity, and the offenders, if arrested, were never convicted. Any man who stood in the way of the organization was quickly murdered in cold blood.

The members of this self-named "Honorable Society" came from the most destitute regions of Palermo, Sicily's capital city.[10] Recruits were physically tough, fearless, and vicious. They used guerrilla tactics on unsuspecting victims and had no problem committing murder for the slightest offense.

Different groups were loosely organized under various bosses; they committed crimes and extorted money in very creative ways.

Kidnappings, maimings, and murders ran rampant. Members infiltrated every aspect of Sicilian society. The members were obedient to their leaders or were murdered. Groups met in secret, spoke in code, and went completely silent after committing horrific crimes.

A criminal code of honor developed called "Omertà."[11] *No member must give evidence in any court of law against a criminal but must conceal and protect him.* It wasn't only the Mafia rank and file that followed Omertà, but private citizens as well: *If someone kills my husband right in front of me, telling the police who I saw or testifying against his murderer in court means that I will be killed, too.* Once you were in the Mafia's crosshairs and slated for execution, survival was nearly impossible.

Realizing the criminals were becoming all-powerful and ruling the island, in the late 1860s, the Italian government sent troops to Sicily. In the mountains above Palermo, Italian soldiers shot and killed presumed criminals without any due process at all. Those who escaped the death squads feared being captured and imprisoned in this new era of national law enforcement. Staying in Sicily seemed like a losing proposition, so many criminals left for America.

They immigrated by the thousands. The influx of émigrés from the Italian mainland and Sicily was so overwhelming to the United States government in the late 1800s that regular immigration procedures completely fell by the wayside. New Hampshire senator William Chandler testified in 1893 that about seven thousand papers were issued to Italian immigrants in New York City in one month by one judge.[12] The judge looked over each application and signed immigration forms at the rate of two per minute. During the Tammany Hall early years, beginning in 1889 in New York City, the courts allegedly issued sixty-eight thousand naturalization certificates, many of them blank, to be filled out by whoever could afford them. In one New York court, thousands of Italians were naturalized by an interpreter. In 1904, the U.S. Immigration Bureau discovered an Italian counterfeiting operation in New Jersey forging naturalization papers.[13]

Back in Rome, the king of Italy was not happy about the damage to Italy's international reputation done by these emigrant criminals.

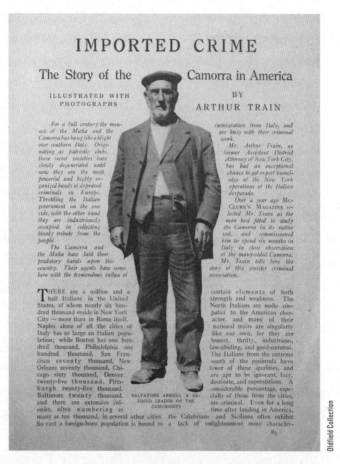

Salvatore Arrigo enjoyed a lifetime career in organized crime in both Italy and the United States. He acted as the first "Boss" of the Society of the Banana and was retired and replaced with Francesco Spadaro by the Society in 1909. He was convicted in 1910 and served his sentence at the Federal Penitentiary at Fort Leavenworth. Sensational articles about The Black Hand were written in magazines of the period. Article from *McClure's Magazine*, 1910.

He preferred that Italy be judged by her useful, industrious sons and daughters. King Victor Emmanuel proclaimed the country would exert her fullest powers to limit emigration to the latter class.[14] However, there appeared to be little done to stem the wave of criminals leaving Sicily.

Many Americans were not happy about the massive influx of Italian-speaking immigrants either. Most didn't differentiate between the upstanding Sicilian and Italian citizens making positive contributions to society and the criminals who preyed upon them. Americans who did distinguish between the groups held a harsh opinion of the southerners. "These filthy paupers massed themselves in certain localities and were classed as Italians though really, they were Sicilians, a people distinct in race, character, and language from the inhabitants of Northern Italy," wrote Margaret Adams in her 1924 doctoral thesis. "This degraded people, refuse of prisons, became in a short time American citizens owing to easy naturalization laws."[15]

One of the sons of Sicily who undoubtedly fell into the category of those tarnishing Italy's international reputation was Sam Lima. His conspirators; his father, the longtime mob boss Antonio Lima, who had come from New Orleans; his brother-in-law, Sebastian Lima; and the directorate of Lima's "Society of the Banana" were not doing Italy any favors either.

While Sam Lima was by far the most motivated Mafioso in his organization in the fall of 1908, he was not the group's official leader. The position of de facto "Godfather" was held by the group's founder, Salvatore Arrigo, a sixty-seven-year-old ex-con living in Cincinnati. Arrigo immigrated to the United States around 1880 with an already long history of crime in the mountains above Palermo. He soon earned a criminal pedigree in the United States as well. He started out with a couple of fruit stands in 1876 in Louisville and Cynthiana, Kentucky.

He had a fruit stand in Cleveland for a few years. When he set up shop in Washington, D.C., in 1884, Treasury agents found that bananas and apples weren't Arrigo's only concern, and he was arrested for counterfeiting. He was convicted in federal court and served two years at the Auburn maximum-security prison in upstate New York.[16] After that, Arrigo settled down in Cincinnati, where the big city afforded him enough anonymity to start from scratch.

Counterfeiting was a risky game if one wanted to stay out of prison, so Arrigo decided on a career change. This time, he'd go into the protection business. He'd make Italian businessmen pay him to make sure that they didn't get their legs broken, a knife slash to the face, or perhaps something worse.

Over time, Arrigo's business grew. He met other Sicilians with similar operations and began to form coalitions. He enlisted the ruthless Antonio Lima—Lima had been a customs agent in Sicily who had escaped prison to land in America and pursue a life of crime across the United States and Canada. Arrigo combined forces with the baby-faced Vicario brothers in Bellefontaine, Ohio. He connected with the dashing fruit vendor Pippino Galbo in Meadville, Pennsylvania. He found Orazio Runfola, a curly-haired stogie maker with a quaint shop in Pittsburgh. He recruited Severio Ventola, a fellow ex-con counterfeiter, from Cincinnati, and a handful of others from Buffalo, Cleveland, Toledo, Dennison, and Columbus.

Together they embarked on a reign of terror. Their coalition gave them the ability to maneuver even more secretly, to leave a trail complicated and convoluted, so that they were never in fear of being found out. They did their research on the best possible victims. They developed plans of attack. They recruited young Sicilian men from West Virginia, Maryland, and Pennsylvania as foot soldiers and hit men. Those who didn't join were killed. In the back room of Marcino's saloon in Columbus, they carved victims' faces for refusing to pay extortion demands, creating walking billboards in Italian neighborhoods announcing their serious commitment to their mission.

Family photo of Annunziata Cancilla and Antonio Lima, parents of Salvatore "Sam" Lima, circa 1900. Annunziata Cancilla Lima was the recipient of dozens of money orders sent to Sicily by Sam Lima. Frank Oldfield obtained an arrest warrant for Antonio Lima, but Antonio disappeared before Oldfield could apprehend him. Antonio escaped to Sicily and was never caught. Courtesy of Melanie Butera, DVM (descendant of Sebastian Lima).

Around 1906, a New York reporter from the *Herald Tribune* coined a general term for Italian criminals based on a case in which a death threat letter was signed *The Black Hand*.[17] Afterward, the term was adopted by different Mafia gangs as well as by copycat criminals looking to place blame on the Italians. Although "Black Hand" was a term used broadly in sensational news articles about Italian immigrant crimes, an organized crime ring was something that almost no one in law enforcement believed existed on American soil. "Experienced policemen say there is no Black Hand: that it is simply a convenient name adopted by any group of Italian criminals who wish to strike terror into their prospective victims," reported the *New York Times* in 1910.[18] "None of these groups, the old-line policeman say, has any relation with each other, and the impression that there is a national or international society of criminals under that name is nonsense."

To Salvatore Arrigo and his business partners, who also used The Black Hand as the signatory on extortion letters, American cops were a joke. They were able to terrorize their fellow immigrants only because law enforcement was so ignorant about their activities. It wasn't only the local cops; federal law enforcement like the Secret Service, formed in 1865, and U.S. Marshals, formed in 1789, also denied there were organized criminal gangs in America.[19] With government forces blind to crimes in the Italian neighborhoods, the gang's web grew. Still, they played it safe, communicating among themselves in code to better protect their organization.

Arrigo, with his own fruit shop, baptized his successful criminal ring The Society of the Banana. It was a name for internal use only, of course, as he had no desire for mainstream publicity. Keeping with the theme, the group adopted a lexicon from the produce business for their clandestine communications.[20] A "car load of lemons" was a large amount of money. "Boxes of lemons" meant a smaller amount. When one member wanted to tell another that he'd sent an extortion letter to a certain mark, he wrote or wired, *So and so is very old. I have just consulted a physician and that he has advised to eat bananas.*

By 1908, after a long and successful career in crime, Arrigo was slowing down. At sixty-seven years old, his hair was shaggy and gray, his face deeply weathered, and he walked slowly with a hunched back and a cane. The Society members began to notice that Arrigo was starting to lack ingenuity and drive as well. He cared less about money, and more about wine, women, and pasta. With the threat of the Society losing its stranglehold on the region, senior members overwhelmingly agreed that Sam Lima was a natural choice to take the leadership role.

Lima's promotion to what was the equivalent of the Society of the Banana CEO couldn't have come too soon. He was getting tired of all the small fish on Arrigo's roster. Lima was not interested in extorting thirty dollars from a railroad worker here or forty dollars from a longshoreman there. Lima had bigger vision and bigger greed, and he did not shy away from terror or violence. He was Al Capone at a time when Al Capone was still a ten-year-old causing trouble on Brooklyn playgrounds.

Lima did not bother separating his Black Hand activities from his fruit store operation. He managed both from his desk in the back room of his shop. A thick blotter underneath his stationery recorded the pressure of his pen as he wrote. Lima's handwriting was not elegant like the writing of Pippino Galbo, the dynamic Pennsylvania mobster who obviously had some postprimary education. Lima's writing was blocky. His *d*'s and *p*'s were square and awkward. His cartoons were silly-looking skulls with black dot pupils inside comically round eyeballs; a decorative dagger piercing a cartoon human heart with drips of blood. Sometimes, though, he was quite eloquent and must have been rather pleased with his prose:

We have silently removed emperors, kings and princes and have been as fearless of apprehension as if we were the wind sighing in the trees

The Society of the Banana distributed its ill-gotten profits through innocent-looking checks and money orders written on local banks and mailed to the cover businesses of its members in the United States and to their families in Italy. These checks are written from the Lima brothers' business accounts at the Marion County Bank (Ohio).

90

at night. We revel in bloodshed, we smile at tears and pleadings and our field of operation is bounded only by the universe. We scoff at the police. We push them aside as we would a child.

No matter the style of his writing, it proved effective. Fred Cianciolo, a successful Cincinnati fruit dealer, paid several thousand dollars on penalty of death for himself and family. Cianciolo originally refused, but changed his mind after a bomb exploded in the doorway of his home. Joseph Annarino, another Cincinnati produce dealer, made payments on a ten-thousand-dollar demand under the threat his child would be kidnapped.[21]

Once Sam Lima had a mark on the books and the letters were sent, he would stop at nothing to track the victim down. After Augustino Anario's home was dynamited for his failure to make an extortion payment, Anario left Columbus and went back to Sicily, where he received another "Black Hand" letter at his home in Palermo. Lima also had no problem going after friends who crossed him. Pete Marcino's saloon in Columbus was a favorite spot for the gang to play cards and gamble in the back room. One day, Lima's cut apparently wasn't what it should have been. That night, the saloon exploded, sending Marcino and his wife and baby running for their lives. The saloon was reduced to rubble.

Then there were those who paid the final price. In January 1909, Antonio Nuzzo ignored the threatening letters. A week later, a man, possibly someone he knew, offered him a banana on the street. Nuzzo began to froth at the mouth and went into severe convulsions. He was dead that evening. Another victim, shot to death in front of his family after refusing to pay the extortion demands, was being prepared for burial in a Columbus funeral home. To make very sure the family knew how serious The Black Hand was about Omertà, someone snuck in and poured kerosene on the coffin and set it ablaze.

Under Lima's unofficial control throughout 1908 into 1909, the society thrived like never before. Each member's cut of the proceeds was bigger than the last. Most members sent money back to Sicily in amounts that surely piqued the interest of the postal clerks. In one month alone, veteran boss and Sam's father Antonio Lima sent nineteen international money orders, each for one hundred dollars, to his wife (and

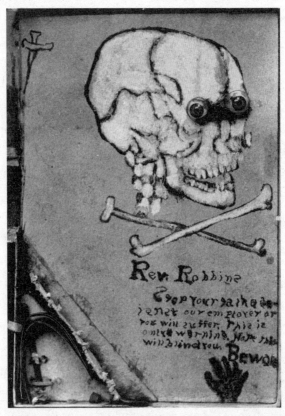

Flash bomb sent by the Society of the Banana to Reverend Robbins of the Lincoln Baptist Church of Cincinnati. Note the actual human eyes attached to the skull-and-bones graphic painted on the box. The reverend roused the ire of the Society due to his fire-and-brimstone sermons identifying and criticizing the criminal gambling and prostitution operations owned by some of the members.
The flash bomb was used by Post Office inspectors as a trial exhibit.

Sam's mother), Annunziata Cancilla, in Palermo. There was so much work that Sam Lima hired subcontractors. He paid Salvatore Luicini to write extortion letters. When Luicini got sloppy and was arrested for a petty crime, Lima hired Luicini's teenage daughter, Maria, to do the job.

Lima's reach was growing, and he was become infamous in the criminal underground for his tactics and power. Some on the outside who dared call him out lived to regret it. A Baptist minister named Reverend Robbins of the Lincoln Baptist Church took the Sicilians to task for their criminal ways and the sins of liquor, gambling, and various other vices. He published his sermons in various Ohio newspapers. Lima was furious. The owners of pubs, liquor distributors, and whorehouses were some of his best "friends." Lima did not want God or any of his minions getting between him and his percentage of the profits. One Sunday, Robbins noticed an olive-skinned man seething in the back pew in his Cincinnati church. The following day, the reverend received a delivery from his postman. He opened the package to find a box with a drawing of a skull on the cover. In place of the skull's drawn eye sockets were human eyeballs. *"Stop your sermons against our employer or you will suffer. . . . Beware. I hope this will blind you."* A clerk at the church opened the box. Inside, a charge ignited packed flash powder, exploding and burning the man's face and hands.

On November 5, 1908, Pippino Galbo sent a letter to Sam Lima from the post office in Meadville, Pennsylvania. "Your next call will be nothing more than to reorganize and make yourself the boss," Galbo wrote. "In case you do not wish to be the boss, we will approve of your choice at any time you make it known." Lima's uncontested leadership of the Society of the Banana was soon to be official. He felt the time was finally right to go after the biggest mark of his career: the Banana Kings. Charles and John Amicon of Columbus had become millionaires with their colossal fruit business, called Amicon Brothers & Company. The brothers were intelligent, fair-minded, and well-respected members of the community. They were devoted to their wives and children and gave copious amounts of money to charity and the local Catholic church. They were exactly the type of men whom Sam Lima despised.

Even worse in Lima's eyes, John Amicon had been very vocal around Columbus after Lima's terrifying visit to Mary Fasone. The Fasone shop was just three blocks from the Amicon Brothers' store, and the couple were friends and customers of the Amicons. Amicon publicly derided The Black Hand and called on friends, neighbors, and colleagues not to pay the extortionists. He chided the Blackhanders as lazy cowards, losers too ignorant and pathetic to work, instead leeching off hardworking men. The Black Hand gave all Italians a bad name. "Let me be very clear," Amicon said to anyone who would listen. "If anyone tries to get money from me, they will have to kill me first."[22]

This seemed to infuriate Lima. He just could not bear the thought that John Amicon was not afraid of him. He had to call Amicon's bluff. He sent off a letter to Giovanni Amicone, John Amicon's Italian name, that sealed Lima's fate. In his desperation to show John Amicon who was boss, Lima would set in motion the toppling of his empire and expose his international crime syndicate to the world.

CHAPTER 5

THE INSPECTOR

In March 1899, thirty-two-year-old Frank Oldfield left for Chatta- nooga, Tennessee, for his first assignment as a United States Post Office inspector. While he was quite excited about the job, he was not happy about the post. Although the southern city experienced a thriving postwar industrial boom and Republicans were in the majority after pushing out leftover Confederate political regimes, to Oldfield, Chattanooga felt like a backwater town. Rather than move his family to a city he couldn't see making a future in, he decided to commute home on occasion. About once a month, he'd take a twenty-hour train ride to spend time with Margaret Galena, who was busy with a toddler and a baby on the way. Oldfield hoped for a transfer up north in the next year or so.

Out of his element for the first time in his life, Oldfield tried to find his bearings. It turned out that his new job had a lot of what Oldfield didn't much care for: *rules*. There were guidelines, expectations, and procedures. There were documents to read, forms to fill out, and reports to detail. There was a long list of things to learn. And although he'd been a mediocre student in school, in the art of investigation, he excelled. He studied the intricate elements of mail fraud. He learned the ins and outs of past cases solved by famous inspectors. He learned how to dig up clues and tease out confessions. He reviewed burglar- ies and train car robberies cracked by lauded inspectors. Then he took a class in the use and care of firearms, a class that emphasized defensive shooting.

Frank's job was to investigate any crime that used the mail, but inspectors also did a fair number of internal investigations. He was on call twenty-four hours a day. His duty was to go wherever he was needed. He had the authority to enlist any law enforcement agency he felt could help, including local cops, Secret Service, and U.S. Marshals. He could even hire private detectives.

The government was not stingy with the inspectors' budgets. For instance, in 1922, $424,000 of travel expenses was budgeted to solve "important fraud cases."[1] Frank was likely most happy to learn that there was no need to go to the local inspector-in-charge for permission to start an investigation, and that there was often a great amount of travel involved. This would get him out of the office and out from under the thumb of those who had power over him. He loved the freedom of being on the road, the anonymity.

There was a downside. Every day, he was required to submit a report on his work, detailing where he traveled, what he did, and his plans for the following three days. The inspectors-in-charge argued that if they didn't get the reports, they couldn't transmit vital information or reassign agents to more urgent work. The inspector-in-charge would also worry that his agent might have met with disaster. Worst of all, Frank was told, *Failure to submit daily reports may result in severe disciplinary action.* Frank despised writing reports.

Feeling controlled by another human being tied Oldfield's stomach in knots. It may have been a Napoleon complex, as he was barely 145 pounds and scarcely five foot four inches tall. Even so, having to constantly report to a supervisor wasn't the worst part of his new job. What caused Oldfield the most consternation was a dire clause in his new job description: Post Office inspectors must maintain political neutrality. Frank Oldfield, dedicated disciple of the Republican Party of Howard County, Maryland, from the time he was a teenager, was forbidden to actively engage in political campaigns. He must resign from his chairmanship of the Howard County Republican Central Committee and his seat on the state committee.

At the time, Chattanooga was the southern headquarters for the Post Office Inspection Service.[2] Frank had a new office in the stately federal office building on East Eleventh Street. The pay was superb. His salary was sixteen hundred dollars a year for a minimum fifty-hour workweek that could easily go to twenty-four hours a day when he was on assignment. He spent money only on nice clothes and cigars. Food was an afterthought, and if he ate while on assignment, he expensed his meals. The rest of his salary he sent home to Margaret Galena. As the newest investigator on the job, though, Oldfield was passed up for many of the larger and more interesting cases. He worked an investigation where contractors repainted mailboxes they'd just painted and the postmaster paid the tab with the government's money in return for a kickback. A postal carrier tried to bribe a Post Office inspector with fifty dollars to get an inspector job. One unique crime out of the Chattanooga office involved an expensive watch stolen in China and recovered in Alabama.[3] He mostly looked into complaints of mail being lifted from someone's mailbox, and he was tasked with developing rural routes in the middle of nowhere, America, a carryover from the Constitutional Post of William Goddard.

While Frank did learn a great deal from the other investigators, including techniques that would help him later in his career, neither his heart nor his mind was on the job. He wanted to be back in Ellicott City. He missed his wife and two sons, but what was nearly impossible for Frank to be without on a daily basis was his politics. In August, Oldfield's brother Clarence, now a customs official in Baltimore, threw in his hat for Frank's soon-to-be-vacated chair on the Howard County Central Committee. (Frank had been emotionally unable to resign from the post and kept his chairmanship even after leaving for Tennessee, much to the annoyance of his political rivals. However, if he could make sure that Clarence got the seat, he would officially resign.) The letter from Clarence made Frank feel isolated and out of the game. How could he possibly not be there for his brother, his best friend and cohort since *forever*. If Clarence won the election, the Oldfields would keep their influence and help push their candidates for office all the way up to the governorship. At the time Frank had signed his bonded employment contract and promised to stay out of politics, the high salary temporarily eased the pain. Now it felt as if he'd made a deal with the devil. The U.S. Department of the Post Office trapped him in golden handcuffs.

Without so much as a word to his bosses in Tennessee, on Wednesday, August 9, 1899, Frank hopped on a Western Atlantic railcar, flashed his inspector badge to ride for free, and headed home to Ellicott City. The town was abuzz. As usual, Republican factions were brutally campaigning against each other ahead of the primary election the coming Saturday. Frank jumped right into the fray, going door-to-door, pushing for Clarence's candidacy and the candidates he and his family supported. Unfortunately for Frank, news got around to his enemies that he was back in town. His political rivals also knew that Post Office inspectors were not allowed to actively engage in politics.

On August 10, Oldfield received a telegram from William E. Cochran, the chief Post Office inspector in Washington, D.C.: *Return to your post in Chattanooga. Immediately.* Frank was so furious he thought he would explode. He didn't want to think about going back, and he didn't want to think about what it would mean if he didn't. He decided to ignore the telegram for a night and continue campaigning, harder than he ever had. He went about town virulently denouncing the Republican primary opponents and building up Clarence for the central committee post. He especially went after the Speaker of the Maryland House of Delegates, Sydney Mudd, whom Oldfield despised. He was sure that Mudd was behind his getting recalled to Tennessee.

1904 photo of the staff of the U.S. Customs House in Baltimore, Maryland. Customs Inspector Clarence Oldfield (front, second from left), Margaret Galena Oldfield (wife of Frank Oldfield; front, third from right), and William Hamilton Oldfield (son of Frank Oldfield; front, right, sitting on counter).

For his part, Mudd denied having a hand in exposing Oldfield to the postal authorities. "I have never sought to have Mr. Oldfield dismissed or transferred, nor did I request that he be directed to return to his work in Tennessee," the Speaker told the *Baltimore Sun*.

"While he has always opposed me, I have done nothing to injure him with the Post Office Department."[4] While many assumed that Mudd wanted Oldfield fired, the truth was that Mudd wanted him out of Maryland. It would be much better for Mudd's side if the powerful rabble-rouser for the opposition kept his job in Tennessee.

Frank couldn't decide what to do. The primary election was two days away. He could stay and campaign, but doing so would probably get him fired. Somehow, Hamilton Oldfield convinced his son that the situation was dire. Frank needed to leave town before the election or risk his very new and very well-paid career. While Hamilton likely breathed a sigh of relief watching the train roll out of Ellicott's B&O station with his sullen son on the car, it was too late. Back in Tennessee, Paul E. Williams, inspector-in-charge in Chattanooga, with pressure from the chief Post Office inspector, was filling out Frank's dismissal forms.

Clarence lost the election, but he still held a seat on the Howard County Republican Committee.[5] On August 14, 1899, furious about the outing of his brother to the Post Office authorities five days earlier, Clarence introduced a resolution to the Howard County group. The wording sounded like something Frank probably wrote himself.

"We condemn the infamous conduct of those persons who have participated in the ignominious attempt, by them made, to disenfranchise and prevent one of our ablest and truest Republican workers from expressing the right and privilege of the elective franchise," Clarence read out loud, took a breath, and finished the sentence, "and deplore the fact that such cowardly and un-American principle has prevailed to the extent of depriving us of his presence here at the beginnings of a campaign wherein the common enemy is to be met."

After his six-month stint with the world's most elite detective service, Frank came back home to Ellicott City. If he was embarrassed or felt like a failure, he didn't show it. Every morning he washed, put on his perfectly fitted suit, combed his hair with a perfect part on the left, and went to the barber for a shave and mustache trim. It was as if he had never left.

Rather than keep a low profile, Oldfield made sure that he had a say in all the important bills introduced in the Maryland General Assembly. He also made sure to be elected as a delegate to the national Republican convention.[6]

After the legislative session ended in the summer of 1900, things got quiet around Howard County, and Oldfield likely realized he'd blown a good thing. He had kids to feed, and Margaret Galena, pregnant with a third child, was not one to live frugally. She loved china and fancy dresses. She adored dressing up and taking the carriage to dine in Ellicott City, Baltimore, and Washington. She loved to travel. Frank was running out of money. He went to his father for help. Hamilton, always hoping that there would be a tipping point that would keep Frank on a stable career path, pulled some strings and was able to get his thirty-three-year-old son one final chance. On February 15, 1901, Frank Oldfield's employee personnel pages were opened from the official Record Book of Inspectors. The word *REMOVED* was crossed out and underneath was scribbled *Reinstated*. It shows he took a four-hundred-dollar-per-year pay cut.

This time, Oldfield was sent west to Ohio to report to the Cincinnati Post Office. Frank and Margaret Galena packed up their three boys and moved the family to Athens, a university town with rolling hills that reminded Oldfield of Ellicott City. He rented a brand-new three-story brick house high above town on North Congress Street, bought the lot next door, and started to build a fine, stately home. Both house lots had expansive backyards leading to a woody ravine below where the boys could play all day long. Then he went to find a place to live near his assignment location at the United States Custom House and Post Office in Cincinnati. Like many of his fellow Post Office inspectors, Oldfield set up a family home in a different city from his work headquarters. Being involved in so many criminal arrests was a dangerous way to make a living, and many inspectors received threats to themselves and their families long after criminals were convicted.

Margaret Galena was not worried about living alone even though she was far away from her family back in Maryland. While the situation may not have been ideal for some wives, Mrs. Frank Oldfield thrived. Between her husband's high profile in Maryland politics and his prestigious job as a Post Office inspector, Margaret Galena lived large. She socialized with wives of high political leaders and was invited to all the best parties. By all accounts, she lived a life of luxury. Margaret Galena was not what you would call beautiful. She was a solidly built woman who loved to eat and each year added a few more pounds. She fancied herself a bit of a princess and wore long taffeta skirts, wide flowing capes, and ornate hats of the current style.

While her husband was away during the week, Margaret Galena often received cards and letters with romantic poems in Frank's flowing penmanship. On the weekends when he wasn't traveling for an investigation, Frank came home to Athens to be with his family. As much as he loved being home, Athens was a sleepy town. Plus, Margaret Galena dragged him to every social event she could, which was not to his liking. On Monday morning, he relished being back at work in the Custom House and Post Office building. Just entering the massive four-story Gothic structure must have made him feel powerful and confident.

In Ohio, Oldfield was given much more autonomy and far better cases than he'd had in Chattanooga. He still despised all the paperwork that went with the job. But the truth was, for Oldfield, being a federal lawman fit his mindset and his lifestyle. At work, his eye for detail converged with a chaotic mind that could work multiple inquiries at once and compartmentalize them all. He showed up for work each morning looking as if he'd stepped out of a men's fashion catalogue. He was meticulous about his clothing, his hygiene, and his appearance. His office was something else altogether. On his desk were his trusted tools: a big magnifying glass, a pair of fragile wire-rimmed reading glasses, his derby hat that made him look a few inches taller, and a giant ashtray with an almost always smoldering cigar. Papers and notebooks and reports covered every surface. He couldn't care less about keeping his office organized.

When Frank investigated a crime, he often went undercover. And with carte blanche to plan his own strategies, he came up with a variety of clever ideas to catch criminals. Frank made Margaret Galena homicidally furious after one of his antics. To bust a notorious robber who stole thousands of dollars from mail pouches on a mail train car, Frank decided to go along, looking like a typical father out for a ride on the train. To complete the picture, he brought along his second son. William Hamilton was four years old at the time. When the robber saw Oldfield, smelled a lawman, and realized he'd been caught, the sight of the father and son gave him such pause that he offered his wrists without a fight. On the ride back, Hamilton sat wide-eyed across from his father and the handcuffed prisoner.

Many of the investigations Frank worked were internal to the Post Office. Oldfield tracked down a rural letter carrier stealing money and packages in Kentucky. He was involved in capturing several postal employees who were stealing money from Post Office ledgers. It was much more exciting than mapping out rural postal routes. He enjoyed the internal investigations and found them challenging, but they weren't usually the biggest crimes. Six months into his time in

Cincinnati, in the fall of 1902, Oldfield was assigned his first big file. Something shady was going on with the Brandt-Dent Automatic Cashier Company out of Wisconsin. For some reason, a deal was made whereby 253 cash registers, each costing $150, sat collecting dust in post offices across the country. It appeared that a few prominent people in New York were involved, and there were rumors of bribes and kickbacks going to some Post Office higher-ups.

During some of Frank Oldfield's investigations, he brought along his second son, William Hamilton, and his brother Clarence. This 1907 photo was taken on the shore of the Niagara River in Buffalo, New York. Back row: Clarence Oldfield, left; Frank Oldfield, right. Front row: William Hamilton Oldfield, left; two unknown Post Office inspectors, right.

Assistant Postmaster General Joseph Bristow was assigned to conduct a widespread investigation under direct order of President Teddy Roosevelt. Because local officials might be implicated in the scandal, Bristow appointed an outsider, Frank Oldfield from Cincinnati, to dig into the Brandt-Dent Cashier case. Oldfield left Cincinnati for New York City. As was typical when inspectors worked in other locations, he set up an office. In the City Hall building in lower Manhattan, the federal government rented the third and fourth floors for the Post Office, the U.S. district attorney for Southern New York, and other federal agencies. The building, an ornate Victorian monstrosity designed by architect Alfred B. Mullett, looked like a wedding cake with a bulbous roof and was considered a giant eyesore. It was also completely unwieldy to use as a post office. Frank didn't mind. His new digs suited him fine.

Some Washington lawmakers believed the Brandt-Dent Automatic Cashier scandal was part of widespread corruption in multiple Post Office departments. Since 1893, money had been disappearing. Over a decade, it appeared that inside and outside players had swindled the public coffers out of millions. Corruption was something Oldfield loathed, both with lawmakers and with civil servants. He could understand why someone would make underhanded deals to gain power. In fact, some of his best political ploys were not executed with the utmost scruples. But to Frank, money was something that anyone could get. Money was easy. Money wasn't important to him, so he found it sordid that men would break the law for financial gain.

Oldfield started interviewing postal clerks about the cash registers. They couldn't stand the complicated Brandt machines, they said, and couldn't figure out how to use them. Some were broken, and some had never been taken out of the packaging.[7] Oldfield sat down with Brandt-Dent bookkeepers and audited company records. There were thousands of documents. While he had never been much for numbers in school, it turned out he was an excellent auditor of complicated financial schemes. After several weeks on the job, he and Frank Little, a Brooklyn inspector assigned to work with him, found a smoking gun linked to some very big names.

Frank was thrilled. It appeared that a U.S. congressman from Brooklyn named Edmund Driggs had taken a bribe of $12,500 to convince his buddies at the Post Office to order 253 machines. Part of the money ended up in the bank account of the assistant United States district attorney for the Southern District of New York, Ernest E. Baldwin, who was also the company attorney for Brandt-Dent, and whose son-in-law was a salesman for the company.

When the news broke that their machines were part of a widespread scandal in the Post Office, Edward J. Brandt, the company president who'd won awards for his automatic cashier design (even though it didn't work well in actuality), signed a written order for Oldfield and Little: *The firm of Boothby & Baldwin, of which Ernest E. Baldwin is a member, must give the inspectors access to any papers in their possession bearing upon the subject.*[8]

Oldfield and Little shared an office just one floor away from where Assistant District Attorney Baldwin (who also retained his private practice, Boothby & Baldwin) conducted business for his federal government work. They took the stairs to the floor below and barged into Baldwin's office.

"There are certain supplies that were purchased by the Post Office from the Brandt-Dent company that we wish to trace," Oldfield said icily, handing the letter to Baldwin.

Baldwin knew who Oldfield was. It was a poorly kept secret that there was an inspector from Cincinnati in the building poking around. He snatched the letter and read it quickly. The attorney's face turned red.

"You need to get the hell out of my office. *Now!*"

Oldfield was used to getting the information he wanted and told the attorney in no uncertain terms that he was not leaving.[9] "We have evidence you're involved in a matter of corruption with the United States Post Office," Oldfield said.

Baldwin was furious. "I have nothing to do with this. You're a God damn liar."

Oldfield was about to lose it. There was nothing he hated more than being called names.

Feeling helpless to deescalate the situation, Inspector Little ran down the hall to get Baldwin's boss. The U.S. district attorney, Henry Burnett, a former Union army general in the Civil War now in his sixties, was a giant man who walked with a cane. Burnett tried his best to make peace between the two. Oldfield and Baldwin ignored Burnett and continued to hurl insults. Both looked about to come to blows. Finally, Burnett got a federal marshal from down the hall, who came and ordered Oldfield to get out.

Oldfield still refused. "I'm here on government business, and I have every right to be here."

The marshal and Burnett finally succeeded in getting Oldfield to go. Little was waiting outside down the hall, trying to stay out of the fray and playing good cop.

With the nasty meeting over, and Oldfield and Little gone, Baldwin and Burnett started out for lunch. When they got off the elevator on the ground floor, Oldfield was there waiting for them. He demanded an apology from Baldwin. But Baldwin just stomped past him.

Inspector Little probably thought Oldfield would drop it after a while. But he'd never worked with Oldfield before. He didn't know Oldfield's history. From the time Frank was a small boy, he could never let an insult go unpunished. Showing disrespect to Frank Oldfield infused him with a need for blood.

Ninety minutes later, Frank was still stewing. He left his office and went down to the lobby to wait for Baldwin to return from lunch. When

Baldwin walked in, Oldfield was immediately in his face. Baldwin put his hand in his pocket, and Oldfield yelled, accusing Baldwin of drawing a knife. It was a ruse. Oldfield wanted an excuse to start a fight.

The next second, Oldfield's fist shot like a bullet toward Baldwin's face. Baldwin dodged and Oldfield hit him hard in the chest.[10] The attorney fell back, then quickly retaliated with a blow to Oldfield's jaw.

The *New York Times* reported the rest from eyewitness accounts:

> Men and women who happened into the east corridor of the Post Office at one o'clock yesterday afternoon were surprised to see a rather small-sized man with black hair and mustache and another rather small-sized man with red hair and mustache, rolling about over the marble floor in angry embrace. Over the writhing antagonists towered a tall, distinguished-looking man with gray hair and mustache, who waved his cane authoritatively and called upon the contestants to "let go."[11]
>
> Half a dozen watchmen and other officials of the Federal Building were soon on the scene and pulled the fighters apart by main strength. Then it was learned that he of the red hair was Assistant United States District Attorney Ernest E. Baldwin, and his antagonist was Post Office Inspector J. F. Oldfield of Cincinnati. The tall man who had stood over them was United States District Attorney Burnett.

When the combatants were finally torn apart, Oldfield was bruised and bloodied and had a large lump on his jaw. Baldwin's eye was swollen shut. General Burnett thought he might charge Oldfield with assault, but after a brief discussion with Oldfield in low voices in the corridor, Burnett chose to avoid any legal procedure. Oldfield walked away at his normal clip without uttering a word about the incident. But there is no doubt that on his face appeared a highly satisfied grin.

By the time Oldfield's bruises and cuts healed, the federal grand jury had delivered fifty indictments for corruption in the United States Post Office. Nearly half were due to the work of Oldfield and Little. The alleged criminals ranged from a former postmaster general to a lowly clerk. There were both Republicans and Democrats indicted. Oldfield and Little testified to the grand jury about their findings in the Brandt-Dent investigation. It turned out to be one of dozens of kickback schemes orchestrated in the highest ranks of the Post Office procurement office: the Division of Salaries and Allowances. Frank and Little, with the help of other investigators, found that over a decade, Secretary George W. Beavers, head of that division, gave away contracts worth millions to buy worthless merchandise. Beavers raised salaries for his cohorts far over what they should have made. He over-ordered things post offices didn't need. On top of the Brandt-Dent machines, he bought more than a thousand Bundy Time Recorder clocks that went unused. Once, seventy-five clocks appeared in one post office. He bought money counters that didn't work and hundreds of Elliott and Hatch typewriters that sat idle. Beavers was by no means alone. First Assistant Postmaster General Perry S. Heath received $20,000 in Doremus Company stock for buying one hundred canceling machines and promising to order three hundred more.[12] The chief of the Free-Mail Delivery Department, Arnold Machen, got $26,000 from Goff Fasteners after signing a $130,000 contract. The fasteners were supposed to hold a mailbox to a post, but they didn't work at all. Indictments piled up for conspiracy against the government, bribery, and accepting bribes. On September 9, 1903, the worst offender in the widespread scandal, George W. Beavers, turned himself in.[13] Days later, he unexpectedly took a plea deal and confessed to one count of defrauding the government. His sentence was two years in prison.[14] On November 29, Fourth Assistant Postmaster General Joseph Bristow released his final report.[15] The corruption, it was found, "began in 1893 and continued until stopped by this investigation." Bristow said that corrupt officials and their business partners embezzled an estimated $300,000 to $400,000, an insignificant amount in comparison with the real losses to the government that handed millions in taxpayer dollars to corrupt contractors.

Oldfield was not satisfied. Assistant District Attorney Baldwin, whom he'd tackled in the City Hall Post Office corridor, was not indicted. In the end, Oldfield didn't have enough evidence for the grand jury.[16] He and Little did, however, drive a nail into Congressman Driggs's political career. The Brooklyn lawmaker, who'd received $12,500 from the Brandt-Dent deal, was ordered to pay a $10,000 fine and spend one day in jail. He arrived in the wardens' office at 3:00 p.m., smoked cigars and played chess, then left a minute after midnight.[17] Oldfield was happy to be part of putting an end to Driggs's political aspirations, but he would have loved to see him go to prison for a good long time.

The team of inspectors, who deciphered the complex web of corruption, received a lot of recognition. "I cannot speak in too high praise of the industry and intelligence of the Inspectors and their loyalty to the interests of the service," read Bristow's report, which came out at the end of 1903. "The success of the investigation is largely due to them. They have sought the truth with eagerness and skill. No accounts have been too intricate for them to unravel, no labor too burdensome to undertake.[18] On Bristow's list of lauded investigators was *John Frank Oldfield, Cincinnati*.

President Teddy Roosevelt, who'd called for the investigation, said he believed the arrests and convictions purged the agency of wrongdoers. However, there was a feeling in the inspector ranks and in the news media that the postmaster general, Henry Clay Payne, shared some of the blame and perhaps colluded with some of those caught in the sting.[19] Payne was also the chairman of the Republican Party, and in the end, Roosevelt did not remove his ally from his powerful post of postmaster general, which was a cabinet position at the time.[20] In all likelihood, Roosevelt was mistaken about the corrupt players in the agency being completely cleaned out.

While most of the feedback from fellow inspectors was also congratulatory, Frank unexpectedly caught the ire of Abraham Holmes, his colleague in the Cincinnati office. Holmes, who was senior to Oldfield and nearly twenty years older, was given only a small role in the massive internal fraud investigations, and Bristow's report didn't name Holmes at all except in a list in the appendix of all the inspectors involved.[21] If the omission bothered Holmes, Oldfield didn't know it. What did bother Holmes, though, and what he had a hard time concealing his disdain for, was how Oldfield conducted himself on the job.

Holmes was the polar opposite of Oldfield. He was calm and thoughtful. He was described as speaking softly and having kind eyes. He was bald, with overgrown sideburns that came down to his chin. He paid intense attention to detail and was fastidious about rules and regulations. He had a stellar reputation for cracking cases, and at the turn of the century was known as one of the best inspectors in the service.[22] Admirers called him "Old Abe" or "Sherlock Holmes," after the famous fictional detective.

Holmes had a reputation for never sensationalizing his work. He did not approve of Oldfield's antics. Getting headlines for punching out suspects was tawdry and embarrassing. This was supposed to be the silent service. Oldfield was an egotistical hothead who thumbed his nose at rules and procedures. His desk looked like a tornado had come through his office. He turned in sloppy reports late or never. His expense reports never added up to the penny, as Holmes's did. And yet, Frank Oldfield was quickly becoming one of the most famous and lauded inspectors in the United States Post Office Inspection Service. Frank Oldfield was Abraham Holmes's worst nightmare.

Colonel Abraham R. Holmes had a distinguished career with the U.S. Post Office Department. While inspector-in-charge of the Cincinnati Division, responsible for Indiana, Kentucky, and Ohio, Inspector Holmes managed Inspector Oldfield's team during the 1909 investigation of the Society of the Banana. Unknown newspaper photo, 1910.

No matter how well things were going with his career in Ohio, Oldfield could not resist the lure of his Maryland hometown and his need to be in the center of the local political storm. Unbeknownst to his superiors and colleagues, Oldfield had never given up his chairmanship in the Howard County Republican Central Committee.

While Assistant Postmaster General Bristow was busy finalizing his report and the grand jury was laying out indictments across the ranks of corrupt Post Office employees, Oldfield took an emergency trip home.

A few weeks earlier, he had gotten wind that former state senator George Day, whom Oldfield supported for an upcoming gubernatorial bid, filed the names of candidates for Howard County judges and clerks. When Oldfield found out who they were, he went ballistic. As chair of the Howard County Republicans, he refused to appoint the nominees. A furious Day asked the board of appeals to force Frank to make the appointments, but he still wouldn't. Oldfield arrived in Ellicott City just in time to publicly refuse the nominees and tell everyone why he was doing so. "These two men are not only *not* Republicans," he said, "but a lot of toughs and murderers."[23] One of the men was Frank Higginbotham, Oldfield's father's longtime rival and claimant to the Howard County Republican Central Committee chairmanship during Frank Oldfield's absence in Ohio. The other was James Melvin, publisher of the *Democrat*, who Oldfield was certain was responsible for inciting the mob lynching of Jacob Henson in 1895.

To settle the dispute between Oldfield and Higginbotham about who was the legitimate chairman, the Maryland Republican Party Central Committee decided to hold a combined meeting on neutral territory at a church in Baltimore. From the start, the meeting was unruly. Each supporting faction had its own muscle waiting outside the windows on each side of the church, in case things went south. Each side was allowed to speak its support for *its* chairman. When it was Higginbotham's turn, he went to the church pulpit, aggressively leaned forward, and furiously waved a finger toward Oldfield. "This man has cost the taxpayers of Howard County more than four thousand dollars, and he could not live without politics." He turned to a snarling Oldfield. "*You rogue*," he screamed. "*You thug. You wife beater!*"

That was it. Oldfield pulled a small lead-filled leather blackjack from his pocket and leaped from his seat in the pews toward the giant Higginbotham. Thugs from both factions leaped in through the windows of the sanctuary. "In less than a second there was a struggling mass of men in the center of the room," a reporter from nearby Frederick, Maryland, wrote. "The row lasted only a few minutes and only one man—Eugene Keith, of Howard County, got hit in the face by Oldfield."[24]

Frank's political career and all the enjoyment he got from it abruptly came to an end in fall 1904. The two Republican factions, fighting each other in Maryland since before the Civil War, called a truce. The bitter adversaries finally decided they would be better at keeping Democrats at bay if they joined forces. Frank would never be far from Republican politics, but it wouldn't be a year-round sport without the party's titanic split. With nonstop active files at work, four tireless boys, and a wife who would love to see him more at home, there would be plenty to keep him occupied. He vowed to enjoy some downtime, and with a heavy heart, resigned from his chairmanship of the Howard County Republican Central Committee. For real, this time.

While he no longer held an official political office, Frank was always up for helping Republicans get into positions of power. About a year later, in the fall of 1905, he had his next chance. Assistant Postmaster General Bristow, who had taken a liking to Frank Oldfield during the corruption investigation, wanted to pull some strings for a Republican running in Georgia's Ninth Congressional District. It was very likely a favor to a lawmaker already on Capitol Hill. It wouldn't be the first time he'd done the bidding of a congressman. Bristow had been chastised for not going after the corrupt Secretary George Beavers early on in the widespread corruption investigation. The congressman had personally asked Bristow to back off his inquiry.[25] Why Bristow would do so was something he explained in his later report. "Congressmen frequently ask executive officers to do things which they themselves would refuse to do if the responsibility of decision was upon them. The traditions of American politics afford many instances of this kind."

When Bristow was asked to do a favor for someone at the end of 1904, he knew just who to put on the job. Bristow told Oldfield that he needed the postmaster of Gainesville, Georgia, relieved of his position. The powers-that-be wanted to replace him with James M. Ashley, the candidate running for Congress in that district. Holding the postmaster position would give Ashley a huge edge on his Democratic competitor, as postmasters were held in very high esteem. Oldfield was sent to find some dirt on the postmaster, Colonel Henry P. Farrow.[26] Farrow, a hardened Civil War veteran with a foot-long white beard and a perpetual scowl, was furious. He told the *Atlanta Constitution* that it was a conspiracy. Why was this guy from Ohio sniffing around *his* post office?

What Oldfield thought would be a slam dunk wasn't at all. Oldfield did not find a dime out of place. Farrow was running a tight ship, and could account for every cent, every money order, every stamp. Every *t* was crossed, every *i* dotted on every report. All Frank could come up with was that Farrow was too generous with his "franking," meaning he was signing his name in lieu of postage on a significant amount of mail. This was not enough to have him removed from his office, so Oldfield tried a new tactic. Colonel Farrow doesn't live in Gainesville, Oldfield reported to the superiors in Washington, D.C. Farrow argued that this was preposterous. He'd been a resident of the city for twenty years, he said. An enraged Farrow gave a long interview to the *Atlanta Journal and Constitution*:

> Who is Inspector Oldfield? Yes, that is the question. Who is he, what is he and where is he from? When Ashley [the Republican candidate] wanted some dishonorable and corrupt work done in putting up a job on me, he went to Fourth Assistant Postmaster General Bristow or some of his subordinates, and instead of ordering the chief inspector of the division (this division is composed of Tennessee, Georgia, Florida, Alabama, and possibly another state or two with headquarters at Chattanooga), to send an inspector here to ascertain and report the facts, they lent themselves and the power of the government to Ashley's scheme by permitting him to name this man Oldfield, way up there in Ohio, to come down here to do Ashley's dirty work. Yes, they sent way off to Ohio for an unscrupulous and pliant tool to do the dirty work. It would be a compliment to him to call him a dog.[27]

Farrow lost his postmastership. Oldfield was back at work in Ohio when the article came out, or he might have gone after Farrow, fists flying.

Frank's career thrived with his focus now entirely on investigations. By late 1907, he had transferred to Columbus, Ohio, to the enormous four-story post office on Third and State Streets behind the state capitol. It was a relief. The new inspector-in-charge of Ohio and the Midwest region of the United States was Abraham Holmes. This meant Holmes was Frank's immediate supervisor, and he had to answer to Holmes on a daily basis. Things had never been good between the two since the 1903 Post Office scandal wrapped, and it seemed that every high-profile investigation Oldfield cracked made the relationship worse. Oldfield would still work under Holmes from Columbus, but there would be no way Holmes could micromanage his work.

The Columbus, Ohio, post office on Third and State Streets was Frank Oldfield's last station during his career as an inspector. It is from here that he began his investigation of The Black Hand. Harry Krumm was postmaster. The post office doubled as a headquarters for other federal offices in Columbus. This photo was taken on Independence Day 1906.

Oldfield Collection

Frank hadn't been on his new beat for long when he got a call from the nearby railroad town of Bellefontaine. The call was from the police. It was about a murder. On the night of April 18, 1908, the police found Salvatore Cira, a fruit seller originally from Pittsburgh, shot to death on the floor of Demar's Fruit Importers, the store he co-owned with his nephew, Charles Demar. His wife discovered the body among crates of apples and bananas spattered with her husband's blood. When the police tried to question her, Signora Cira appeared not to understand English, or at least she pretended not to. Cira's fourteen-year-old daughter, Maria, was beside herself and wouldn't talk to the police either. The police learned that Cira was fifty years old and prominent in Italian circles. Italians from Pittsburgh, Cincinnati, Cleveland, and Buffalo often came to visit. The police had always suspected Cira of being engaged in nefarious practices, but could never connect him with anything.

Two Bellefontaine cops searched the premises and collected evidence. There was no sign of forced entry. In a drawer, they found a stash of money untouched. There appeared to be no reason for the killing until they searched Cira's body. In his pockets were two letters written in blocky Italian and signed *La Mano Nera*. Knowing they had no chance of getting anywhere by interviewing friends or relatives of Cira, the police hoped the letters might lead to a break in the case. It also meant that the investigation was out of their hands. Anything having to do with the U.S. mails went straight to the Post Office Inspection Service.

The police took the letters to Columbus to Inspector J. F. Oldfield at the Post Office and described the crime scene and what they'd learned about the case. Frank pushed some papers and files aside and opened the large envelope to find the two Black Hand letters. He asked around until he found a Sicilian translator and hired her to decipher the contents of the letters. The first letter called Cira a "friend" and offered to let him live in exchange for two thousand dollars. The second letter was a warning and an admonition for failure to pay. This was his last chance, it said. Both letters were written in black ink with angular letters, the *d* and the *b* just squares on sticks, really. Both had cartoon black hands and a crude drawing of a heart being stabbed by a dagger and dripping blood. Apparently, Cira had ignored the second letter, too. Now he was a bullet-riddled corpse.

Oldfield left the next day for Bellefontaine, about an hour's train ride north. He was anxious to start this investigation. It would be unlike anything he'd done before. No Post Office inspector had yet had a single break into the crimes of The Black Hand Society. Roaming around the Italian neighborhood where Cira had been killed, Oldfield stood out, pale and gaunt in his three-piece suit. No one would have anything to do with him. The locals pegged him as a "buzzard" straightaway. Still, he watched, scribbled notes, and collected evidence. He learned a few details from a pub owner. When someone in the community dies, he was told, the men grow their beards for thirty days as a sign of reverence and mourning. In Cira's case, all the men shaved after just two weeks, possibly indicating a lack of respect for the dead man. It was a tidbit of information that didn't do him much good at all. Oldfield, who considered himself among the country's best detectives, was fast coming up with zero.[28]

Months went by and Frank strained to hear news leaking out of Ohio's Italian neighborhoods. He couldn't get the community to trust him, but he did learn that many immigrant business owners and their families were rocked by murders, dynamite explosions, and kidnappings for ransom that they almost never reported to police. This disturbed him greatly. While Frank began to believe that the Black Hand crimes were interconnected, at least those in Ohio that connected back to Palermo, he didn't have support from witnesses or others in law enforcement or the press.

Police and politicians all over the country dismissed the idea of organized Sicilian criminals as a fairy tale. The media took their cue from the authorities and played down crimes. The caption of a 1909 newspaper photo of Marcino's Italian-owned saloon in Columbus blown to a million pieces says that the building appears to have "collapsed." Everyone from the NYPD to sheriffs in Texas to the mayor of Chicago—even U.S. Secret Service agents and the U.S. attorney general—declared that The Black Hand was simply a scary name co-opted by disorganized local criminal bands and "anarchists." In his gut, Oldfield believed that they were dead wrong. He just had no evidence to prove it.

There were two men, whom Oldfield knew by their reputations, who had more insight than anyone about Italian crime in America. The first was NYPD detective Joseph Petrosino, the second man was a Pinkerton detective from Pittsburgh, Francis Dimaio. After Mafia crime in Manhattan's Lower East Side bled into surrounding neighborhoods, the NYPD formed a five-member "Italian Squad," under Petrosino. Petrosino cracked several high-profile bombing, kidnapping, and murder cases and became a celebrity of sorts. He also became a wanted target of the criminals. While Dimaio tried his best to *not* get headlines, lawmen around the country knew of his incredible undercover stint in the New Orleans Parish Prison, working to solve the murder of Police Chief Hennessy. Over the next two decades, Dimaio infiltrated Mafia gangs that terrorized steelworkers and miners in Pennsylvania, New York, New Jersey, and Ohio. Both Petrosino and Dimaio also saw The Black Hand as something more interconnected than the authorities would admit. Frank had a twinge of jealousy toward both Italian-Americans, because there was no way he could ever go undercover on a Black Hand investigation. The idea that he could break into what he believed was an internationally organized Sicilian crime ring seemed more unlikely with each passing month.

A year went by, and Frank was no closer to finding out where the letters in Cira's pocket came from. Stacks of evidence and notebooks grew a foot tall on his desk. He solved dozens of other cases, but his failure to crack into The Black Hand Society and to protect innocent immigrants from the horrifying Mafia crimes left a hole in his gut.

Then, one frigid day in January 1909, a portly Italian with a massive mustache and expensive fedora burst into the Columbus post office with a letter.[29] He approached the first clerk he saw. "I want to see Uncle Samma," he demanded, using the term Italian immigrants had coined for federal law officers. The clerk called for Postmaster Harry Krumm, who sized up his visitor and looked over the letter. Then Krumm led the man down the hall to the office of Inspector Frank Oldfield.

Oldfield's eyes narrowed at the large Italian. He took the letter from Krumm. He couldn't read a word, but the blocky penmanship and the ridiculous cartoon drawing of a black hand and a bleeding heart made him catch his breath. For the inspector who never gave up trying to solve a crime, it was the most beautiful thing he'd ever seen.

CHAPTER 6

THE IMMIGRANT

Columbus was specifically chosen as the Ohio state capital in 1816 due to its perfect location as a national transportation hub between industry and agriculture in the West and markets in the East. It was little more than an outpost until the construction of a feeder canal connected the city to the Ohio and Erie Canals in 1831. The new waterway was a windfall for lumber and agriculture. Two years later, the National Road—the first federally funded highway and the brain-child of Thomas Jefferson—arrived from Cumberland, Maryland.[1] By 1839, the road linked Columbus all the way to Springfield, Ohio, but Congress abandoned the project that year and left the road into Illinois unfinished. By the middle of the century, railroads and telegraph lines raced like giant tentacles 360 degrees from the heart of the city. By the late 1800s, mammoth commercial buildings of granite, sandstone, and marble five stories tall lined High Street, and consumers flush with cash bought everything from cigars to saddles to firearms.

The city was alive and rich with food, theater, politics, and com-merce. There were nearly two hundred factories in operation. The population of the city was more than fifty thousand, and almost every person depended on goods from the Central Market House, a massive commercial center covering an entire city block on Fourth Street between Town and Rich Streets.[2] The two-story brick building was once the Columbus City Hall, and the upper floor the mayor's office.

It became a market in 1872, and stalls surrounded the outside for merchants to sell their wares.[3] Every day except Sunday, most vendors were up by 4:00 a.m., ready for the 6:00 a.m. opening.[4] Thousands poured into the market stalls to shop for clothing, farm tools and machinery, furniture, carriages, and clothing. In the summer, there were cherries, blackberries, peaches, pears, apples, and delicious cider. Year-round, pigeons, doves, quail, rabbits, and squirrels were sold dressed for cooking, or cooked on the spot for eating in the street.

Wealthy Columbus merchants took great pride in their city and together paid to illuminate huge arches across the canal and commercial district. One such business owner was forty-one-year-old John Amicon, among the most successful men in Columbus. Amicon owned half of Amicon Brothers & Company, a twenty-year-old wholesale fruit distributor, the biggest fruit dealer in the United States at the time. The headquarters of Amicon Brothers, "The Banana Kings," on their company stationery, was on Third and Naghten Streets, just ten blocks north of the federal building and the post office where Inspector Frank Oldfield had his office. The three-story building spread an entire city block and employed hundreds of laborers, managers, drivers, and salesmen. Capitalizing on refrigerated train cars and the new popularity of bananas, considered a luxury fruit and an exotic status symbol, the Amicons thrived.[5] Their empire reached from New York to California to South America and back. At a time when the average worker's salary was thirty dollars per month, the Amicon Brothers' business brought in a cool million dollars a year.

John Amicon did not see himself as an immigrant who had one foot in the old country and one in the new. With his successful company, he felt part of the American story and equal to other community and business leaders in Columbus. His house at 51 Rich Street was about a half-mile south of his warehouse.[6] It was a giant stone home with ample room for his family of ten. Most evenings after leaving his office, Amicon shed the stress of the day on the short walk home, then ate dinner with his wife, his seven children, and his teenage niece, who lived with the family.

This January evening in 1909 was different. Amicon had only one thing on his mind. In the morning, before he left home for his office, the mail carrier handed him a letter. The letter had no return address, and Amicon didn't recognize the handwriting. The letter, written in his native Italian, was direct and to the point.

Dear Sir, You must give us $10,000, and nothing bad will happen to you. We are confident you will not go to the police. The letter ordered Amicon to send an "honorable" man to Pittsburgh with the money. It was signed: *La Mano Nera*, or The Black Hand.

Amicon felt hot rage well up in his body. In truth, Amicon was not surprised by the extortion letter. On Sundays at mass at the Italian Catholic church, in the local pubs, in the neighborhoods, Amicon heard whispers and gossip. The shoemaker, the saloon owner, the grocer . . . they were already paying "tribute" to The Black Hand. Some said that a local saloon owner was paying monthly "protection" to some Sicilian "friends." But he also heard that the mob men played cards in the saloon, and the saloon owner was on their payroll. In a shop near his warehouse, two of his wholesale customers, Mary and Ignazio Fasone, had been terrorized by a group of Sicilians just a year before. He believed that the Fasones were now paying for the right to stay alive.

Other Italian businessmen could be trapped in an endless cycle of extortion. Amicon would not. "I'm not afraid of any man in the United States," he later told a reporter.[7] "I wouldn't give them a cent if it cost me my life." There was no way he would give in to these demands.

Teresa Amicon was terrified when her husband confessed he'd received a Black Hand letter. Amicon's brother and business partner, Charles, also received a letter with the same demand, and he was very alarmed. Charles was married and had eight children. Both Teresa and Charles pleaded for John to pay, or at least try to negotiate for a smaller amount than the ridiculous ten thousand dollars. But neither of them was surprised when Amicon angrily swore he would never in his life pay a single dime. Living in fear and poverty was what had driven him from Italy a quarter-century before. He was an American now, living in the land of the free, the land of opportunity. He swore he would never give in to a bunch of criminals leeching off honest workers.

The year Giovanni Amicone was born, in 1868, Italy had been a nation for only seven years. The infant country was weakly held together under King Victor Emmanuel II, and the forceful unification of independent states left a lot of uncertainty and insecurity. Bandits preyed on working people and farm laborers. Famine followed, and disease ravaged the population. The political system was authoritarian. Anyone against the new government could be subject to abuse by the gendarmes and jailed. Property of dissenters was commonly seized by the government and given over to loyalists.

In 1882, with his parents' blessing and likely great worry, at just fourteen years old, Giovanni Amicone left his home in the northern Italian city of Fiori with almost no possessions and only a few lira. The ship he took passage on was full of frightened youthful faces like his—boys and young men heading to a foreign land with only their labor to sell. Many of them had few skills, and less than half could read or write. Giovanni was one of seventy thousand migrant workers who left Italy for America that year.[8]

Amicone arrived at Ellis Island in 1882, the first year it opened as an immigrant processing destination.[9] He got wind of jobs in New York and Chicago where Italians were doing extremely hard labor and sleeping in overcrowded rooms in squalid tenements. Almost 100 percent of public works employees in New York were Italian, as were an estimated 90 percent of street sweepers in Chicago.[10] Amicone was told there was plenty of work on the railroads, and although it would be backbreaking, he would be out in the country rather than in the squalor of a big city, which suited him much better. The Baltimore & Ohio Railroad had just purchased the Marietta & Cincinnati Railroad and the Ohio & Mississippi Railroad and was laying thousands of miles of track through the industrial belt.

Amicone landed in Midland, Ohio, where he took a job serving water to workers on a "section gang" of the B&O.[11] He worked mostly among Irish and Eastern European immigrants. The pay was two dollars a day, which he considered quite a lot of money. In 1909, Amicone told a Columbus newspaper that carrying the heavy water bucket was "okay," at first. Then, a year into the job, the crew began building a viaduct across a steep valley. The scaffolding was a hundred feet up. And as brave as he had been leaving his family and crossing the Atlantic Ocean, his fear of heights got the best of him. Amicone was terrified to step out on the rickety framework. The day the construction reached halfway across the valley, Amicone stepped gingerly onto the trellis with his heavy, sloshing bucket. Then he did something he had avoided doing before: He looked down. Below him a horse and buggy appeared so tiny that Amicone felt his head spin. He froze, unable to move until several workers guided him off the platform. He quit that very day.[12]

The thrifty teenager had saved up twenty dollars, which got him as far as the town of Chillicothe with a few dollars to spare. Chillicothe was once the capital of Ohio and a lively town of about twelve thousand. The modern city boasted public "Water Works" and electric streetlights. There were any number of businesses looking for workers. There was a giant ironworks factory, several machine shops, a hay stacker and rake factory, factories that made gloves, cigars, candy, and ice. There were companies that produced bricks and tile, flour mills, and the largest gunstock factory in America.

Amicone didn't see himself working for any one of them. Instead, the enterprising teenager decided that Chillicothe was the perfect place to start a business. His first investment: one large bag of peanuts. He split the bag in two and resold the nuts, earned a little profit, then bought another bag. In no time, Giovanni Amicone became John Amicon and set up a small stand to sell fruit and nuts near the public square. Soon he had a store on Chillicothe's Main Street. He got so busy, he needed trusted help, so he sent for his older brother, Charles, who had come to America a few years before, and who was working a section gang up north.

John Amicon (right) walking with a U.S. Marshal in Columbus, Ohio, during the Black Hand investigation.

John and Charles figured out how to import produce from Mexico and Brazil so they could sell Chillicothe residents fresh fruit and vegetables late into the fall. The two made such a prosperous team that Chillicothe began to feel too small for their ambitions. John was twenty-one when the two men set their sights due north on the capital city of Columbus. Together they had about thirty thousand dollars—enough to launch Amicon Brothers & Co. They rented a building on Town Street in the heart of Columbus's commission house district near the Central Market, where companies bought and sold commodities of all kinds and made a percentage of the profit on the deals. At the time, the majority of immigrants in Columbus were from Germany. There were some Brits and Irish and a few from Eastern Europe. There were only a handful of Italians in Columbus. Most worked at low-paying factory jobs as day laborers, or as waiters, waitresses, and cooks in restaurants.

At first, vendors in the market district were skeptical of the Italian brothers. "Other commission firms nearby laughed and made remarks about 'another Dago firm in town,'" one newspaper reported.[13] But John was shrewd and had foresight, and Charles had a head for business. "When the Amicons did not go under in two months, the merchants in the neighborhood were astonished," the paper said. Soon, John and Charles made a game-changing hire in manager Herman Holland, who had several years of experience in the commission business.

"Holland helped steer them into the channels that made their business grow into an enormous affair," wrote the paper. And by the early 1900s, Amicon Brothers & Co. was one of the biggest fruit distributors in the United States. Its four-story brick Columbus warehouse covered half a city block next to the B&O railway station on Naghten and Third Streets. Twenty-four hours a day, horse-drawn trucks and carts pulled up to loading docks with citrus fruit, bananas, strawberries, turnips, and cabbage for Columbus's stores and restaurants. Wooden crates with logos from companies all over the world were stacked six feet high on the sidewalk. Carts and trucks moved shipments to refrigerated railcars with wooden slats on the bottom to drain melting ice on the way to distant destinations.

The Amicons bought two other distribution houses, one in West Virginia and one in Michigan, a giant storage house for cabbage in Illinois, one for apples in Seneca, New York, and another for onions in Ohio. The brothers oversaw every aspect of the business. Nothing was too exotic for their commission house. They imported fruit and vegetables from as far away as Hawaii and South America. Bountiful harvests of oranges, lemons, and apricots from Amicon ranches in Colorado and California traveled by train across America. For the first time, Americans in the Northeast and Midwest could have fresh fruit and vegetables all winter long. By 1908, Amicon Brothers & Co. was a million-dollar-a-year business.[14]

Amicon was determined to resist the Black Hand demands, but the stress was eating him alive. He imagined someone kidnapping one of his children or blowing up their entire home with all of them inside. He was well aware of how things could turn out.

Amicon ignored the letter and tried to carry on as usual. Then another letter came . . . then another—all written in the same handwriting. Most came with a Pennsylvania postmark, each one more menacing than the last:

We have put you down in the register of the dead, nasty brute—that for money you are content to be killed. No one escapes from under our hands. We have stabbed many in Italy. Consider that I, who write this, has a price of 14,000 lire on my head, for eight years was followed by the police, and know not how many I have killed with my trusty carbine which has never failed me. Either money or your blood—The Black Hand.[15]

After a few weeks and several more letters ignored by Amicon (who implored his brother, Charles, not to pay the extortionists either), the criminals became brazen. One morning, Charles's wife found a rolled-up Pittsburgh newspaper on her front porch with a note and a stick of dynamite inside. It was obviously hand delivered by the criminals themselves, who had come right up to their porch. The note demanded ten thousand dollars, or the house and its entire contents, including the children inside, would be blown to a million pieces. Charles gave the notes to company manager Herman Holland, who carried them to Cincinnati to request help from the Italian consulate. The consulate diplomat there basically shrugged his shoulders and told him there was nothing they could do. The American authorities were in charge.

A few days later, John Amicon stepped out onto the front porch of his home and found a shiny narrow dagger, a stiletto, wrapped in a note. The stiletto was a duplicate—the letter said—*the other will soon be in your back, Mr. Amicon.*

Amicon did share one trait with fellow Italian immigrants: He had no faith in the police. So he hired a local private detective named Charlie McLees to escort him home in the evenings and to guard his house at night. The third night of his employment, McLees was on watch in the shadow of the grape arbor at the Amicon home when he heard the rear gate open.[16] He spotted a man approaching the back of the house from the alley. In the glare of the streetlight, McLees recognized him as the same man he'd seen loitering around the saloon across the street from the Amicon Brothers' warehouse that day. He'd also done a lot of investigating in the Italian community, with John Amicon's blessing, about who could be sending the letters. McLees yelled at the man, but the man kept coming toward the house. McLees fired two shots, and the suspect took off down the alley with two others. It was dark, but from what he described, Amicon had an idea who they might be—two fruit sellers from Marion, Ohio, named Sam and Sebastian Lima and their henchman, an ex-con in his sixties named Severio Ventola.

A week later, on January 20, 1909, after getting all of her children started with their morning routines, Teresa found a package on the back porch. Just like the one her brother-in-law Charlie received, it was enclosed in a Pittsburgh newspaper. Trembling, she unwrapped the package to find a stick of dynamite and a letter. She didn't dare read it, but sent her son to fetch Amicon at the warehouse.

Dear John Amicon

By the blood of God we are in back of you. We have killed kings and emperors. Consider a fly like you! If you wish to avert your death, you will search for an honorable person to come to Pittsburg [sic] and while he is searching for us, he will be found. We advise you that if you go to the police, you can count yourself dead.[17]

That was the last straw. Gripping the letter in his hand, red-faced and steaming, Amicon marched three blocks to the massive four-story Federal Post Office and Custom House building on North Third and State Streets and barreled through the door. Under a portrait of round-faced, bespectacled President Theodore Roosevelt, he slammed the note down on the counter demanding to see "Uncle Samma."[18]

When Amicon was led by Postmaster Harry Krumm to Inspector

Frank Oldfield's office, Amicon unraveled his story in broken English.
Oldfield listened intently and scribbled in his notebook. They were
after both him and Charles for twenty thousand dollars together, he
said. Amicon gave Oldfield names of other victims he knew of. He
also told Oldfield about the man he suspected of writing the letters,
one Sam Lima from Marion. He said he had a stack of more letters
back home to hand over to Oldfield and would absolutely testify
against the criminals in a United States courtroom. It was his duty
as an American citizen.[19]

Oldfield, who'd been stymied by the Salvatore Cira murder in
Bellefontaine for over a year, immediately understood the signifi-
cance of Amicon's visit. The portly millionaire with the enormous
mustache was the first witness to come forward, and one who wielded
enough power in town to not be dismissed. Amicon, however, was
not confident in Oldfield at all. He sized up the rail-thin inspector—
his close-trimmed hair perfectly flat and divided by a razor-straight
part, his tidy mustache neatly waxed, his expensively tailored suit
without a hint of lint. Amicon sighed. "The network is vast and secret
and ruthless. Plus, no one else will talk to you," he warned Oldfield.
Amicon was almost certain that other victims would say nothing to
this pale and unimpressive-looking government agent. Frank wasn't
worried. In fact, he took Amicon's sentiment as a welcome challenge.
Being underestimated by the criminals was an asset, not a liability.

CHAPTER 7

STAKEOUT

In late February 1909, Sebastian Lima left the Society of the Banana headquarters in the back of his brother-in-law Sam Lima's fruit shop and walked three blocks south. He arrived at the Marion post office, a corner storefront in the Masonic Temple building at 173 South Main Street, with a stack of letters addressed to cities in Ohio, Pennsylvania, and New York. He asked the clerk for stamps and received tiny two-cent rectangles with perforated edges. The image on the stamp was a portrait in profile of George Washington, his face created from a series of minute strokes and dots. Thin horizontal lines crossed the backdrop and laurel leaves framed the president's image. To prevent counterfeiting, the U.S. Post Office printed the stamps in bright red ink from a highly detailed engraving. What Lima did not notice about the stamps the clerk gave him that day was that each one had a tiny red dot inside the letter *o* in the word "two."

After the letters were ready to mail, Lima, dressed like a laborer in baggy pants and suspenders, dug into his bag and handed the clerk nine hundred dollars in neatly stacked bills. Even though this was about twice the clerk's annual salary, it did not surprise him. In fact, the clerk was already taking out a money order form for Sebastian to fill out. Transferring enormous amounts of money from the Marion post office to Sicily was a nearly everyday occurrence for Sam and Sebastian Lima, who the clerk, and everyone else, believed were brothers. It was assumed by many in the Italian community as well as throughout the city that the two had some kind of criminal business on the side, but the hefty influx of the Lima money into the economy and the Marion County Bank Company kept the gossipers at bay. The two Limas also were careful to never make victims out of anyone in Marion, so no one could be sure where the incredible amounts of money came from. Sebastian filled out the money order. The recipient was his mother, Signora Carmella Barbara Lima in Palermo. He paid for the transfer and left.

When Lima was out of sight, the clerk took the copy of Lima's money order and put it aside to give to the Post Office inspector who'd come to work in the back office. Then he got out a sheet of stamps, put tiny dots in the *o* as he had been instructed, and put the sheets away so he wouldn't accidentally use them on the next customer.

Tracking every letter out of Lima's shop was part of Inspector Frank Oldfield's complex strategy to bust open The Black Hand Society. Over the past nine years, since coming to Ohio after his embarrassing tenure in Chattanooga, Oldfield had greatly matured as an investigator and as a man. His resume now included some of the most harrowing crime busts in the Post Office Inspection Service's history. Working internal Post Office investigations, he had helped uncover millions of dollars in fraud and theft and recovered substantial bounties, to the delight of the chief Post Office inspector.

Oldfield had earned a reputation for being a master interrogator of suspects and an equally savvy interviewer of victims and witnesses. For criminal suspects, different Oldfield personas would appear. On some occasions, Oldfield's blue eyes narrowed and turned to steel. He sucked his cheeks deeper into his narrow skeleton, and he drilled a suspect with demands for answers. Other times, he turned on the charm. *I'm really impressed by how you figured out how to work this crime*, he'd say thoughtfully, to the delight of an egotistical suspect.

When those methods didn't work, Oldfield would turn into the worst five-foot-four-inch, 145-pound nightmare you ever saw. With skills honed back in the hills of Maryland, he'd beat the daylights out of a suspect until the details he was looking for were spat out in blood with the suspect's broken teeth. He was equally good at all methods.

Oldfield's reputation gave him the respect of most other lawmen, but what fueled his ego even more was that bad guys were in awe of his methods, too. No one wanted to get "sweated out" by Inspector Oldfield. His colleagues and newspapermen were incredulous that even after people took a beating from Oldfield or he put them away in prison, Frank somehow made himself irresistible, trustworthy. They couldn't help but like him. Criminals captured by Oldfield often corresponded with him for many years from prison. Many sent Christmas and birthday greetings to Oldfield's family long after his death. Oldfield's wife and sons graciously returned the courtesy to the families of the convicts. One safe-cracking thief carved an intricate marquetry box in his cell. He sent it as a gift to Oldfield from the Ohio Penitentiary.

One newspaper later reported on Frank's curiously chummy relationship with "Burglar Jim" Anderson, a highly productive thief Oldfield captured in 1902 after Anderson robbed nine Ohio post offices:[1]

> Inspector Oldfield, who worked up the major portion of the case against the Society of the Banana, is absolutely without fear. For years "Burglar Jim" Anderson, who died in prison was known to be camping on the trail of Oldfield. But that did not seem to bother Oldfield in the least. Burglar Jim had sworn to kill Oldfield, and Oldfield knew that Anderson wanted his scalp, so when he last arrested him on a charge of dynamiting and robbing a post office safe, Oldfield took no chances. He located Burglar Jim in a hotel

in Lancaster Pennsylvania and invaded his room at night when Anderson was known to be in bed, if not sound asleep. Oldfield had a sleuth companion with him at the time, but did not need his services. Quietly unlocking with a duplicate key the locked Anderson's room, Oldfield bounded in with a revolver in his hand and said to the aroused crook: "Jim, if you move a muscle I am going to kill you."

Jim did not move a muscle. Oldfield's assistant removed from under burglar Jim's pillow two busty looking revolvers, and then the inspector slipped the handcuffs on Jim's wrist. Anderson was planted in the Ohio Penitentiary, and Oldfield had occasion many times after that to visit Jim in the state prison to get a line on others that Oldfield was trailing and whom he subsequently landed. Oldfield has a way about him of smoothing out wrinkles that made a hit with Anderson, and the two got along very well together, despite the ambition in Jim's heart to slaughter Oldfield for past offenses.

In a small, leather-bound notebook, in hurried cursive handwriting, Oldfield recorded hundreds of addresses, names, and phone numbers. He had dozens of sources who gave him insight into criminal activity. He cultivated relationships with informants, or "snitches," and kept them close, often inviting them out for a whisky or a meal in a low-key location. He kept friendly relationships with the families of men he'd sent to prison, making sure wives and children did not go hungry with the family breadwinner locked up. Because he didn't have a wife and children to go home to during the week, he was out most evenings at restaurants and pubs, catching up on his buddies' case files or playing cards. He didn't have much of a taste for alcohol, but he liked an occasional beer and was seldom seen without a smoldering stogie in hand.

The political and networking skills that Frank honed in the hills of Ellicott City before the turn of the century served him well in Ohio's big cities and across the Northeast. From top newspaper editors to state and U.S. lawmakers, to shoemakers and saloon owners, Frank had connections. He had friends in the Secret Service, which was the law arm of the Treasury Department, and friends who were federal marshals serving under the Department of Justice in jurisdictions not covered by local law enforcement agencies. Frank had close ties to local sheriffs and police, to circuit court magistrates, federal judges, and prosecutors. Even defense attorneys who fought to free the criminals Frank wanted convicted were quick to have a drink with Oldfield and hash over past battles. He still held tight to his political roots and was always on board to help make sure that Republicans got all the best political appointments.

Oldfield's closest work relationships tended to be within his own agency and with his fellow inspectors. Often, those in the Post Office bureaucratic ranks were wary of inspectors, knowing that it was the detectives' job to keep an eye out for internal corruption by postmasters or general malpractice by any of the rank and file. That didn't keep Frank from becoming great friends with Postmaster Harry Krumm after Oldfield transferred to Krumm's Columbus post office full-time in 1907. Krumm was a rising star in the department, and Frank was immediately impressed with Krumm's credentials and his confidence. Krumm was one of the youngest postmasters in the service, but he looked older than his thirty-five years, with a protruding forehead and thick black eyebrows shading heavily lidded eyes.[2] He also carried himself with the self-assurance of someone a decade older. Krumm not only ran a tight ship in his massive Columbus post office, he also loved taking part in active investigations run by the inspectors who were domiciled there. Sometimes, he took the lead himself. In 1907, Krumm made national news when he busted one of his cashiers, a top Ohio Republican named William C. Wallace, for stealing. When Krumm and his inspectors audited the office finances, they found twelve thousand dollars missing and a paper trail leading to Wallace. Krumm went to Wallace's home to confront him, but it was too late. Minutes before, Wallace had loaded his pistol and blown out his brains. Krumm was left consoling Wallace's hysterical widow.[3]

Although younger than Oldfield by six years, Krumm played the part of older sibling in a fraternal relationship with Frank. He was supportive of Oldfield's work and personal life. He was a buffer between Frank and Inspector-in-Charge Abraham Holmes and other higher-ups who scoffed at Frank's public grandstanding and his hot temper, which still got him in trouble on occasion. Krumm even had a nickname for Oldfield: He called him *Barney*, after a famous race car driver of the time, the first man to go a mile in under a minute, Barney Oldfield.

There were several other inspectors working out of the Columbus federal building. Many, like Frank, had their families living outside Columbus. The men would spend late evenings together in Krumm's big office hashing out the details of investigations or chatting about their lives and gossiping about political goings-on. Mostly, though, they worked. The caseloads for Post Office inspectors were staggering. In fiscal year 1909, which ran from July 1908 to June 1909, the Post Office Inspection Service, with about one hundred inspectors in its ranks, had approximately 280,000 cases on its plate. The enormous load included "All complaints concerning depredations upon the mails and losses or irregularities therein and violations of the postal laws and regulations and many questions arising in the other offices or bureaus of the department regarding the service are referred to this office for investigation," wrote Acting Chief Inspector Theodore Ingalls in his 1909 annual report.[4]

Crimes and losses against the mails were "jacketed," meaning given a file number, categorized, and assigned to an inspector, who would decide if the matter could be dealt with through correspondence or if the inspector would have to take to the field. "A" cases were things like complaints about someone having tampered with or rifled through someone's registered mail, delays of delivery, or the wrong delivery altogether. "B" cases were the same, but for ordinary, nonregistered mail. "C" cases were miscellaneous complaints, including mistakes in money orders, complaints against employees, and failures to remit customs duties on packages coming into the country.

All three categories were big yawns to Oldfield. He would commonly shove "A" through "C" files under a stack of folders or pass them off to a junior inspector. Then he would attack his pile of "D" (robberies) and "E" (mail fraud) with gusto. These were the crimes that Frank salivated over, and there was no shortage of them. In 1909 alone, nearly 2,000 post offices were robbed. The Railway Post Office Service was robbed 36 times. There were 1,631 robberies of rural and street letterboxes. One hundred and twenty-two mail cars were wrecked or burned. Six hundred post offices were burned partially or to the ground. There were 4,787 mail pouches that were lost or stolen and were not recovered. For the "E" cases, where suspects used the mails to defraud, transmit illegal lottery tickets, or send "obscene and scurrilous matter," the Post Office Inspection Service created a new category for 1909 because of the sheer volume. In 1909 there were 7,686 such crimes. (One of them was the extortion of fruit merchant John Amicon.) Post offices were robbed another 1,615 times by outsiders, and by the end of the year, there were 1,093 convictions. The amount of capital lost in 1909 to the Post Office Department was nearly half a million dollars. In one Indiana post office alone, $131,942.69 worth of stamps, postal funds, and money order funds disappeared.[5]

Frank's relationship with Harry Krumm notwithstanding, post-masters were not always comfortable with the investigators among them. It was an inspector's job to dig deep into the financial goings-on in each post office in America. Audits were commonplace and tedious, and discrepancies could cost someone his job. Still, the limitless influx of cash was sometimes too tempting even for those making a good salary from the federal government. In 1909, 107 postmasters were arrested for stealing or corruption. There were 45 assistant postmasters, 80 clerks, 24 railway postal clerks, 45 city letter carriers, 43 rural letter carriers, and 22 mail carriers also arrested by Post Office inspectors.[6]

Aside from all the fun, the endless work, and the sleepless nights, the job of Post Office inspector was also very dangerous. It was something Frank rarely thought about, but certainly Margaret Galena did often. One day in September 1908, the danger of the job hit home for everyone in the service and their families. Charles Fitzgerald, a Post Office inspector from Jackson, Mississippi, was shot and killed by Will Sorsby, the assistant postmaster of a train depot post office. Fitzgerald had discovered a shortage in the office accounts and tied it to Sorsby. The suspect begged and pleaded for Fitzgerald not to turn him in, but the inspector refused. Sorsby shot Fitzgerald in the back. "The assassination was unprovoked, cold-blooded, and a most wanton act," wrote the chief Post Office inspector.[7] Sorsby was apprehended, tried, convicted, and sentenced to life imprisonment.

In Athens on most weekends, Frank lived a completely different life than he did as a federal detective in Columbus during the work-week. Margaret Galena dragged him to concerts and fancy parties where she coerced him to chat with her society friends. She wore her fanciest dresses and he wore his best suits. He tied his bow ties and Margaret Galena fixed his agate cuff links. They went to events at Ohio University and garden parties at the College Green. They ate lavish dinners at the fancy Elk Hotel on Union Street. At parties, Frank mainly stayed close to other detectives, lawmen, and politicians, mostly refusing Margaret Galena's demand that he mingle with the university elite. They were not Frank's type of people.

Frank Oldfield owned two homes in Athens, Ohio. He occasionally posed for a casual photo on the front lawn after some coaxing by his sons. This photo was taken in 1909.

At home with his four sons, who ranged in age from nine to fifteen years old in 1909, Frank was not an openly demonstrative father. There were no warm hugs or vocal expressions of love. But as the boys grew, there was no shortage of fun. He took the boys hunting for deer, squirrel, rabbit, and pheasant. The five went fishing together most summer weekends down at the eddy on the Hocking River next to White's Mill. Frank didn't roughhouse with his boys, but in the vein of his own childhood, he never chastised his sons for going at one another, even to the point of blood and bruises. They needed to be tough. He also demanded they look presentable. Oldfield was emphatic about the boys' personal hygiene and appearance. Each boy was inspected up and down for scruffiness or grime when their father was home. He admonished them less about their schoolwork. That was Margaret Galena's job.

Several times a year, Frank took the boys back to Ellicott City to see Granddaddy Hamilton and Grandma Wilhelmina (until Wilhelmina passed away in 1907), Margaret Galena's parents, and the boys' aunts, uncles, and cousins who still lived in the mill town. The sibling Frank missed the most, of course, was Clarence, his favorite brother and partner in crime. Clarence had become a top boss at the U.S. Customs House in Baltimore and a major player in the Maryland Republican Party.

The last weekend in January 1909, just after he'd encountered the furious John Amicon and his fistful of extortion letters, Frank went to Athens. He was distracted, but he tried to make the most of the time with his family. He didn't know how long it would be before he could take a weekend at home again. As with other massive and complex investigations, he was bound to end up sleeping in his office chair rather than heading back to his rented house when he finished work at 3:00 a.m., his eyes too blurry to read any more. He would have his clothes taken out by clerks to be washed and pressed at the laundry and returned to his office. He would probably forget to eat breakfast or lunch, and skip meals until he was so hungry he would gorge himself at the local diner. He would burn out lightbulbs writing late into the night and empty bottles and bottles of ink into his inkwell.

In the early morning of February 1, 1909, Margaret Galena and the boys waved good-bye as Frank disappeared in a carriage down the street for the train depot. Margaret Galena had probably been told enough to know that her husband wouldn't be around much for a while. The case of The Black Hand was about to consume Frank's every waking moment for a long time to come. He stopped only briefly in Columbus to drop his bags. John Amicon had tipped Oldfield off that the letter writer was possibly his fruit customer Sam Lima from Marion. He hopped on a train to Marion, an hour's ride, and went to the post office in the Masonic Temple building. Postmaster Milton Dickerson was expecting him, and Oldfield immediately took over a back room to use as a part-time headquarters. He instructed the clerks and Dickerson to monitor all mail sent by the Lima "brothers" and to give him all the money order receipts. Marion was a small town. The Lima store was just down the street. Oldfield emphasized to Dickerson and the clerk that his comings and goings must be as clandestine as possible and that not a word should escape the Marion post office.

Back in Columbus, Oldfield gathered everything he could on Sam and Sebastian Lima. He called the Italian consulate in Cincinnati and asked for any information the Palermo government had about Salvatore and Sebastian Lima. He dug into customs and immigration records and queried other law enforcement agencies for clues. He learned that Sam had spent time in New Orleans after coming to America twenty years before. Sebastian was much newer to the country. Oldfield got hold of a copy of Sebastian Lima's naturalization certificate. He'd come to the United States in 1900, arriving in Boston Harbor from Sicily, and became an American citizen in 1907. Sebastian filled in the blanks on the immigration form himself:

It is my bona fied [*sic*] intention to renounce forever all allegiance and fidelity to any foreign prince, potentate state or sovereignty, and particularly to *[Victor Emmanuel, III King of Italy]*, of which I am now a citizen/subject; I arrived at the port of *[Boston]*, in the State of *[Massachusetts]* on or about the *[14]* day of *[October]*, anno Domini *[1900]*; I am not an anarchist; I am not a polygamist nor a believer in the practice of polygamy; and it is my intention in good faith to become a citizen of the United States of America and to permanently reside therin [*sic*]: SO HELP ME GOD.

    [SEBASTIANO LIMA]

    Subscribed and sworn to before me this *[6th]* day of *[November]*, anno Domini 19*[07]*[8]

Postmaster Krumm knew how much Oldfield wanted to land The Black Hand. He'd seen Oldfield struggle and fail to uncover the conspiracy behind the murder of Salvatore Cira. Like Oldfield, Krumm believed that many of the Ohio Black Hand crimes were connected and spread far beyond the extortion crimes against Cira, John Amicon, and his brother Charlie. Krumm also knew that a big Black Hand bust would bring a lot of prestige to his Columbus post office. Krumm promised Oldfield 100 percent cooperation with the investigation. He generously offered Oldfield his giant office for Oldfield's team, even knowing Oldfield would surely trash the place.

With Krumm fully in, Oldfield wanted three additional inspectors to work with him on the initial investigation. He needed men whom he trusted implicitly and who were brilliant and tough investigators who could unravel complicated crimes. His first call was to Edward Hutches, who was stationed in Chillicothe, the small town fifty miles south of Columbus where John Amicon got his start in the fruit business. Hutches was tall, cocky, and handsome, with ice-blue eyes and a dashing grin. He was also fearless and was not a desk jockey. He had no problem going after armed, violent criminals. Originally from Urbana, Ohio, Hutches had spent the last several years in Chillicothe, where he did more surveying of rural free delivery routes than catching crooks. Oldfield, who had worked investigations with Hutches in the past, wanted to give his friend an opportunity that would raise his profile and get him a better future post. Hutches also had close ties to Washington through his brother-in-law, and Frank never missed an opportunity to make political connections.[9]

Inspector Edward F. Hutches was supervised from the Cincinnati post office by Inspector-in-Charge Abraham Holmes. Hutches's stationing was normally in the Chillicothe, Ohio, area. Oldfield selected Hutches for his investigative team against The Black Hand in 1909.

Oldfield's next pick was George Pate from the Cincinnati office. Another good friend, Pate was a cunning detective with the look of an amiable family man, and was terrific at "blending in" when undercover. Oldfield knew that Pate, like Hutches, had suffered numerous boring assignments mapping routes in the rural free delivery system. Each time, he had to spend two to three months in some one-horse town. Half the time, the roads were in such poor shape that Pate couldn't commit the Post Office Department to delivering the mail unless the residents could get their acts together and make the roads drivable.[10] Oldfield knew Pate's talents were being wasted, and Pate was thrilled when he got Oldfield's call.

Frank's final pick was Raleigh Hosford, the inspector responsible for Cincinnati and surrounding areas.[11] Like Oldfield, Hosford was infamous in the service. He had a lot of successful crime busts under his belt, but he had also had some run-ins with the law. In February 1904, Hosford shaved off his mustache to look like a mild-mannered professor and coerced a woman he'd arrested into unknowingly signing a confession. When the woman realized what she'd done, she threw herself at Hosford, who blocked her and pushed her to the ground. The woman told police that Hosford kicked her, and she filed charges. Hosford was arrested, tried, and exonerated a few months later.[12] The following year, Hosford got a tip that a mother and daughter in Indiana were bilking lonely men out of cash, promising marriage. When Hosford grabbed the women's letters without a warrant, the mother called the local police, who arrested Hosford and threw him in jail. Hosford beat the charges again and both women went to prison. Oldfield was delighted when Hosford was free to help, and he knew he could use Hosford's sometimes unscrupulous tactics on the Black Hand investigation.

While the Fourteenth Amendment's due process clause officially prohibited law enforcement officers from depriving "any person of life, liberty, or property, without due process of law," police brutality by law enforcement was commonplace in the age. The term was first used publicly in an 1872 headline in the *Chicago Daily Tribune*: "Police Brutality: A Prisoner Shamefully Mal. treated by Officers. Kicked and Pounded in a Cell—Probably Fatally Injured."[13] In the late 1800s, large-scale riots involving police and workers erupted during labor strikes. For federal lawmen, including Post Office inspectors, Secret Service agents, and federal marshals, there was no real worry about lawsuits or recourse by victims of violent or overzealous officers. For Frank and his fellow inspectors it was a matter of "qualified immunity"; they could always argue they were acting in good faith in their discretion as peace officers. It would not be until *Bivens* v. *Six Unknown Federal Agents* in 1972 that the Supreme Court extended liability for bad acts of federal agents.[14]

With his team of inspectors in Columbus working out of Krumm's office, Oldfield began to imagine himself like his father's hero, Ulysses S. Grant. He spread out the four Amicon threat letters and their typed translations on his desk, pinned maps and notes to the walls, and scratched flow charts connecting the dots of what he already knew. With federal support and an unconstrained budget that no one would question, at least for a while, Oldfield built a strategic and ambitious plan that pulled in information from Columbus, Ohio, to Palermo, Sicily, and across dozens of cities in between. On top of monitoring the Marion post office, Oldfield sent undercover agents to watch Sam Lima's store, report who came and went, and tail the "brothers" everywhere.

If anything happened to Amicon, Oldfield's case would crumble, so throughout February 1909, Oldfield had Charlie and John Amicon's warehouse under surveillance, as well as both of their homes. He hired undercover Pinkerton detectives to do everything they could to protect the Amicon brothers and their families. It wasn't an easy task. There were eight children in Charlie's house, and John had seven kids plus his niece living with him. Oldfield also dispatched a plainclothes detective to hang out in the saloon next door to the Amicons' business.

Then he sent word to every post office around the country where the Lima letters were going to keep an eye out for suspicious characters checking post office boxes. He ordered mail carriers to report back on who was receiving the letters, and what they did after the letters were received. Did they look Italian? Did they live alone or with a family? Frank called the Pinkerton Detective Agency in Cleveland and hired more undercover detectives to follow and track those sending and receiving the letters.

With what was sure to be a flurry of activity among detectives, clerks, postmasters, and mail carriers, Oldfield had a major concern. The newspapermen in Columbus were some of the best sleuths in the state. They were sharks that circled Oldfield's office daily, looking for a sensational story. Oldfield normally loved the attention. From the beginning of his time in Columbus, Oldfield made fast friends with the city's reporters and correspondents. The newsmen soon learned that his door was always open. Sometimes, they could get him to leak a little info on something coming up. And often he would just sit them down and narrate while the newsmen scribbled furiously. Often, the next day's copy was almost verbatim Oldfield. But in this case, it would be a liability if his strategies were leaked too soon.

Frank knew that it was vitally important to keep the reporters on his side. It was a symbiotic relationship. They fed his ego and helped him get attention from the higher-ups in Washington. He also used them as a tool, at times leaking fake details to throw suspects off guard. Oldfield's cozy relationship with the reporters in Ohio annoyed

Abraham Holmes, Oldfield's longtime adversary and his immediate superior, to no end. Holmes, like many senior law enforcement officials, refused to believe that there was any real organized Black Hand crime. Oldfield, Holmes believed, was on a very expensive wild-goose chase.

The criminal gangs appeared to be widespread, and Oldfield believed there were Black Hand suspects and victims all over the United States, with criminal cohorts all the way back to Sicily. If even a hint got out, Oldfield believed, the Blackhanders would scatter like roaches, burning all the evidence in their wake. Victims would go into hiding, knowing they were tailed by the criminals, and be of no use to the investigation at all.

Oldfield came up with a plan. He called his reporter friends from the biggest newswires and papers:[15] the Associated Press, the *Cincinnati Enquirer*, the *Chicago Tribune*, the *New York Times*, the *Washington Post* and *Evening Star*, and the *New Orleans Picayune*.

"Listen," he told the newspapermen. "I need to swear you all to secrecy."

They all leaned in, hovering over Krumm's desk as Oldfield's voice resonated with a conspiratorial undertone. He gave them rousing hints about what he was up to. He let them in on his plans for the case and what they could expect to see over the next month or so. Then he became deadly serious: "Anything that you print can critically derail this investigation," he warned. "These homicidal tyrants prey on innocent victims. I'm asking all of you to give me your promise, right here and now, that you will not breathe a word of it, that nothing leaves this room. If you swear to do this for me, I will tell you every detail the moment we make a move to capture the suspects. There will be no one paper scooping the story, but you will all have every last fact about how this investigation progresses." While the newspapermen genuinely seemed to like Oldfield, they mostly didn't want to risk being cut off from future access to the inside information on what was sure to be a sensational story. Every one of the newspapermen gave his word.[16] It was a risky move for Oldfield, but it was his best shot for keeping his plan under wraps.

Even with his investigative team in place and the newsmen at bay, Oldfield knew the cards were still stacked in favor of the criminals. One thing that tied Oldfield's hands was this: Any letter or package traveling from a person's hands all the way to its final destination was completely protected from warrantless search and seizure by the federal government. This was why Hosford got into hot water for grabbing the letters from the mother and daughter swindlers. While Oldfield could inspect the envelopes from Sam Lima's fruit store and note the addressee, there was no legal way to see if Sam Lima was penning death threats, scribbling cartoon coffins, or demanding a hit on a victim who failed to pay. Opening a piece of mail without a warrant had been strictly forbidden since 1878 and the Supreme Court decision on ex Parte Jackson:

> Letters and sealed packages . . . in the mail are as fully guaranteed from examination and inspection, except to their outward form and weight, as if they were retained by the parties forwarding them in their own domiciles. The constitutional guarantee of the people to be secure in their papers against unreasonable searches and seizures extends to their papers, thus closed against inspection, wherever they may be. . . . No law of Congress can place in the hands of officials connected with the postal service any authority to invade the secrecy of letters, and such sealed packages in the mail; and all regulation adopted as to mail matter of this kind must be in subordination to the great principle embodied in the Fourth Amendment to the Constitution.[17]

◄ The house where Frank Oldfield was raised on Main Street in Ellicott City, Maryland. The first floor was used as the city's post office during the period when Frank's father, Hamilton, was postmaster.

► Frank Oldfield in 1909, during the Black Hand investigation.

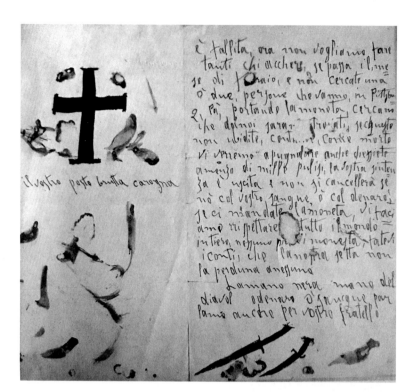

▲ Original fourth threatening letter sent to John Amicon in spring 1909. The letters were used by Oldfield to secure an indictment against Sam Lima and other members of The Black Hand.

▶ Translation of fourth threatening letter to John Amicon in spring 1909. Oldfield hired several Sicilian translators to translate correspondence during the Black Hand investigation.

And the Grand Jurors say that a translation of the words of said letter and communication into English is as follows:—

Finally you play deaf, but if you think we are fooling. No!Ugly carrion that you are. You will believe it when you see two or more with daggers in their hands which we will plunge into your heart. In that moment you will call for help, but there will be no remedy, it will be useless. We have put you down in the register of the dead, nasty brute, that for money you are content to be killed, do not think you can free yourself. No! No! no one escapes from under our hands. We have stabbed many in Italy, and consider that I, who write this, had a price of 14,000 lire on my head for eight years, was followed by the police, and know not how many I have killed with my trusty carbine, which has never failed me.

Now we do not wish to have too much idle talk. If the month of February passes and you do not search for one or two persons to come to Pittsburgh, Pa., bringing the money and searching and who will be found by us, if you do not obey this, count yourself as dead. We will come and stab you even if you are in the midst of a thousand police. Your sentence is passed, and it cannot be cancelled. Either your blood or your money. If you send the money, you will be well respected, and we will have you respected over all the world; no one will molest you. Consider well that our band pardons no one.

The Black Hand.
Hand of the Devil.
Either your money or blood.
We speak also to your brother.

Your place, Ugly Wretch.

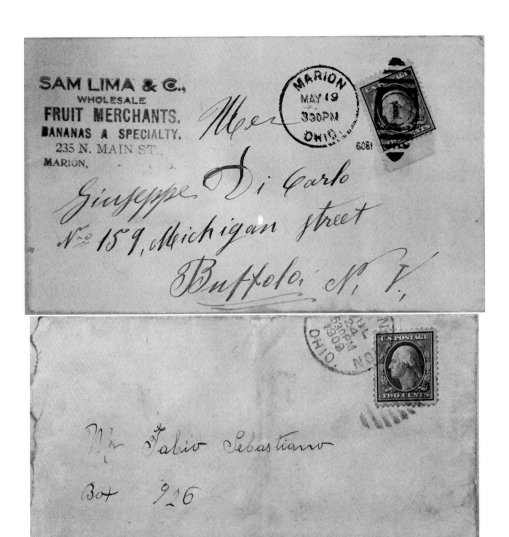

SAM LIMA & C.,
WHOLESALE
FRUIT MERCHANTS.
BANANAS A SPECIALTY.
235 N. MAIN ST.,
MARION,

Giuseppe Di Carlo
N°. 159, Michigan street
Buffalo, N. Y.

Mr. Fabio Sebastiano
Box 926

▲ An undercover letter sent by Sam Lima from Marion, Ohio. The addressee is meant to open the first letter, finding an extortion letter within with instructions to forward this extortion letter to a victim (hence the term "undercover").

► Original stamp marked by Post Office inspectors during the Black Hand investigation. The letter "O" was filled in with red ink to mark stamps on letters sent by members of the Society of the Banana.

◄ Frank Oldfield, R. M. C. Hosford, and George Pate in 1909 in the Columbus, Ohio, office of Postmaster Harry Krumm. The inspectors had just seized a large cache of weapons from the Black Hand suspects.

► Editorial newspaper photographs taken after the capture of Sam Lima and other Black Hand members. Inspector Oldfield, Columbus postmaster Harry Krumm, and Inspector Hutches (top left). Oldfield at his desk (top right). Postmaster Krumm, Oldfield, and Hutches with mountains of Black Hand evidence (lower right). *Commercial Tribune*, Cincinnati, 1909.

◄ There were many editorial cartoons about the Black Hand investigation. This cartoon from the *Cleveland Leader* was published during the capture. *Cleveland Leader*, June 11, 1909.

◄ Mug shots commissioned by Frank Oldfield after the Black Hand captures. From top left: Sam Lima, Marion, Ohio; Guiseppe Ignoffo, Marion, Ohio; Severio Ventola, Cincinnati, Ohio; Sebastian Lima, Marion, Ohio; Salvatore Arrigo, Cincinnati, Ohio; Vincenzo Arrigo, Cincinnati, Ohio; Francesco Spadaro, Cincinnati, Ohio; Augustino Marfisi, Dennison, Ohio.

► Mug shots commissioned by Frank Oldfield after the Black Hand captures. From top left: Pippino Galbo, Meadville, Pennsylvania; Orazio Runfola, Pittsburgh, Pennsylvania; Cologero Viccario, Bellefontaine, Ohio; Antonio Viccario, Dennison, Ohio; Salvatore Demma, Columbus, Ohio; Salvatore Rizzo; Marion, Ohio.

◄ Newspaper headline including courtroom sketch of Sam Lima on trial and photos of other Black Hand defendants. *Cleveland Leader*, January 15, 1910.

▼ Newspaper photograph of Toledo, Ohio, defense attorney John O'Leary, who defended Sam Lima and others from Marion, Ohio, in the Black Hand trial. Unknown newspaper, 1910.

◄ Newspaper article during trial showing photographs of (from left) Assistant U.S. Attorney Thomas Gary, U.S. Attorney William Day, U.S. Federal Judge Robert Tayler. Unknown newspaper, 1910.

◄ Trial exhibit storyboard with seized weapons of Black Hand members, including rifles, revolvers, knives, ammunition, and brass knuckles.

► Bertillon card of Salvatore Arrigo, December 1909. Bertillon cards were used by law enforcement to record physical attributes and other data about convicted criminals at the turn of the twentieth century.

▼ Oldfield family portrait taken December 1910 in Athens, Ohio. Top row (left to right): John Frank, Jr.; Frank Oldfield; Robert Fulton. Second row (left to right); Laura Oldfield-Noss (Frank's sister); Hamilton Noss; Hamilton Oldfield (Frank's father); Margaret Noss; Margaret Galena Oldfield. Bottom row (left to right): William Hamilton; Harry Edward.

▲ Vacation photo during the Panama Pacific Exposition in San Diego in 1915 showing Frank Oldfield and sons (left to right): William Hamilton; Robert Fulton; Frank Oldfield; Frances Foster (daughter of Congressman Foster); Harry Edward "Gist."

▲ Vacation photo of the Oldfield family from 1915 on the Mexico–United States border showing (left to right): Frank; William Hamilton "Hammy"; Margaret Galena; John Frank, Jr., "Barney"; Robert Fulton "Fulton"; Harry Edward "Gist"; and driver.

Oldfield had nothing yet on which to base a warrant to search Lima's letters. He had only Amicon's supposition that the Limas were somehow involved. If Frank did open a letter from Sam Lima or Sebastian Lima during the Black Hand investigation, he never admitted it publicly or in his correspondence. But what is certain from his case notes is that he did get a big break that opened up a window into The Black Hand organization.[18]

A Sicilian informant from the inside was feeding Oldfield information. In Oldfield's notes from April 1909, he describes what he had learned:

> Investigation was begun, and through the assistance of a Sicilian, it was learned that Salvatore Lima, Antonio Lima, Salvatore Rizzo, and Sebastian Lima of Marion Ohio and Severio Ventola of Columbus, Ohio were hanging around Amicon's place of business and the Saloon of Petro [*sic*] Marsini [*sic*] which is located just across the street from Amicon's expansive operations, for a day or two after each letter was received. Through the same party it was learned that Sicilians were in the habit of holding meetings at Salvatore Lima's store, 235 N. Main St. Marion, Ohio, and it was learned that on March 9, 1909, there was to be a meeting held at the above place, Sicilians from Cincinnati, Pittsburg, Cleveland, Columbus and other places to be present.[19]

Oldfield also learned that the letters Sebastian Lima sent from the Marion post office in late February were actually invitations to fellow members of the Society of the Banana. The invitation was for a March 9, 1909, meeting at Sam Lima's headquarters in Marion. That night, Oldfield was told by his informant that the Society would choose a new president and retire the old boss, Salvatore Arrigo.

Working out of his Columbus office, Oldfield compiled a list of addressees on the Limas' invitations. He asked the postmasters of the cities where the letters were sent to have mail carriers get some intelligence on the letter recipients. More than a dozen mail carriers now had extra duty as they walked neighborhood streets delivering letters and packages and picking up outgoing mail. Often, mailmen already knew a lot about every person at each address on their routes. They knew how many people were in their families, if they received letters from family abroad. They knew what type of goods they ordered by mail, and what type of bills they needed to pay. Now they would be looking to commit some of these details to memory and report back to their boss. *What did this particular person look like? Was he a business owner? Was there gossip in the neighborhood he might be some kind of criminal? Did he look poor or well-to-do? Did he seem at all suspicious?* Oldfield also reached out to police departments, Secret Service agents, and U.S. Marshals looking for anyone who had information on those receiving Lima's invitation.

Reports poured in. In order to get a handle on the logistical distribution of the recipients, Oldfield spread his notes across Harry Krumm's desk and office floor. Working with Hutches, Pate, and Hosford, Oldfield divided the men by city and created a detailed dossier on each Society member who received an invitation in the Ohio and Pennsylvania areas.

Columbus, Ohio

In Columbus, a man named Salvatore Demma received an invitation at his house on 296 East Naghten Street, just down the street from the Amicon Brothers' massive warehouse. There was nothing Oldfield could find on Demma as far as criminal background. A letter carrier on Demma's route described him as short, about five foot three inches, in his late twenties, with straight brown hair, a square jaw, several facial scars, a neat mustache, and a mini pompadour.[20] The other Columbus man receiving an invitation was Severio Ventola at 326 East Spring Street, two blocks south of Demma's house. The same letter carrier reported that Ventola was an old man in his sixties with a soft, sagging face, unkempt white hair, and matching ratty mustache. For Ventola, Oldfield's criminal background check turned up a twenty-five-year-long rap sheet, including a two-year stint in the Ohio State Penitentiary for forgery.

Cincinnati, Ohio

A man named Salvatore Arrigo received an invitation at 1637 Hughes Street in Cincinnati, where he lived with his wife, Ameka. The mail carrier described Arrigo as speaking Italian, in his sixties, about five foot six inches, perhaps taller if he wasn't so stooped over. Arrigo was slow-moving and walked with a cane, and his bulbous nose betrayed a life of heavy drinking. He didn't seem to care about his appearance, as his clothes were rumpled, his hair was disheveled, and he had a ratty beard down his neck.

With the help of the Cincinnati police, Oldfield discovered that a decade earlier, Arrigo had served two years at a maximum-security prison in upstate New York for a counterfeiting conviction. The Italian consulate told Oldfield that Arrigo had a criminal record back in Sicily, where he'd been a customs officer. The Cincinnati police suspected Arrigo was up to no good but could never pin anything on him without witnesses or victims. Another letter recipient, named Vincenzo Arrigo, was Salvatore's son. Vincenzo and his wife, Girolima, had a fruit stand at 19 West Twelfth Street, about a half-mile south from Salvatore Arrigo's house, where the couple lived with their six children. The postman described the younger Arrigo as very tall and muscular "for a Sicilian," midforties, balding, clean-shaven, with a narrow nose and lips so thin that his mouth was just a straight horizontal line beneath his nose. Frank found no criminal history on Vincenzo.

Finally, with a Cincinnati saloon owner who received a Lima invitation, Oldfield hit the jackpot. Francesco Spadaro was a true gangster. According to the Italian consulate, in the late 1880s, twenty-year-old Spadaro came from Termini Imerese, a city home to a massive government warehouse complex near Palermo. Spadaro's father was a hardened criminal who died in a straitjacket in the Palermo penitentiary. Oldfield learned that Spadaro first settled in Boston after emigrating from Sicily, then partnered in a saloon business with an Italian named Joseph Ciro.[21] Within a few months, Ciro was dead, stabbed to death by Spadaro, who took the whole business interest and all of Ciro's belongings. Spadaro was arrested, tried, and acquitted on a witness's perjured testimony. His next stop was Cincinnati, where he opened a saloon and low-budget boardinghouse at 227 West Sixth Street.[22] He was soon in trouble again, and on March 15, 1887, he was sentenced to serve two years for forgery in the Ohio State Penitentiary.

Oldfield sent undercover agents to Cincinnati to stake out Spadaro's saloon and the surrounding neighborhood. They reported that many respected Italians kept their distance from the steely-eyed mobster in his forties, but there was a constant stream of Sicilian and Italian laborers in and out of the boardinghouse and saloon.

Dennison, Ohio

In Dennison, the mail carrier described Antonio "Tony" Vicario, another Lima invitee, as in his late teens. A handsome boy, he had a round face with full lips and strong features. He always dressed casually and either shaved often or had little facial hair. Vicario worked for Augustino Marfisi, a local merchant in his midforties who owned a saloon, candy store, and fruit shop, and whom the police suspected of Black Hand involvement. The mail carrier said that Marfisi was married to a woman named Gerolama and the couple had five daughters and were active in Dennison's Immaculate Conception Catholic Church.[23] Again, there were no arrest records or immigration records on Vicario or Marfisi.

Bellefontaine, Ohio

From the Italian consulate, Oldfield learned that Cologero "Charlie" Vicario, the brother of Antonio, came from the city of Messina on the northeastern tip of Sicily. After Vicario's mother and brother were killed in a massive earthquake in 1908, twenty-seven-year-old Vicario left for the United States. At the time he left, he was a suspect in the mutilation killing of one of his enemies. According to the post office in Bellefontaine, Vicario, a clean-shaven man with a hairy mole on his right cheek and a bum right arm with limited range, arrived sometime in 1908 and had sent money back to Sicily regularly since.[24]

What really got Oldfield's interest was that Vicario was a partner in the Demar Fruit Company, the business where Salvatore Cira was murdered in cold blood with two extortion letters in his pocket. Bellefontaine police, who still had the Cira file open, told Oldfield that Vicario was living in Cira's house with Cira's widow, and it appeared he was romantically involved with the murdered man's fourteen-year-old daughter.

Meadville and Pittsburgh, Pennsylvania

There were two invitations that went to Pennsylvania. One went to Orazio Runfola, a Sicilian in his thirties with brown curly hair who owned a cigar shop at 2207 Pennsylvania Avenue, Pittsburgh. Another went to Meadville, to a fruit vendor named Pippino Galbo. Frank found immigration records showing Galbo came to the United States from Sicily in 1899.[25] The postal carrier reported that Galbo lived in a house in back of his shop with his wife, Angeline Leon, and their four young children, two girls and two boys.[26] Galbo had arched eyebrows and a protruding chin and dressed impeccably, with diamond stick pins and jeweled cuff links. The postman also said that Galbo was well-known and well-liked around Meadville and was known to own more than ten thousand dollars in real estate around town. Several invitations went to New York State, but for the time being, Oldfield knew he had his hands full. He would make his first assault on the suspects in Ohio and Pennsylvania.

Inspector George Pate was supervised from the Cincinnati post office by Inspector-in-Charge Abraham Holmes. Pate's stationing was normally in the rural southern Ohio area. Oldfield selected Pate for his investigative team against The Black Hand in 1909.

On March 8, the day before the meeting was supposed to take place at Lima's store, Oldfield called inspectors George Pate, Edward Hutches, and Raleigh Hosford and his friend from Athens, a Post Office employee named John Gist, to meet him in Marion. The men strategized all day and into the night. Pate would cover the railway station, they decided, as he was the least conspicuous of the four. Oldfield and Hosford would watch Lima's store from different vantage points. Hutches would cover the back of the Lima residence in the alley behind Main Street. The team went over and over their notes, letters from the Italian embassy, and physical descriptions of the suspects from the mail carriers. They committed everything to memory, hoping to be able to identify the attendees arriving from out of town.

There were very few relationships between the public at large and the insular Italian community, so word of Oldfield's queries had not yet reached the gang. Most Sicilians still lived by the law of Omertà, had a high level of distrust for American institutions, and did not have personal relationships or friendships outside their own communities. Sam Lima and his cohorts had no idea what was brewing.

CHAPTER 8

THE BOSS

Late in the afternoon of March 9, 1909, George Pate, wearing a slouchy suit with his jacket unbuttoned, loitered in the arched entryway of the Marion train station and waited. The Sicilians came on different trains from all different directions. On the Cincinnati inbound, an old man walked especially slowly: Salvatore Arrigo. With him came another, younger man, who Pate knew must be Vincenzo Arrigo, the old man's son. On the line from Pittsburgh came an impeccably dressed man in a well-tailored suit with a diamond stickpin sparkling in his silk tie: Orazio Runfola. Another on a Pittsburgh train was inordinately good-looking, with black eyes and chiseled cheekbones, his black hair perfectly slicked back from his handsome forehead and a scar running from his ear halfway to his mustache: Pippino Galbo. A kid, maybe in his late teens, about five foot two inches, with no facial hair, arrived from Dennison: Tony Vicario.

Francesco Spadaro, the saloon owner from Cincinnati, arrived next. He was impossible to miss, with a huge walrus mustache and ample second chin. He came not by the regular B&O line, but by the Ohio Electric Railway from Columbus. He was accompanied by another Sicilian, who Pate assumed must be Salvatore Demar. Both went into the station and sat down, evidently waiting for someone else. After a short while they left and headed in the direction of Main Street and Sam Lima's fruit store.

A short man with a dimple in his chin and thick, straight hair got off the regular train from Cincinnati. Pate checked off the list in his head: Salvatore Rizzo. On the inbound from Columbus came two older men: the white-haired Severio Ventola and a large-waisted, well-dressed Sicilian with a long graying beard: Antonio Lima, Sam Lima's father.

Hosford and Oldfield waited across from Lima's store inside the lobby of the Pilgrim Inn, a two-story hotel. They could see through the giant window but remain hidden from the street. They watched the men enter Lima's store one by one. Soon after, a few of them left and came back carrying cots, which they must have purchased from the local hardware store. It would be a long night.

When it was completely dark, all four inspectors took to the streets to monitor the store from four different vantage points. It was a cold March evening and all of the windows were closed in the store. Oldfield wished he could hear what was going on, but even if he could have, there was no way to understand what was being said without a translator.

The lights at Lima's burned on and flickered, and Frank assumed that the Society of the Banana meeting was in full swing late into the night. He was right. The men had a lot of current business to cover. There was new ground to break as well. This was not an ad hoc gang of criminals haphazardly going after one victim, then the next. This was an interstate and intercontinental coalition. This was a covert and tight-knit confederation. And best of all to Sam Lima, the new and improved Society of the Banana was just like a corporation, just like Amicon Brothers & Co.

Sam Lima no longer saw himself as a criminal. He saw himself as a CEO, and he was about to be elected along those lines by the men at the meeting. He saw these regional leaders as his board of directors. He fancied himself like the shipping magnates in the Great Lakes or the oil and steel barons who built skyscrapers and put their names on top. He was just as smart as they were, he knew. Even smarter. Who among Mather, Bolton, Rockefeller, or Carnegie had the government subsidize their entire profit with the nearly free logistical services of the Post Office? The only overhead to Lima's organization was a few hundred two-cent stamps per year and a bit of travel to meet up with marks.

Fourteen Mafiosi sat cramped in Lima's back room on chairs and fruit crates amid the smoke of a dozen cigars. Commanding his audience, Salvatore Lima called the meeting to order. First order of business, a vote to elect a new "Boss" of the Society of the Banana. Arrigo, everyone knew, was too decrepit and unmotivated to remain in the position. A unanimous vote made Cincinnati saloon owner Francesco Spadaro the successor. Spadaro agreed to the title, happy to collect checks and use his saloon as cover for the group's illegal activities. The real control was to go to the Society's new director.

All in favor of Salvatore Lima to be the new director of the Society of the Banana?

Thirteen hands rose.

Lima's first order of business was to hammer out the Society's new bylaws.[1] There would be no insubordination, none at all. Over the evening, a brutal and sinister list of sixteen articles was proposed and agreed upon.

By Laws and Regulations of the Society of the Bananas

Art. 1. The person who tries to reveal the secrets of this society will be punished with death;

Art. 2. A member who offends one of his companions, staining his honor, will be punished according to article 1;

Art. 3. The member who tries to do harm to another branch of the society, or to the family of other companions, if this harm shall have been grave, will be undressed and marked on his body with the mark of infamy and called with word of contempt, "Swindler," and if the offense is more grave, he will be stabbed;

Art. 4. The person who is a coward and does not sustain the punishment assigned to him by the Society, he will be punished in accordance with Art. 3;

Art. 5. The member who profits by the opportunity of the plan of another member, is punished as prescribed in Art. 3; if the misdeamor [sic] is less grave he must make restitution within 24 hours of that which he caused to be lost, and he will be out off from his share of the profits for two months;

Art. 6. The member who offends another companion with offensive titles, if the offense is considered grave, will not only lose his right of membership but will also be stabbed. If the offense is less grave, he will be cut off from his share of the profits for 3 months and at the same time must do his duty;

Art. 7. The member who has received the insult and resents it himself, without notifying the Society, is punished according to Art. 3;

Art. 8. The member who abandons one of his companions in the time of need will be held to be a traitor, and then punished according to Art. 3;

Art. 9. The person appointed to inspect must always go around and maintain good order as it is prescribed, passing all the news around. Failing in this for the first time, he will be cut off from his share of the profits for 3 months, then second time he will be stabbed;

Art. 10. A reunion of the society cannot be called for a visiting member if he is not known;

Art. 11. The person who goes away must pass the news and tell the "local" in the place where he goes how long he will be there, and if he carries a message he must leave his pledge. Failing to do this he will be punished according to Art.6;

Art. 12. The person who shall have been called to use the knife and does not go through fear, will be punished according to Art. 3;

Art 13. The person who deals sparingly, (does not do his duty) will be punished according to Art. 3 at a convenient place by the society with a brand on his face;

Art. 14. The person who refutes the call of command will, for the first time be deprived of his share for 3 months; for the second time, from one to two cuts with the knife, for the third time, from two to five cust [sic], as the society thinks best, and to follow his work as prescribed if it is grave, he will be punished according to Art. 3 without having any benefits from the society.

Art. 15. The person who is sent somewhere by the society will be paid by the day and for the journey;

Art. 16. There can be no excuse for failures or penalties in conformity with the articles. However there may be extenuating circumstances in case of drunkenness.[2]

With that squared away, Lima got down to the main business at hand. Each man came to the meeting with a list of "friends" for the Society to persecute. Having done their background research on the marks, they estimated net worth and monthly income and put a price on the victim's "friendship." Most of the proposed victims were fruit dealers or other merchants whom the Blackhanders did business with. Some were doctors or other professionals. All were Italian or Sicilian. In a leather-bound ledger, Sam Lima listed all the names. In the next column, he wrote the person's address. In the third column was the amount of money the Society would require in order to let the victim and his family live. The fourth column he left blank to fill in once payment or partial payment was made. If no payment was made, there would eventually be an *x* in that spot. They then set about creating an intricate plan to deliver their demands, not directly, but in a convoluted scheme of "under cover" letters sent to victims by other victims. There were forty-three human targets on the list. The sums they would owe ranged from $200 to $20,000, for an initial payment. If all went as planned, in the next month, the Society of the Banana would rake in $118,000.

The last thing on the agenda to discuss was something eating at Sam Lima: the defiant, dismissive John Amicon. *How dare he disrespect the Society and publicly belittle us?* Lima called on baby-faced Charlie Vicario from Bellefontaine, his favorite go-to hit man. When Lima said the word, Vicario would take a stiletto and put it into Amicon's heart. Lima would give Amicon one more chance to pay. In the meantime, Lima ordered another man to go and light a stick of dynamite under the back porch of Charlie Amicon's house. That should encourage both brothers to come up with the money.

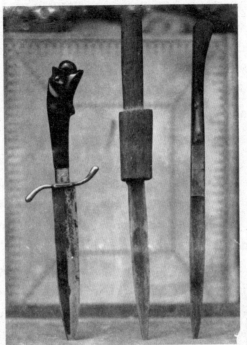

Stilettos, also known as "dirks," were carried by all members of the Society of the Banana and other Sicilian Mafia gang members of the era. These examples were seized from Society members and used as trial exhibits.

Outside Lima's store at daybreak, the inspectors waited. The Sicilians emerged from the shop one or two at a time. Some came out bleary-eyed. Some looked just as dapper as they had the night before. Over the next few days, without any clue they were being watched at every turn, the Society of the Banana began its new reign of terror: an all-out assault on forty-three victims all at once. Within a week of the meeting, the post office clerks and postmasters in Marion, Cincinnati,

Columbus, and a half-dozen other cities were tracking letters sent to a half-dozen states. Every post office where the letters left the hands of Society members was watched. Oldfield engaged local policemen, federal marshals, Secret Service, and Pinkertons to help investigate the letters' final recipients. Frank and his fellow inspectors were completely overwhelmed. It was a tornado of activity on the part of the Society of the Banana that Oldfield didn't have the manpower to match.

Still, they tried. Oldfield, Pate, Hutches, Hosford, and another inspector from Canton, Ohio, named A. P. Owen went city to city, knocking on doors. Terrified Italians and Sicilians answered, wide-eyed and stuttering. "We know you just got a letter. What did it say?" the detectives asked. The inspectors were in plain clothes but had the unmistakable look of lawmen. Time and again, the immigrants denied that they had received a letter. Many said they didn't speak English and gestured that they had no idea what was being asked of them. In one case, Hosford got information that a certain victim paid off The Black Hand with a check. "Can we have the endorsed check?" Oldfield asked him after tracking him down at home. The canceled check bearing the endorsement of one of the blackmailers would be critical evidence. The victim shook as though breaking a fever, and flatly refused to give it up.[3]

Two weeks went by and the Black Hand case wasn't getting anywhere even though Frank was blowing through an enormous amount of resources. With his army engaged all across Ohio and into Pennsylvania, travel expenses piled up. The inspectors were given promissory notes that paid for hotels, meals, travel, and other necessities. Oldfield hired dozens of private detectives from the Pinkerton bureau in Cleveland. Their expenses went on the Black Hand case tab as well as their contracted salaries. There were two translators working nonstop, charging by the hour, and Frank was about to hire more.[4]

Local police and sheriffs' departments billed Oldfield for their man-hours, including document retrievals, copies of documents, mug shots, and time on the streets. The team sent hundreds of telegrams, and there were dozens of long-distance phone calls to pay for. There were freelance camera operators hired for stakeouts and camera equipment for inspectors. And there was one line item in Oldfield's budget with a significant cash outlay: *informant*. No name given. Inspector-in-Charge Holmes grumbled about Oldfield's endless spending to the higher-ups in Washington, especially with the money going out to some unnamed source. But Frank was so sure that he'd have dozens of victims stepping up and willing to testify in court that all of the expense would be worth it.

In truth, he had zero.

It was like the Cira fiasco all over again, but now Oldfield's entire career was on the line. John Amicon was the only victim who had agreed to testify in court against The Black Hand. How could Frank prove there was a highly organized band of criminals with only one single victim coming forward?

Time for plan B. If he couldn't pressure the victims to come forward working behind the scenes, then he would smoke the criminals out right in the open. In late March, Oldfield, Pate, and Hutches set up a camera on a tripod directly across the street from Lima's fruit store. The surveillance photo taken of Salvatore Lima and family that day shows a completely unintimidated Lima. In fact, when Lima saw the camera, he gathered the family, his wife, Mary, and their three little girls and baby boy, his sister Caterina with her husband, Sebastian Lima, and their donkeys and cart. Then the Lima family stood as if they were having a professional portrait done for posterity. The girls were in pretty white dresses. Sam Lima's wife and sister looked deadpan into the camera. Sebastian appeared annoyed. Looking as

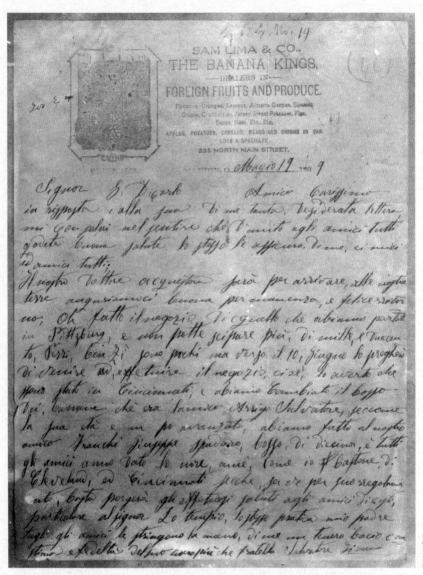

Internal Society communication in Italian between members Salvatore Lima of Marion, Ohio, and Giuseppe DiCarlo of Buffalo, New York, after the March 9, 1909, meeting of Society members, informing DiCarlo that "friend" Dr. Vincenzo Purpura of Cincinnati, Ohio, has begun paying extortion money to the Society, Salvatore Arrigo is retired as "Boss of the Bananas," Franchi "Frankie" Spadaro is the new "Boss," and that Lima has been elected "Overseer of Cleveland and Cincinnati" by the "Aen" (brotherhood). Used as a trial exhibit.

Oldfield Collection

Buffalo, N.Y.

Mr.G. Dicarlo,

Dearest friend:

Our Doctor by this time will have arrived
in our land and let us wish him a happy voyage and safe
return.   I have closed the deal with him of whom we
spoke in Pittsburg, and he could not ship more than 1200 -
this is little, but by the 10th of June, I will ask him to
complete the deal.

I advise you that I was in Cincinnati and that we
changed the Boss of the Bananas which was the friend
Arrigo Salvatore, as he is well advanced in years, and
we have made our friend Franchi Guiseppi Spadaro Boss
of the "Acn", and all the friends honored me as overseer
Of Cleveland and Cincinnati, and this will serve for your
guidance.

Nothing more.

Salutes, etc.

Salvatore Lima.

Internal Society communication in English between members Salvatore Lima
of Marion, Ohio, and Giuseppe DiCarlo of Buffalo, New York. Translated from the
original letter by Italians hired by Inspector Frank Oldfield.

Oldfield Collection

if he hasn't a care in the world, dressed in baggy work clothes with his hair high in a curling pompadour, Sam stared at the camera and nearly smiled. It was the look of a calculating criminal who believed he was ten times smarter than any of the buzzard lawmen stalking him.

But as much as Lima looked cavalier, he was definitely disturbed. Soon after the stakeout, on a tree by the Marion courthouse, a sign appeared written in blood. *Unless the investigation into the Italians is called off, we will burn down this city.*[5] He'd never found himself in the crosshairs of the law before. Most of his colleagues had done time in jail or prison, some many times. But he was too smart. The letters he sent were untraceable. He spun a web so tangled and intricate no one could follow his tracks. Still, he couldn't help feeling that the cops were closing in.

With Oldfield's team staking out the homes and businesses of all fourteen men from Lima's meeting, it was obvious that something was up. It wasn't only Lima who was getting nervous. On March 25, three weeks after the gang's meeting, Orazio Runfola wrote Lima a letter to tell him that he had left his wife, Nunzia, and kids at home and was in hiding.[6] He was trying to conduct business from a hideout because he knew he was being tracked by detectives. Lima, like a mouse catching the scent of a cat, sent off a frenzy of letters to his board of directors warning members to lie low and watch their backs.

It was a warning that went out a little too late. There were forty-three "cover letters" containing forty-three extortion letters traveling on mail cars and mail pouches in every direction across the Great Lakes, New York, Pennsylvania, West Virginia, and Chicago. Letters even went as far as Oregon, where Lima had a brother, Michelangelo, with a Portland operation identifying victims on the West Coast.

On March 29, postal clerks at Marion reported that Sam Lima dropped off a stack of letters.[7] As he was instructed, the mail clerk gave the unknowing Lima marked stamps and called Oldfield, who inspected the addressees on all the envelopes. Oldfield's biggest hope was that the final recipient of the extortion letter inside one of those letters was John Amicon. Because without seeing a letter through its journey from Lima's hands all the way to a victim who would testify, Oldfield had nothing on which to base an arrest warrant.

One was addressed to Tony Vicario, so Edward Hutches went to Dennison to trail the young gangster. While Hutches was following Vicario, the same scenario was unfolding all across the region, with other inspectors, postmasters, mailmen, and lawmen watching the Blackhanders as they sent and received letters.

On March 30, Vicario arrived at the Dennison post office and checked his post office box. There were two letters. From behind two-way glass, D. C. Mann, the Dennison postmaster, and Inspector Hutches watched the young Sicilian open the envelopes and read the letters.[8]

Then Postmaster Mann came out from behind the counter. "Wait, Vicario, there is some more mail for you."

Mann handed Vicario the Lima letter.

Vicario opened it, took out another sealed letter and a slip of paper. From the angle where he was behind the glass, Hutches saw "Columbus, Ohio" on the address of the second letter but could not make out the name of the addressee.

When Vicario looked up, Mann was back behind the glass with Hutches. Vicario appeared to see them, stuffed the letters in his pocket, and ran out of the building.

Later that day, Vicario ran into Postmaster Mann on the street. In broken English, Vicario demanded to know what the detectives were doing at the post office. Mann pretended not to understand the Sicilian's thick accent. Vicario, frustrated, took out his pen and on a paper sack he was carrying wrote the word "detectives."

"There are no detectives at the post office," Mann casually told Vicario. "Occasionally, an inspector drops in to look over my accounts."

Mann walked away smiling, happy to be part of something so suspenseful in his sleepy little town with a population of less than four thousand. As soon as he was back in his office, Mann marked more stamps with red dots specifically for Vicario and his boss, saloon owner Augustino Marfisi.

On April 1, a rattled Tony Vicario wrote a letter to his comrade Giuseppe Nuzzo in Cleveland. Nuzzo was another Society of the Banana member, but had not been at the March meeting.

Dear Friend Nuzzo:

Some persons came on purpose to find some banana bills, and I warn you to be sure and not make any shipments, for these buzzards will get you for sure. I am sure you are convinced of what I say.

Saluting you together with your brother, Your Friend, A. Vicario

The Post Office inspectors were interfering with Sam Lima's bottom line, and he was determined to put a stop to the investigation. In the first week of April, Sebastian and Sam loitered around the Amicon warehouse and watched the brothers come and go from Pete Marsino's saloon across the street.[9] Amicon's air was nonchalant. Rather than snarl at the Limas as he had before, John Amicon pretended not to notice them at all. That made Sam Lima all the more furious. There was still no money coming from either Amicon brother, so Lima made a decision. The time was right for a little reminder. The next day, a dynamite explosion blew the back porch off Charlie Amicon's home. Apparently, Lima had a beef with saloon owner Pete Marcino, too,

Pietro "Pete" Marcino's saloon in Columbus, Ohio, was across the street from John and Charles Amicon's expansive produce distribution warehouse on the corner of Sixth and Naghten Streets. Members of the Society of the Banana used the saloon as a meeting place and to stake out the Amicon brothers for extortion.

Unknown newspaper photo of Pietro "Peter" Marcino's saloon in Columbus, Ohio, after it was bombed in 1909 by the Society of the Banana. The saloon was destroyed after Marcino declined to continue to allow their activities in his business and was also intended to intimidate the Amicon brothers, whose warehouse was across the street. The newspapers of the day described the "Collapse of the Saloon," in denial of its complete destruction by a dynamite blast.

because not long after, Marcino's saloon was blown into a million pieces.

One day after the explosion, Columbus members of the Society of the Banana, the white-haired Severio Ventola and the young Salvatore Demma, went to the Amicon Brothers' giant warehouse on Naghten Street to further intimidate the brothers.[10]

The Amicons knew who they were. Demma was in the fruit business and Ventola worked for Sam Lima's fruit company when he wasn't working a section gang. John and Charlie stood in the doorway unmoving, their arms crossed.

"What do you want?" John demanded icily.

"Now, John, if you suspect me of sending you threat letters, why don't you have me arrested?" Ventola asked.

"If I knew positively that you sent me that kind of a letter, I would take a gun and kill you, and you wouldn't have to go to court."

The warehouse manager called John to the telephone, and he left Charlie with Ventola and Demma.

"If you boys will let those fellows alone now and not bother with this investigation, you won't receive any more letters or have any more trouble," Ventola told Charlie.

Charlie knew that proposing that his brother back off was fruitless. But he was so rattled by the explosion at his house that he made a futile attempt to get his brother to let it all go. John Amicon refused to even discuss it.[11]

A week went by with John and Charles Amicon at odds on how to handle their predicament. It had been a month since the Society of the Banana meeting. Money was rolling in. Sam Lima, once again, felt unstoppable.

Then on April 8, a letter from Dennison, Ohio, came by mail carrier to Columbus, addressed to Signore Giovanni Amicone, John

Amicon's Italian name. Amicon immediately called Oldfield. When the inspector came, Amicon handed him the letter. Oldfield took out his magnifying glass and looked closely at the stamp. Inside the letter *o* in "two" was a tiny red dot.

Amicon opened the letter. Inside was a threat to his life written in Italian and a demand for payment of ten thousand dollars. He translated the message to Oldfield. It was in the same handwriting as the letter that had left Sam Lima's shop for Dennison ten days before.

Amicon studied the letter and then studied the small inspector, who looked as if he was so excited he might explode. The tiny, pale man with deep blue eyes and a ridiculously tall derby hat was finally proving everything he promised he'd be.

After nearly three grueling months, Inspector Oldfield now had enough evidence to report to U.S. Attorney William Day and have a federal judge sign a warrant to arrest Sam Lima.

CHAPTER 9

THE TAKEDOWN

With a solid trail of evidence linking the perpetrator, Sam Lima, to the victim, John Amicon, Frank Oldfield finally felt confident he was about to take the Society of the Banana down. The second week of April 1909, he took his notes, the paperwork, and the extortion letters directly to the U.S. attorney for the Northern District of Ohio.[1] He found William L. Day in his Cleveland office in the federal building on Superior Avenue. Although he was one of the youngest federal prosecutors in the country at thirty-three years old, Day had quite a pedigree in the criminal justice system. Most notably, he was the son of Supreme Court Justice William R. Day. The elder Day had a superlative reputation and was known on the Court as a "very conservative thinker, a man who abhors everything in the nature of 'fireworks,' a safe and reliable counselor in every national crisis."[2] The same year that President Teddy Roosevelt nominated William R. to the bench, William L., also a prominent Ohio Republican, was appointed U.S. attorney. The young Day was incredibly well respected, both as a prosecutor and as a man about town. He was tall, handsome, and clean-shaven, with a deep cleft in his chin. He was a family man as well, and the day Oldfield walked into his office, he had a third child on the way.

Before Oldfield could arrest Lima on charges of mail fraud, he needed Day to agree to prosecute the case as a federal crime. Frank laid the evidence on Day's desk. He pointed out the letters he said were sent by Sam Lima. He showed how the handwriting matched in all of them. He offered Day the transcriptions typed up by his secretary after being translated by the Sicilians he'd hired. He told Day all about the meeting on March 9, the first meeting of Mafiosi ever witnessed by law enforcement. "This is the biggest crime ring Ohio and the Northeast has ever seen," Oldfield told Day, practically jumping on top of the prosecutor's desk. Lima appeared to be the boss, Oldfield said, but there were at least fourteen others whom he could tie to the mail fraud conspiracy. Dozens more would fall once he had a chance to coerce confessions out of the suspects. All Frank needed now was an arrest warrant for Sam and Sebastian Lima.

Day looked over the evidence and listened intently to Oldfield. It was the beginnings of a good case with the threatening letters and the English translations, but he was not yet ready to give Oldfield what he wanted. He told Oldfield that he just didn't have nearly enough to prosecute.

Oldfield felt his face grow hot and his ears turn red. He'd spent every waking hour for almost three months to make a direct connection between Lima and Amicon. He knew that federal mail fraud charges were hard for prosecutors to make stick, but he was positive that this clear-cut evidence linking the two men, a letter marked and monitored throughout its entire journey from suspect to victim, would be enough.

Still, if Oldfield was right about how much money the Society of the Banana was worth, he knew that Day would be up against some of the most cunning defense attorneys in the business. So far, Oldfield had only one witness who would testify, a witness whose English was broken at best, a fact that would likely prejudice the jurors against him with the help of a shrewd defense. It was a chance the calculating William Day did not want to take. Oldfield was not one to beg or plead. Seeing Day wasn't likely to budge, he stomped out of the Cleveland federal building and caught the next train back to Columbus.

On the ride home, Oldfield's shrewd mind worked on a new plan. In truth, Frank knew that the young prosecutor was right. With only Amicon's testimony and one letter, he didn't have enough evidence. Oldfield began to shore up his case in his head. All of Amicon's letters had to be translated, transcribed, and decoded, as well as any other correspondence Oldfield's team could get their hands on. Then he and his team would systematically build a dossier on every suspected member of the Society of the Banana and the forty-three suspected victims.

With a long list, Oldfield and his detectives went out into the field. In Dennison, a nervous Italian businessman named Fabio Sebastiano received a letter from Lima via a Giuseppe DiCarlo in Buffalo. Oldfield tailed Sebastiano to Steubenville, Ohio, where he observed him meet with a man and transfer a fabric sack of something. When Oldfield approached Sebastiano, he refused to talk. Frank had no way of know- ing at the time, but the last letter Sebastiano had received warned him that going to the police would result in his death. It included a cartoon coffin with the ominous caption "If you do not fulfill all that we seek from you, your bones will be in here."[3]

Inspector Raleigh Hosford followed a letter mailed from Sam Lima to Orazio Runfola in Pittsburgh. From there, the letter inside was sent to a Vincenzo Purpura at 614 East First Street in Cincinnati. Purpura was a wealthy doctor with a thriving practice. He was also very vocal about shutting down illegal immigration from Italy and Sicily. Hosford tailed Purpura. He watched the doctor meet a man on a bridge and exchange something that Hosford couldn't make out. When Hosford approached Purpura after the man left and asked him what it was he gave the man, Purpura claimed that it was a gift. He knew nothing about any letters, and no, he was not being threatened by The Black Hand.

On April 3, 1909, a letter was sent from Meadville to Gaetano DeCamilli at his saloon on Eighty-Ninth Street in Cleveland.[4] DeCamilli was furious. It was the third letter. He had ignored the first two, and like Amicon, he vowed not to pay the extortionists. He went to the Cleveland police for help and showed them the letters. The police watched his saloon but did not see anything suspicious. Afterward, DeCamilli received another letter. The police in Cleveland shared it with Oldfield, who they knew was looking for information on The Black Hand. DeCamilli handed the letter over to the Post Office inspectors. It read "From one of our secret spies we have learned that you have informed the police, contrary to our warning. Therefore it is time to die, and on the first occasion you will feel a bullet in your stomach. Coward. You have willed it and you will die like a dog." DeCamilli told Oldfield that he didn't know who the letters were coming from, and to Frank's chagrin, not in a million years would he testify in court.

Also on April 3, another letter was sent from Newcastle, Pennsylvania, to Giuseppe Gatto in Blairsville, Pennsylvania. When a Pinkerton detective knocked on Gatto's door and asked about the letter, he denied receiving any letter at all, even though the detective had just watched him take it from his mailbox. Gatto was stuck. He wanted help from the federal officers, but didn't trust them. He did, however, trust that The Black Hand would make good on its promises. The letter told him in no uncertain terms, "If you go to the police, your head will fly in the air."[5]

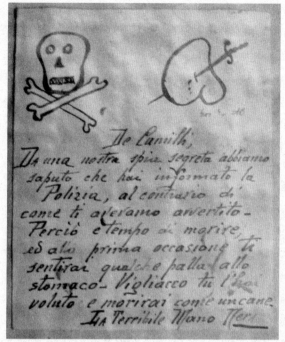

Gaetano DeCamilli of Cleveland, Ohio, received numerous Black Hand letters from the Society of the Banana. This example in Italian has graphics of a skull and a dagger in a heart drawn in human blood. Used as a trial exhibit.

Gov. Ex. #10.

De Camilli:-

From one of our secret spies we have learned that you have informed the police, contrary to our warning. Therefore it is time to die, and on the first occasion you will feel a bullet on your stomach. Coward. You have willed it and you will die like a dog.

The Terrible Black Hand.

Gaetano DeCamilli Black Hand letter in English. Translated from the original letter by Italians hired by Inspector Frank Oldfield.

While the tedious work of following up with victims and staking out the homes of those sending letters was going on, Frank sent agents to scour post offices and banks and collect all of the financial evidence they could. He dispatched deputies and secretaries to dig into immigration records and enlisted clerks to dig through dusty files in county courthouses for records on the gang. He hoped to tie the band to cohorts in Sicily to prove the vast scope of their operation. Once they had enough evidence, Frank would convince Mayor Louis Scherff of Marion to write search and arrest warrants for Sam Lima. Then Frank would follow with arrest warrants for all the rest. He and his team would sweep every last one of the Black Hand businesses and homes and build the biggest and tightest case that any federal prosecutor had ever seen.

With all that, Oldfield knew he still had a critical missing link that he couldn't find on his own. Although he had a secret informant, he didn't have a single Mafia insider who would turn state's evidence. How could he? There wasn't one Italian detective in the Post Office inspector ranks; probably not anyone who could even speak the language, and who could try to infiltrate The Black Hand. In fact, in the history of the United States of America, there were only two men Frank Oldfield knew of who could bring him a witness from inside The Black Hand. The first was the celebrated detective Joe Petrosino of the New York Police Department's Italian Squad. But it was too late for help from Petrosino. After making headway stamping out Italian crime in New York for several years, Petrosino traveled to Sicily to track down a killer. There, on March 12, 1909, just three days after Sam Lima's meeting in Marion, the world's most famous Italian police detective died in front of the Café Oreto on the Piazza Marina in Termini Imerese, Sicily. He was gunned down by two Mafia assassins.[6] After Petrosino's murder, there was no leadership left in

Giuseppe Gatto of Blairsville, Pennsylvania, received numerous Black Hand letters from the Society of the Banana. This example in Italian asks Gatto for ten thousand dollars (a tremendous sum in 1909). Used as a trial exhibit.

Giuseppe Gatto Black Hand letter in English. Translated from the original letter by Italians hired by Inspector Frank Oldfield.

the New York Italian Squad, only a few scattered detectives with zero budget and little support from the NYPD.

The only Italian detective left standing with the skills Oldfield needed was Francis Dimaio of the Pinkerton Detective Agency. In the twenty years since Dimaio went undercover in the New Orleans Parish Prison, he'd become one of the Pinkertons' most important operatives and was now the director of the Pittsburgh bureau. Often working for coal mining or steel interests, Dimaio still loved to do undercover work. Dressed as a laborer, he went to mob meetings around Pittsburgh. And in 1909, Dimaio's investigation landed dozens of Mafiosi in jail for extorting money from laborers in various coal mines. Oldfield knew that Dimaio could be a huge help. He excelled at extracting information from Italian victims and Sicilian criminals alike—all without the bureaucratic constraints that loosely tied Frank's hands.

Having a contemporary so competent and legendary in ways that Oldfield was not must have weighed on Oldfield's fragile ego. Likely with some hesitation, but not having any other option, Frank made the call to the Pinkertons' Pittsburgh headquarters where Dimaio was the superintendent. He described the case to Dimaio in all its complicated detail and asked if he could hire Dimaio and some of his top Pinkerton men who specialized in Italian crime. It would be another expense that Inspector-in-Charge Abraham Holmes would be furious about, but Oldfield couldn't move forward without Dimaio. Oldfield needed the Italian detective to come along on takedowns, to interrogate suspects who didn't speak English or pretended not to, and by whatever means necessary, to help bring down the Society of the Banana. The most important thing that Oldfield needed, he told Dimaio, was an informant from inside the Society who would testify against Sam Lima and his confederates. Dimaio waited for a break in Oldfield's monologue and calmly responded, "Not a problem."

The Pinkerton detective already had the perfect mark, a young kid named Orazio Parabelli, newly initiated into The Society of the Banana in Pittsburgh. Dimaio had met Parabelli a few months earlier while undercover at a mob meeting in a dark Pittsburgh saloon. He was just a kid, nineteen years old, nervous and obviously not there on his own accord. Instinctively knowing he could use the kid somehow in the future, Dimaio made friends with Parabelli, acting as a sort of protector to the teenager and gaining his trust. Dimaio learned the anxious young man had come to Pittsburgh, where he worked in the mines after landing in America. After months of being harassed to join the gang, he was forced to join the Society of the Banana under penalty of death, he said, unless he could pay twenty-five dollars.[7] He didn't have twenty-five dollars. His role in the Society was to be on call to murder anyone the bosses told him to. If a "friend" refused to pay tribute to the gang, Parabelli was told he and others would draw cards. If he got the card with the lowest number, he would be the assassin. If he told anyone about the Society or failed to do his job, they would torture him and leave him to die. Nine men initiated him into the Society. One of them was Sam Lima from Ohio. Another was Orazio Runfola, a stogie maker from Pittsburgh.

As soon as Oldfield arranged to put Dimaio and the Pittsburgh Pinkertons on the U.S. government's payroll, Dimaio sent two of his pale, English-speaking heavies to grab Parabelli off the street. They took him to a secret location.

"What are you doing in the Mafia?" one of the men asked, getting inches from Parabelli's face. "We know you're not the type to be an assassin. We know you want a peaceful life."

Parabelli was too terrified to answer.

"Listen, we are with the government. We will protect you if you testify against the Black Hand organization, specifically the Society of the Banana in Ohio and Sam Lima."

"But they'll kill me," said a stuttering Parabelli.

"They won't know anything until the day you testify. Then we will hide you and keep you safe for the rest of your life. You will walk free from the Mafia. Say nothing now and testify later."

Parabelli didn't have much confidence that these pseudo-government thugs could protect him from the murderous likes of Sam Lima, but it didn't matter anymore. It was more horrifying to be marked as a murderer for the Society. He would take his chances with the lawmen. Dimaio made sure word didn't get out about Parabelli's brief chat with his Pinkerton agents. Then he sent the kid back to his job in the mines and told him to keep his trap shut.

Dimaio called Columbus. "Oldfield," he said, "I have your man."

In Postmaster Krumm's office with Hosford, Hutches, and Pate, Oldfield worked on his plan of attack. To be able to nab more than a dozen gangsters in a half-dozen cities, he needed precise execution from different agencies and several dozen operatives. Oldfield made contact with federal Secret Service men and Treasury officers, local police in Marion, Dennison, Columbus, and Bellefontaine, federal marshals, and several more Post Office inspectors. All got the same message: *Get ready.*

The first operation began in Marion, Ohio. At 1:30 a.m. on June 8, 1909,[8] Oldfield, Hutches, Hosford, and an Athens Post Office employee named John Gist, Oldfield's best friend back in Athens, all arrived in the post office. They met Postmaster Harry Krumm and went to get Sheriff Stark at home and two deputies at the sheriff's office. Together the group descended on Mayor Scherff's house, roused him from bed, and had him write a search warrant for Sam Lima's property and arrest warrants for Sam and Sebastian Lima.

With the addition of Pinkerton detective Dimaio, who arrived from Pittsburgh at sunup, they were ready to move.

Tuesday, June 8, 8:00 a.m., Lima's fruit store, Marion Ohio

Without the slightest warning, Dimaio, Oldfield, Hutches, Gist, and Sheriff Stark broke in Lima's front door and burst into the store. Sam Lima ran to the back of the store and escaped out a window, evading Hosford, who was waiting for him in the alley, expecting Lima would come out the back door. Hutches dashed around to the back and intercepted Lima by tackling him to the ground and wrestling a loaded pistol from his grip. Lima's wife and sister came into the store, screaming.[9]

With Hutches holding a gun on Lima, Frank forced the Sicilian to open the safe in the back room. At first, Lima refused, but he was quickly persuaded by Francis Dimaio. When the safe door opened, Oldfield couldn't help but smile. Jackpot. Inside were hundreds of letters and documents. Oldfield and Dimaio quickly went through them. There was a list of dozens of Lima's cohorts in the Society and a stack of accounting books for the extortion business. There were also piles of internal gang communications. The forty-three victims who had recently received extortion letters were all recorded in a leather-bound ledger, as well as the amounts paid. On a separate piece of paper was something that Dimaio, the only one who could read Italian, said were bylaws governing the Society of the Banana.

With Lima muttering threats in Italian, another of Lima's brothers-in-law, Giuseppe Ignoffo, froze to the wall. The inspectors filled two canvas mail pouches with the safe's contents. Gist and Sheriff Stark grabbed a trunk full of weapons and passed it off to deputies outside who kept an eye out for Sebastian Lima. Next, Oldfield and Hutches ripped into the walls. Lima was icily quiet now and showed no expression when, from behind the paneling, thousands of dollars in cash fell to the floor. There was more when Oldfield and Dimaio ripped up the floorboards, more inside the mattress, and stacks more in the back of the safe.[10] The detectives proceeded to tear up the entire home and store with Lima's wife hysterically pleading for them to stop. "We are law-abiding citizens," she screamed. "Sam Lima is a good man!"

When they'd searched every crevice, Frank slammed Lima into a chair. Hutches pointed his pistol at the suspect. Gist watched the entrance.

Frank got in Lima's face. "What do you know about Spadaro, Vicario, Arrigo . . ." he asked.

Lima refused to answer, pretending not to understand, until Dimaio encouraged him to find his English skills.

"Never heard of any," Lima spat, his round eyes narrowing at the detectives.

"What do you know about the Society of the Banana?"

"Never heard of it. I sell bananas. I'm a businessman."

"Aren't you the president of that society?" Dimaio pressed.

"I told you, I *never* heard of it."

"I know you're the chief of the Society," Oldfield told Lima. "I personally witnessed all these men come into this store on March 9. I watched all of your friends bring cots. They all stayed the night."

Lima shrugged and said nothing.

"Where's Antonio Lima?" Frank prodded, assuming that Sam and Sebastian were brothers and Lima both men's father.

"No idea."

Oldfield handcuffed Lima and shoved him outside for the deputies to take him to the Marion jail. In the corner, a cowering Giuseppe Ignoffo muttered about the great character of Salvatore Lima.

Oldfield and his team waited for several hours in the shop with

Lima's family. At 5:00 p.m., when Sebastian Lima came in looking for Sam, he jumped when he saw the destruction and the barrel of a gun pointed in his direction. He refused to answer any questions and was roughly removed by deputies. Salvatore Rizzo was the next to show up. The very tiny man was still in his railroad clothes when Oldfield put him in handcuffs. He knew nothing about the Society of the Banana, he said, and had no idea why he was under arrest.

Oldfield took one last look around the room. It was completely destroyed. Hundreds of one-, five-, and ten-dollar bills covered most of the flat surfaces. Oldfield told his men not to confiscate the cash.[11] It was not important, and would only serve to muddy the waters for the prosecutors. Also, with Lima's family still in the house, Oldfield likely didn't want to put the women and children and the actual fruit business at risk. He did see one item that he wanted, and before he left the building, he went to Sam Lima's desk and peeled off the leather desk blotter.

That night, Frank Oldfield finally made good on his promise and spent the whole evening surrounded by salivating newspapermen furiously scribbling in their notebooks. He unraveled the story theatrically, telling his audience about busting into Lima's fruit store, tackling the fleeing suspect, and finding the ledger in Lima's safe. "Forty-three cases are known to us and forty-three will be prosecuted," he said. "Other Sicilians are to be arrested if we ever lay hands on them. The principal one of these, and the one whom we give credit for planning most of the jobs, is Antonio Lima, who is now at liberty."[12] Rumor had it that Antonio had fled to Sicily. It was Frank's strategy to tell the press that each man he spoke of was a top boss in an effort to divide the clan, whose members were constantly vying for superiority. "We have enough evidence against the men arrested today to keep them in jail for practically the remainder of their lives."

PUT IT DOWN HARD, UNCLE

Oldfield Collection

Editorial cartoons chronicled the investigation and capture of members of the Society of the Banana in newspapers across the United States and overseas. This cartoon illustrates "Uncle Sam" stamping out The Black Hand as a snake. Cartoon from unknown newspaper, 1909.

This last statement, Oldfield knew, was hogwash. In fact, one of the problems of mail fraud cases was the very weak punishments. Each conviction carried a maximum of two years in prison and a five-hundred-dollar fine.[13] Frank lobbied hard for stiffer sentences, but the statute never changed during his tenure. To work around the constraint, Post Office inspectors worked side by side with other law enforcement agencies to bring charges that would receive the longest sentences—felony crimes of robbery, murder, attempted murder, and kidnapping. In this case, with no witnesses coming forward to provide testimony or evidence in Black Hand crimes, it was impossible to put Lima and his men behind bars for good. Even when a Black Hand case did make it to trial, jurors were almost always threatened, killed, or bought off, victims silenced, and judges and juries bribed.

Back in Cincinnati, Inspector-in-Charge Abraham Holmes happily answered press calls. After denying the existence of an organized crime ring for years, Holmes appeared to see the light. "We have found what I believe to be certain proof that the Black Hand outrages, at least in the Middle West, including Pittsburgh, Cincinnati, Cleveland, Chicago, Columbus and other Western cities, were committed by a well-organized society with grips [secret handshakes] and passwords, and that they are not simply sporadic cases of individual extortion."[14] He went on to give details of the crimes. One paper called Oldfield "a pupil of Inspector-in-Charge Abraham Holmes of the Cincinnati office, he knows all the ropes, and he trailed the every movement of the men whom he arrested in the recent raid of the Society of the Banana."

Oldfield had no time to be angry at Holmes, who after being little support on the case was now taking the credit. Still, he managed to be annoyed anyway.

News quickly got out in Marion's Italian community that Sam Lima and Sebastian Lima were in jail. In no time, protesters gathered in the streets to lobby for the release of the law-abiding citizens. "As Lima, a crafty appearing Italian, was being led, handcuffed, from his cell in the Marion jail to a carriage," one paper reported, "he raised his cuffed hands above his head to the crowd of citizens assembled to view his departure, and exclaimed dramatically: 'Black Hand? Black Hand?' See, my hands, they are white. My persecutors have black hands. They try to injure me and my business. They want to ruin me and my family." [15]

Two deputy marshals shoved Sam Lima into the carriage before his friends could move in to free him. In the Marion jail, Lima met his brother-in-law Sebastian and Salvatore Rizzo, the railroad worker who was a subordinate of the Limas. Oldfield was afraid there could be an attempt to free the men, so he put four guards on them at all times. He also feared that Rizzo might be killed in order that he not testify against the Limas or the Society.[16]

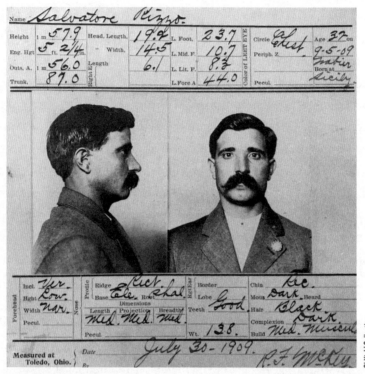

1909 Bertillon card photo and anthropometric data of Society of the Banana member Salvatore Rizzo. Toledo, Ohio, police created the Bertillon card while Rizzo was awaiting trial. Rizzo was convicted and sentenced to the federal penitentiary at Fort Leavenworth, Kansas.

Perhaps Oldfield should have taken the cash in Lima's store, because in no time, Sam Lima and Sebastian Lima secured the most expensive criminal defense lawyers in Ohio with the help of money received from extorted "friends" throughout the region. Frank got word that the attorneys were demanding a return of the confiscated letters and documents, claiming they were obtained illegally. Oldfield braced himself. He tried not to worry about a trial that would be many months away and instead concentrated on the coming days. His men would fan out across Ohio and Pennsylvania over the next week and orchestrate an epic assault on a dozen more top-level Mafiosi.

Wednesday, June 9, 3:00 a.m., Dennison, Ohio

Seventeen hours after busting into Sam Lima's, under Oldfield's direction, the mayor of Dennison and one of his police officers broke into the home of Tony Vicario, the eighteen-year-old who had forwarded Lima's extortion letter to John Amicon.[17] The lawmen pounced on Vicario in his sleep. In his bed were four shotguns, two rifles, eight pistols, twelve knives and dirks (a type of long, narrow dagger), and belts containing cartridges. Officer Poland and Mayor Mahon dragged Vicario to the Dennison jail. While the two went to call Oldfield, Vicario slipped out the door. When the men realized he was gone, they ran after him and tackled him in the street, hauling the kid back to the jail, much the worse for wear.

At 11:15 a.m., Oldfield secured an arrest warrant for Vicario's boss, saloon owner Augustino Marfisi.[18] He wired the Dennison police to arrest Marfisi and hold him until the arrival of the Secret Service agents. When the officers reached Marfisi's quarters, the Italian took to his heels, running through a back door and into an alley. Several shots were fired by the agents, with Marfisi returning the fire. He was captured after a chase of several blocks.[19]

The same time: June 9, 3:00 a.m., Bellefontaine, Ohio

At almost the very moment that Charlie Vicario's brother, Tony, was captured in Dennison, Oldfield and his team descended on Charlie in Bellefontaine. Believing that the twenty-eight-year-old Vicario was the most dangerous of all the Black Hand gang, Oldfield took Hosford and Hutches and enlisted the Bellefontaine chief of police and his deputies. The team surrounded the house of the deceased Salvatore Cira, where Vicario was known to be living. Oldfield knew the house well, having been there many times trying to solve Cira's murder. The officers forced their way in, guns drawn. A half-dozen Sicilian women and children, all heavily armed, ran into the front room, screaming at the invaders. Vicario came downstairs, armed to the teeth, but was quickly neutralized and handcuffed by Hutches and Hosford. The inspectors and deputies tore through the house. They found nearly a thousand dollars under Vicario's pillow, a bucket filled with gold and silver coins in his room, and a roll of money as big as a man's leg. The trunk also contained letters, which Oldfield quickly inspected. Many were signed *La Mano Nera*.

Oldfield desperately wanted to tie Vicario to Petrosino's murder and spent three hours with Vicario in the "sweat box" trying to force a confession. "Why, he actually refused to admit mailing letters that we saw him deposit with our own eyes," Oldfield said to a reporter. "We tripped him up many times and he lied to us right and left. No, he did not give away any of his confederates, nor did he admit that there was such an organization as that of the Society of the Banana." In the end, Oldfield told Charlie Vicario that it didn't matter that he wouldn't talk. One of his confederates in Marion had already ratted him out. Vicario's face went dark and he launched into a tirade of what a smiling Oldfield assumed were Italian curse words.

That afternoon: Wednesday, June 9, Toledo, Ohio

On the afternoon of June 9, federal marshals moved a handcuffed Salvatore Lima and the others to the Toledo jail by train. The newspapers reported the prisoner transfer. Hundreds of Italian and Sicilian protesters clamored to get into the jail. Reporters jockeyed for interviews with the assailants. Never before had a Black Hand criminal been interviewed for a newspaper. It would be the scoop of the decade. The newsmen were let in to see Sam Lima, who sat scowling in his cell. The Sicilian had been under arrest for just over a day, but hadn't been told of the charges against him. One of the reporters handed Lima a newspaper through the cell bars. Lima arose from his cell cot and grabbed it. He could read a little English, and when he learned that he was believed to have instigated the plot against John Amicon, he became furious: "Amicon is jealous," Lima screamed at the line of reporters. "He is jealous of me because I sell more bananas in Ohio than he does. See, my hands are white. They are not black." Lima held up his hands. "I am a hard-working business man. I work every day, night, even Sunday."[20]

The reporters fired off questions.

"How'd ya get all that dough you sent to Italy, Sam?"

"I earned it!"

When the newsmen left, the jailers let visitors in. They were all men, all Sicilian, and all similar in appearance. Some shoved wads of cash through the bars to Sam and Sebastian and to the Vicario brothers. Several of the visitors got up close and spoke in whispers to the Mafioso boss. Go to the "friends," he told them, meaning the victims, and demand money. Lima needed a lot of cash to pay the defense attorneys and for their very high bail amounts, ranging from three thousand dollars for Salvatore Rizzo to ten thousand for Sam Lima. Lima also wanted all of the victims to tell the police of Sam Lima's upstanding ways, that Sam and his brother-in-law, Sebastian, and other friends under arrest were purely hardworking businessmen.

Behind the scenes, Oldfield went to work to turn the members against each other. He told each man that one of his Society brothers had ratted him out. Francis Dimaio came to the interrogations to make sure that there was nothing said in Italian that was missed. The Sicilians growled and sneered. Still, not a single Black Hand suspect would talk. The man most furious of all was Sam Lima. Lima simmered and stewed and plotted revenge. He had been raised by Sicilian brigands, and the law of Omertà coursed through his blood. On the second night in the Toledo jail, he sent a message through a compatriot who came to visit. *Make sure this message gets to that buzzard Oldfield and his Italian stooge Dimaio: We will kill you all.*

The next day: Thursday, June 10, 1909, Columbus, Ohio

On June 10, Oldfield took just one U.S. Marshal, a friend of his named T. H. Huey, and the two went to arrest Lima's henchman, Severio Ventola, the white-haired criminal with the extensive rap sheet. Ventola came without a struggle. Then Oldfield began the monumental task of getting all of the written correspondence he and his team had confiscated translated. He hired two Sicilian translators, one man, one woman, put them in separate secret locations, and partnered each with a secretary to type up the translated letters.[21]

Two days later, on June 12, 1909, Oldfield and fellow inspectors Pate, Hosford, Hutches, and Owen arrived in Cleveland for a planned press conference with U.S. Attorney Day. By now the whole world was watching the unraveling of The Black Hand Society. The handsome Day beamed from the steps of the Cleveland federal building as he described the details of the arrests. A dozen photographers snapped photos, and flash powder smoke filled the air. Reporters scribbled notes and shouted questions. "I believe that we have the right men and that through them we have been able to break up the so-called Black Hand Society which has been preying upon the wealthy Italians in the central states," Day announced. "These letters lead me to believe there is an actual organization among the Italian blackmailers with its headquarters at Marion, and that it had it murderous tendrils reaching as far east as Rochester, N.Y., with more of them in and about Buffalo, Niagara Falls, Pittsburg, Cincinnati, Cleveland, Toledo, Indianapolis and Chicago, with minor agencies in the smaller cities. . . . They are a dangerous lot and should be exterminated. Having charge of the prosecutions, I shall do all possible to wipe them out. They have been responsible for more depredations than the public knows."[22]

Frank and the others were cool as cucumbers, each with cigar in hand, looking every part the detectives of legend they were turning out to be. Frank was especially smug. He'd finally hooked Day on prosecuting the Society of the Banana members as the pervasive conspirators he knew them to be. Oldfield and his team spent the next few days sharing all the evidence they'd collected with Day and planning their next move.

Four days later: Thursday, June 17, 1909, 5:30 p.m.,
Cincinnati, Ohio

The word was out. Francesco Spadaro, the saloon owner from Cincinnati who was the "official" Society of the Banana Godfather, knew what was coming. The Limas' arrest was plastered across the front page of the *Cincinnati Enquirer*. He knew that it was only a matter of time before they'd be coming for him. Rather than wait around to be arrested, he decided to skip town. At 4:30 p.m. on Thursday, June 17, the forty-one-year-old, well-known for his giant droopy mustache, went to the barbershop down the street from his saloon and got a clean shave.

He'd been back in his saloon and boardinghouse for only a few minutes when Post Office inspectors and U.S. Marshals burst into the saloon.[23] A dozen Italians froze. Some were playing cards, others were at the bar. The officers searched every man. None were carrying weapons. They arrested all of them, including the now fresh-faced Spadaro. The marshals confiscated papers, letters, and account books found in wooden "pigeonhole" filing boxes on the wall and emptied the contents of Spadaro's safe.

Two blocks away, Inspectors Hosford and Hutches, with U.S. Marshals, broke into Vincenzo Arrigo's fruit store on West Twelfth Street. They found Arrigo alone, and against the show of force, he grudgingly submitted to arrest. The lawmen confiscated a double-barreled gun with .44-caliber cartridges, a revolver, and several dirks, sharpened to a fine edge. "What do you do with these?" Hosford asked, touching the blade of one of the dirks. "They're used for cutting bananas," Arrigo calmly replied. "And what about this?" Hosford asked, holding up the revolver. Arrigo said nothing. In a hurry to get him to the jail, none of the lawmen searched Arrigo himself. When the prisoner was taken into a private office to be questioned, a loaded long-barreled .32-caliber revolver fell from the pocket of his coat.

Next stop was Arrigo's father's house at 1637 Hughes Street above Liberty. When Hosford and Hutches got there with the marshals, they searched the house. There was no sign of the retired Godfather Salvatore Arrigo. They went to his daughter-in-law's house next door. The woman said she hadn't seen him since the Saturday before. But when Arrigo's granddaughter came out, before her mother could stop her, she told the officers that Grandpa Arrigo was in bed suffering from rheumatism until the day before when he left the house and did not return.

1909 Bertillon card photo and anthropometric data of Society of the Banana member Vincenzo Arrigo. Arrigo was the son of "Boss" Salvatore Arrigo. Toledo, Ohio, police created the Bertillon card while Arrigo was awaiting trial. Arrigo was convicted and sentenced to the federal penitentiary at Fort Leavenworth, Kansas.

Four days later: Monday, June 21, 12:00 a.m., Pittsburgh, Pennsylvania

Four days after the roundup at Spadaro's saloon, Oldfield was ready to go after two suspects in Pennsylvania. This was Francis Dimaio's territory. Oldfield, more trusting now of the Italian detective, let him take charge. At midnight, Oldfield, Dimaio, and several deputies surprised Orazio Runfola in his apartment hideout just outside Pittsburgh.[24] The officers searched Runfola and put him in handcuffs. Then they rifled through his room. There were a ton of letters and incriminating evidence linking him to The Black Hand Society. There were several letters from Sam Lima.[25]

1909 Bertillon card photo and anthropometric data of Society of the Banana member Orazio Runfola. Runfola, from Pittsburgh, was an especially colorful member of the Society. Toledo, Ohio, police created the Bertillon card while Runfola was awaiting trial. Runfola was convicted and sentenced to the federal penitentiary at Fort Leavenworth, Kansas.

Dimaio shoved a letter from Lima in Runfola's face.

"I have no idea who that is," Runfola lied in heavily accented but clear English.

Oldfield showed him letters and telegrams sent to Sam Lima with Runfola's signature.

"We found these in Sam Lima's house. Did you write them?" Frank prodded.

"Yes," Runfola said, visibly unnerved now.

"What are they?" Dimaio asked.

"They're just friendly communications. I met Antonio Lima and Sam Lima in fruit yards at Pittsburgh."

"What is the Society of the Banana?"

"I have no idea."

1910 Bertillon card photo and anthropometric data of Society of the Banana member Pippino Galbo. Galbo was highly successful and quite popular in Meadville, Pennsylvania, and remain so after his term in prison. Toledo, Ohio, police created the Bertillon card while Galbo was awaiting trial. Galbo was convicted and sentenced to the federal penitentiary at Fort Leavenworth, Kansas.

Runfola refused to say why he was in hiding rather than at his cigar shop in Pittsburgh, but he was coming unglued. To Dimaio, who Runfola realized was a private contractor, he begged, "Please, protect me from the government. These letters are all innocent. I'm innocent."

The following day at 1:00 a.m., Oldfield, Dimaio, and several other agents captured Pippino Galbo at his home above his fruit business in Meadville. Galbo got dressed calmly in his expensive suit, put a diamond stickpin in his tie, and left for jail with the inspectors, sure that he would be free in no time.

The next day in the Pittsburgh jail, Dimaio told Orazio Runfola that Galbo believed Runfola was the one who had ratted him out. Runfola, who had remained stoic until then, became white with terror.[26] "They'll kill me! They'll murder me sure!" he shouted at Dimaio. "They will never believe me when I get out!" When Dimaio pressured him on who "they" referred to, Runfola shut down and refused to say anything at all.

After a stunningly successful spree of arrests in Marion, Bellefontaine, Dennison, Cincinnati, Pittsburgh, and Meadville, Oldfield grabbed two more Society suspects in Columbus. Salvatore Demma and Severio Ventola, both involved in shaking down the Amicon brothers, were taken to the Toledo jail. "With the arrest of Marfisi in Dennison and Ventola in Columbus, we fixed two important cogs in the human chain of extortionists managed by Lima and his fruit store cabinet," Oldfield told reporters. "Ventola, I am convinced, is one of the sharpest of the crowd." Still, Frank was furious that two senior Blackhanders, Salvatore Arrigo and Antonio Lima, had slipped through his fingers. Inspector-in-Charge Abraham Holmes, now publicly offering his full support to the investigation, told the press that finding Arrigo and Lima "will be a case of digging them out of their holes."[27]

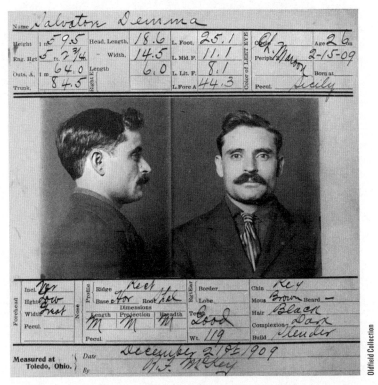

1909 Bertillon card photo and anthropometric data of Society of the Banana member Salvatore Demma. Toledo, Ohio, police created the Bertillon card while Demma was awaiting trial. Demma was convicted and sentenced to the federal penitentiary at Fort Leavenworth, Kansas.

Bail was set at between three and ten thousand dollars for each man. William Day argued there shouldn't be bail at all, while the gaggle of defense attorneys argued they all be released on their own recognizance. Just over a month after his arrest, on July 17, Maria Cira, the teenage girlfriend of Charlie Vicario, arrived at the courthouse, carrying five thousand dollars in cash.[28] The *Mansfield News-Journal* reported the awkwardly romantic story:

Collogero Vicario of Bellefontaine, one of the alleged Black Hand agents, recently captured in the raids by postal inspectors, owes his release on heavy bond to the love of a young woman, also a native of sunny Italy.

When asked if she didn't think Vicario would run away, the answer came quickly. "No, no, Charley won't run away. He loves me."

Ever since his arrest Signora [Cira] of Bellefontaine has been untiring in her efforts to minister to his wants, and when Vicario was held to the federal grand jury, which is to meet in Toledo next December, she immediately undertook the task of securing the $5,000 bond required for his release from custody. Her mother pledged all her property and friends were induced to make up the balance of the bond.

Pippino Galbo, the handsome and popular fruit vendor from Meadville, Pennsylvania, also had friends on the outside working quickly to come up with five thousand dollars for his bail. He was released not long after Charlie Vicario. Fearing Lima and the others would skip the country, William Day successfully lobbied Judge Robert Tayler, who'd just been assigned to try the case if the grand jury chose to indict, to rescind bail for the rest of the men.

With eleven secure in the Toledo jail, Oldfield went after his last big trophy, Salvatore Arrigo. For more than a month, he had no idea where the deposed Godfather was hiding out. Fortunately, Arrigo was used to living well. His hideout was actually a lovely remote farmhouse a few hours east of Cincinnati. The house was so deep in the woods that Oldfield might never have found him, save for the fact that there were some things the old Sicilian couldn't do without. Frank got word that packages of candies, wine, and flowers were being sent to Clermont County from the Cincinnati post office, many addressed in a feminine hand. He also heard that an Italian restaurant was delivering meals to the same address.[29]

Reports came in of locals in the area seeing a strange Italian at the house in the woods of another Italian named Pasquale Scantaliato.[30] Oldfield asked a rural mail carrier to help him pinpoint the location of Scantaliato's cabin and give him an outline of who was living there. By July 22, Oldfield was ready to take down the sixty-seven-year-old retired Godfather. Oldfield, George Pate, and three deputy U.S. Marshals secured a carriage and set out from Cincinnati in the afternoon. They arrived in the small town of Batavia at dusk. From there, a farmer directed them to a path that zigzagged through the wild woods in the dark. Oldfield told the driver to push the horses up and down steep hills at breakneck speed, afraid the old Sicilian would receive warning and escape. Within three-quarters of a mile of the cabin, the driver stopped and tied the horses. The lawmen made the rest of the journey on foot.

From a distance, Oldfield made out the structure by a glimmering lantern on the porch.

When they got closer, they could see and hear three men and three women sitting and chatting in Italian. Oldfield watched as one old man picked up a rifle from the floor, toyed with the weapon, and put it down again. Arrigo. He could see two other guns in one corner of the porch. Oldfield readied himself for a violent shootout.

"Now," whispered Oldfield to his men.

The five lawmen rushed at the group on the porch, revolvers drawn. The surprise attack was such a shock that before Arrigo and friends could regain their wits they were looking into the barrels of three pistols. Grumbling, they all held up their hands.[31] When pressed, Scantaliato said that yes, Arrigo was his guest, but he barely knew the man and certainly didn't know anything about any Society of the Banana. Arrigo looked as if he hadn't bathed in weeks. His baggy clothes were dirty. He was unshaven and his white hair stuck up in all directions. Deputy Marshal Sanderson read the arrest warrant. "What are you doing with those rifles?" Oldfield asked as he led the stooped old man down the road to the carriage. "We've been shooting squirrels," Arrigo said. Then the old man clammed up and refused to say another word.[32] When pressed for more, Arrigo replied, "Me no speak bad English." On the way back to Batavia, Oldfield and his squad got the fright that they didn't get at the cabin. On a steep precipice, the wagon wheels on one side went over a cliff and the entire carriage nearly dropped thirty feet into a ravine. In almost complete darkness, with the utmost respect for the force of gravity, the men unloaded the wagon, quieted the spooked horses, slowly pulled the carriage back to the road, and made their way back down the trail.

That night, a ravenous group of reporters from Cincinnati gathered around Oldfield in Inspector Holmes's office:

"Salvatore Arrigo," said Oldfield, "is one of the fellows who got away from us when we made our first raid on the Sicilian settlements in Cincinnati. We had been close on his heels for more than a month, and we knew his whereabouts for the past three weeks. The old man was betrayed into our hands by his preference for macaroni, spaghetti and ravioli. Arrigo could not subsist on the vegetables and fruits indigenous to Clermont County, where he went to hide. He had to have his macaroni and spaghetti every day, and somebody had to take it to him. We got trace of the somebody, and soon had Arrigo located. He and his two Italian companions just finished eating a lot of macaroni when we pounced upon them. Baskets full of macaroni, spaghetti, Romano cheese, vermouth and Italian wines were in the cabin for feast of some kind. But we spoiled that."

Salvatore Arrigo, first "Boss" of the Society of the Banana, was captured by Post Office inspectors and other agents in late 1909 in a sensational assault on his rural hideout near Goshen, Ohio. Article from *McClure's Magazine*, 1910.

As usual, Oldfield used the reporters to further his goals. He was ready to go back to U.S. Attorney William Day in Cleveland and get him to agree to prosecute Lima and all of the Society of the Banana members now under arrest. He knew that Day, like nearly every living soul in America, was glued to the front page of his daily newspaper, waiting for news in the epic Black Hand takedown. "We have an absolute case," Oldfield told the gaggle of reporters. "The evidence is in the handwriting of the accused, and there are no missing links in the chain."[33]

CHAPTER 10

THE TRIAL

Frank Oldfield spent the second half of 1909 tying the Black Hand case together. The judge had rescinded bail, so all of the captured Black Handers remained in jail except Pippino Galbo and Charlie Vicario. Sam Lima's crew on the outside were still raising money from "friends," to pay the high-priced defense attorneys. Back home in Marion, the wives of Sam and Sebastian were struggling just to buy food for their children.

Oldfield swore a team of translators to secrecy and tasked them with uncovering messages and codes in hundreds of letters. He connected the dots among suspects and victims and those who played both roles. He dug deep into the backgrounds of the criminals. He analyzed the trunk of weapons he referred to as the "pirate's loot," which he stored in the cashier's room at the Columbus post office.

He reached out to postmasters, newspaper editors, and police departments around the country. What he uncovered was startling. The Society of the Banana conspiracy was beyond what he had imagined. The tentacles of the Society reached to San Francisco, New Orleans, and Chicago. Oldfield, who had confiscated letters from a Portland-based nephew in Lima's effects, got wind that the elder Lima might have absconded for the West Coast, rather than back to Sicily. The Post Office inspector there, O. C. Riches, wrote to Oldfield that a man going by the name of Michelangelo Lima had arrived a few months before and moved in with his adult "son," named Antonio Lima.[1] Another Portland inspector, E. C. Clement, followed up in a second letter. Detectives in the Portland police department had been reading about the busts in Ohio and thought the same type of shenanigans might be happening in Portland's Italian quarter.[2] "Yesterday the City Detectives called upon me to know if we had any dope on the case," Clement wrote to Oldfield, "stating that they had been given some tips concerning a set of Italians in the lower end of town who were undoubtedly connected with some such game and were preparing to work it here." He described a disastrous fire in the Portland Italian quarter. Four Italian peddlers nearly lost their lives and lost their horses and wagons. "It now begins to appear that the fire was the work of this gang and that the owner of the buildings had been threatened but refuses to play," Clement wrote.[3]

By August 12, Clement reported that he was able to trace extortion victims in Portland to the letters Oldfield had found in Antonio Lima's house. Clement told Oldfield that he had learned that a man named Antonio Lima left Portland and was headed to San Francisco. However, the man was young. What the lawmen did not figure out was that the young Antonio was actually Sam Lima's nephew and the grandson of the at-large Antonio Lima.

The scope was overwhelming. Throughout the fall of 1909, Frank drew maps and graphs, made lists and flow charts, and shored up evidence. Columbus postmaster Harry Krumm's office was the war room of the entire operation. William Day's U.S. attorney's office in Cleveland was the well-orchestrated brain room. Oldfield and Day worked side by side, hour after hour and day after day, hammering out the details and organizing their notes into what they would present to the grand jury. In the end, the physical evidence filled seven leather-bound steamer trunks. The condensed intellectual evidence

Day and Oldfield put together to present to the grand jury amounted to a 147-page indictment, typed on India paper, and included copies of many of the threatening letters reprinted from photographs on rubber-coated fabric.

By December, the case of The Black Hand had fallen off the collective radar of the nation. There were no hordes of press when William Day led Frank Oldfield, George Pate, Raleigh Hosford, Harry Krumm, Edward Hutches, and John Amicon down the marble hallway of the Toledo Federal Courthouse on December 9, 1909. Day carried the book of evidence, and Oldfield brought his trusty magnifying glass in case it could be useful in presenting their findings to the grand jury for the Northern District of Ohio.

For the entire day, the U.S. attorney dazzled the jurors with titillating evidence. He read the incriminating Black Hand letters and argued that the evidence clearly showed that the Sicilians arrested for Black Hand crimes had colluded to extort money from John Amicon. Each inspector and Postmaster Krumm took the stand to testify under Day's careful direction. Then Day put John Amicon on the stand. Having the actual victim describe the terror he and his family experienced was the clincher. The next day, Oldfield and Day were thrilled and relieved. The grand jury returned "a true bill." The fourteen men had found solid evidence to return an indictment for fifteen counts of illegal use of the mails.

Oldfield immediately sent for warrants and ordered the police to pick up Charlie Vicario in Bellefontaine. In Meadville, Pennsylvania, he didn't have such connections with the local police. Instead, he sent a telegram to the Meadville postmaster:

> Pippino Galbo, indicted by grand jury today. Bond fixed at ten thousand dollars. Court orders immediate arrest. Have your chief

police hold Galbo until arrival capias [arrest warrant]. If possible arrest him at once and wire the U.S. Attorney, Cleveland. Oldfield, Inspector.

Postmaster Earnest Hempstead did what Oldfield asked, but he was very unhappy about it. Hempstead was a by-the-book kind of guy. He should not be telling the police to arrest anyone. He became even more upset two days later when there was still no arrest warrant, and the chief of police, holding Galbo without due process, was breathing down Hempstead's neck. Galbo's lawyer caused a ruckus and got a judge to order Galbo discharged. Hempstead fired off a letter to both the Post Office Department attorney general and Oldfield's boss in Cincinnati, Abraham Holmes. "The whole affair strikes me as open to serious objection, because anyone might easily impersonate a post office inspector and send a telegram ordering the arrest of anyone."[4] Fortunately for Oldfield, he was able to call Pinkerton detective Francis Dimaio to smooth things over, get the warrant, and pick up Galbo before he skipped town. Unfortunately for Frank, Abraham Holmes made sure to ink in this infraction in Oldfield's personnel file with a long list of others.

Frank Oldfield went home to Athens for Christmas in December 1909. The streets of the lovely town were decorated with local pine wreaths and garlands. The four Oldfield boys, on break from school, spent their days sledding down the steep hill in the backyard and crashing into the pine trees in the hollow below. At night, Christmas trees with flickering candles appeared in the windows of the stately homes on North Congress Street. Margaret Galena put out her finest china and decorated the dining room with fancy linens and an elaborate centerpiece. She cooked all day and served her favorite German dishes and pies. By the big fireplace in the living room, the

Frank Oldfield's wife and family, sister Laura Noss and her family, and his father, Hamilton, spent Christmas 1910 in Athens, Ohio. This photo of Frank Oldfield is one of many portraits taken during this holiday season.

four boys gathered around their father. Frank asked his second son, ten-year-old Hamilton, to do the honors. He handed his son a sheet of stationery that said at the top *Post Office Department, Office of Post Office Inspector.* With his father's fancy fountain pen, ten-year-old Hamilton composed a joint letter to Santa.

Dear Santa Claus,

We are all going to bed early and hope you will be here to see us soon and bring us lots of toys. Fulton wants a horse and cart, story books, set of dishes and cupboard, blocks and anything nice you have for me. Gist wants a car, a baby doll, a set of blocks, story books, automobile. Games.

Margaret Galena Oldfield (Inspector Frank Oldfield's wife) enjoyed the finer things in life, especially her dresses. This family photo is of Margaret Galena posing in a country setting in 1909.

After a much-needed week of downtime, Oldfield returned to Columbus briefly on Monday, January 3, then headed straight to Cleveland to meet with William Day. The trial was set for January 10. They had one week. When Oldfield and Day did some research on the judge assigned to the case of *The United States* v. *Salvatore*

Lima et al., they were a bit uneasy. Fifty-seven-year-old U.S. federal judge Robert Tayler was known mostly for trying cases between government and private industry. Oldfield and Day had no idea how Judge Tayler would handle the biggest Mafia case so far in American history. Tayler's only interesting criminal case to date was the wild tale of Cassie Chadwick, a female con artist who embezzled money from the Oberlin National Bank by pretending to be a Rothschild heiress. Tayler coolly presided over the trial, unimpressed with the enormous press interest in the case. In the end, Tayler sentenced Cassie Chadwick, an old woman hard of hearing, to ten years in prison.[5]

More typical of his caseload was a lengthy case involving the Cleveland Street Railway Corporation and the City of Cleveland in a fight over a five-cent fare increase.

Day and Oldfield, both steadfast Republicans, took heart in Tayler's solid conservative credentials. He'd previously served in Congress, representing Ohio's Eighteenth District from 1895 to 1903.[6] In person, Tayler was shy, calm, and understated. He was a small man with sloping shoulders and mouselike features. He parted his hair in the middle and slicked it neatly down the sides. He was never without his delicate eyeglasses. Tayler had a reputation as a fair judge and a kind and honest man. A civil attorney who tried a case with him called him "firm, but gentle—wise and just—courteous to lawyers in a superlative degree—exceptionally kind to the young practitioner."[7] While Tayler was known to have a very cool head on the bench, he went off the rails for America's favorite pastime. Attorneys across Ohio knew he was likely to schedule trials to avoid any conflict with Toledo Mud Hens or Detroit Tigers games.

William Day always believed the Black Hand cases would be tough to win. But when he learned how well the defendants had lawyered up, he lost a chunk of confidence. Fourteen self-described "simple fruit dealers" retained the best defense attorneys in Ohio and Pennsylvania. Defendants from the same cities shared legal teams. All cooperated with the renowned Toledo firm of Taber, Longbrake & O'Leary, which represented Sam and Sebastian Lima. The firm was known in Ohio for handling the biggest and wealthiest corporate clients, including the National Supply Company, the American Metal Wheel & Auto Company, and countless city and county banks.[8] "All the members of the firm are held in the highest esteem by the bar and business men and the people generally," according to one Ohio newspaper. John O'Leary took the lead and went to work immediately doing damage control in the press. Yes, the prisoners are members of the Society of the Banana, O'Leary told the newsmen. "But the Society is an organization formed for controlling the fruit trade, not for Black Hand purposes."

From behind bars in the Toledo jail, Sam Lima wasn't operating like a poor fruit merchant at all. To pay his high-priced attorneys and the counsel of other gang members, Lima made continuing efforts to extort money from his "best" friends, those who paid extortion demands regularly without hesitation. Lima's shakedown was verified by an anonymous letter to Oldfield from a mark being forced to pay three thousand dollars for the defense of his Sicilian "friends." Extortion letters weren't the only communications directed from Lima's cell. On January 8, Frank went to his office on the second floor of the Toledo federal courthouse building. Stuck with a stiletto into his desk was a note: *Five federal government officials prosecuting the "Black Hand," are all under sentence of death*, it said.[9] The letter listed those marked for murder: *Judge Robert Tayler, U.S. Attorney William Day, Assistant U.S. Attorneys Thomas H. Gary and John S. Pratt, and Post Office inspector J. F. Oldfield.*

Oldfield, Day, and the assistant district attorney Thomas Gary shook off the threat. They'd all worked on numerous criminal cases. Being threatened with death was an occasional job hazard. While he'd captured many of the Society's top bosses, Oldfield knew that Lima still had dozens of troops at liberty who were unfalteringly loyal to the Society of the Banana.

Day made sure his team was constantly guarded by federal marshals, police, and Secret Service agents. He did the same for the state's star witness and his family.[10] John Amicon, his wife and children, his brother Charles, and Charles's entire family had detectives, police, and federal marshals protecting them twenty-four hours a day.

On January 10, 1910, the morning the trial was to start, Oldfield had the seven steamer trunks hauled to the courtroom from the storage closet in the Toledo federal building. Inside the trunks were boxes of folders with letters and photographs, communications between law enforcement, mug shots, Bertillon cards, and money order receipts: every bit of evidence they needed for the trial. Jury selection was set to start, but before the trial could begin, the group of nine defense attorneys, led by John O'Leary and his partner, J. J. Sullivan, a former United States district attorney, made a plea to Judge Tayler.[11]

"This is nonsense," argued Sullivan to the judge, whom he knew personally and professionally, as Sullivan had prosecuted the Cassie Chadwick trial to conviction under Judge Tayler. "The mere writing of a letter in no way constitutes collusion or conspiracy. These letters are purely innocent correspondence among businessmen. We respectfully ask the court to throw out this indictment and release the prisoners." Sullivan quoted Tayler's decision in the Cassie Chadwick trial to support his contention. The skillful attorney went on to argue that while the state may have shown that the defendants wrote some of the threatening letters, they hadn't shown the letters had been mailed or received by any of them.[12]

Oldfield's shoulders tensed. It was quite a play, but Sullivan's request was preposterous. Oldfield wanted to laugh out loud, but William Day's look told him an outburst wouldn't be appreciated. Judge Tayler studied the indictment on his bench and thumbed through its pages. Then he looked up, large eyes peering thorough small, round spectacles.

"I will sustain the motion of the defense for all but one of the fifteen counts," Judge Tayler said coolly. "The fourteen charges of conspiracy in the indictment are quashed." Conspiracy was difficult to prove. It was a delicate dance for a prosecutor to tie defendants to a crime when they might not have been present when the crime took place. It was essentially asking a jury to find the suspects guilty by association. Apparently, Tayler was not impressed by what Day was offering up on the conspiracy counts.

Oldfield let out an audible gasp. Tayler went on, "Only the first count that alleges an overt act of placing a threatening letter in the mails is sustained. Trial is postponed until January 18. Adjourned."[13]

Oldfield felt the gavel like a knife to his stomach.

While William Day and Thomas Gary somberly gathered their files, Oldfield glared at Judge Tayler. Frank racked his brain to try to figure out Tayler's motives. Were the corporate defense attorneys so cozy with federal judges that every decision would go to the defense? Had Tayler been bought off? Had Sam Lima gotten to him? Was Tayler actually afraid for his life? The judge was under a death threat along with Oldfield and the prosecutors, true. But was Tayler such a pansy that he'd throw away the case of the century, a case that the U.S. Post Office Inspection Service had spent tens of thousands of dollars and hundreds of man-hours to crack? The one saving grace for the prosecution was that Judge Tayler refused O'Leary's request to free the prisoners until the trial.

Oldfield hadn't slept more than a few hours a night for months. He had been positive that he had enough evidence to get a conviction for conspiracy. Now the trial would begin on January 18 with just one measly count. That one count could get only a maximum two-year sentence and only for one or two of the defendants. Oldfield huddled with Day and Gary to come up with a plan. If Tayler thought they didn't have enough evidence, they would get more. They would build the strongest case this judge had ever seen. The team would revamp the indictment, Day would call a special grand jury, and the prosecution would have a new indictment for conspiracy. Oldfield had only eight days before the January 18 trial to pull off a miracle.

Frank ran back to his office and got on the phone. Over the next few days, he re-enlisted everyone he'd worked with on the case. He made calls to police departments in every city where there were victims or suspects to gather more info on the defendants. He didn't sleep. The main deficiency in their case was that they still had only one victim willing to testify.

When Sam Lima and his conspirators were first arrested seven months earlier, law-abiding Italian victims were greatly relieved, but they weren't public about celebrating. They were well aware that many of the Society members were still on the streets. Perhaps with Lima behind bars for so long, some victims would find nerve they had never had before. Oldfield hoped it would be enough to encourage them to testify in court.

Oldfield re-enlisted Pinkerton detective Francis Dimaio. Since they had worked together to capture the Society of the Banana mob, Oldfield's admiration and respect for Dimaio had grown immeasurably. He still had pangs of envy about the skills Dimaio had as a birthright that Frank could never claim, but he knew that Dimaio was an invaluable asset. Together Dimaio and Oldfield went to Lima's victims. *This is your only chance*, the detectives told them. *Lima and his cohorts are in jail. They can go to prison. But unless you testify, they will be out in the streets and stronger than ever. You will live the rest of your life in fear for the lives of you and your family.*

The gambit worked. Within a few days, Oldfield and Dimaio secured more than a dozen Black Hand victims to testify. Most had no direct knowledge of who'd sent them letters, but their emotional testimony would be an enormous boon to the prosecution. Fred Cianciolo, father of ten children from Cincinnati, would testify he paid fifteen hundred dollars at Frank Spadaro's saloon.[14] Baptisto Vencurio of Columbus would testify to paying eight hundred dollars to someone named Michael Salamona in March 1908. Augustino Anario received a Black Hand letter in Sicily, where he had fled with his family after his house in Columbus was blown up with dynamite. Charles Amicon finally agreed to join his brother on the witness stand and tell of the months of receiving extortion letters and dynamite bombs.

After a week, Oldfield had about twenty victims who would testify. Except for Amicon, none were truly happy about it. Some were even a bit hostile. It didn't matter. The addition of these voices would lend an enormous amount of credibility to the government's conspiracy charge and certainly help sway the jury. The new indictment consisted of 239 pages, furiously typed up on ultrathin India paper by contracted secretaries sworn to secrecy. It was nearly 80 more pages than the first indictment. Once again, there were fifteen counts of conspiracy against each defendant.[15] The charges were violation of section 5480 of the revised statutes of the United States, a law passed in 1872 that made mail fraud a federal crime.[16]

On January 15, U.S. Attorney Day called for a special grand jury session and carried in the new indictment to the sixteen jurors. They had only three days before the start of the trial, which as of right now was an enormous production for only one criminal count. Oldfield, Hosford, Pate, Hutches, and more than a dozen witnesses testified to the grand jurors for two grueling days. On Monday, January 17, the grand jury returned the indictment on all fifteen counts, not a moment too soon.

The next morning, on Tuesday, January 18, 1910, Judge Tayler opened the proceedings in his Toledo courtroom. Dozens of newspaper headlines touted the beginning of the trial of the century. America would not be disappointed.

"A few minutes before 10 o'clock, the half-hundred male spectators, fortunate enough to run the gauntlet of guards that covered all entrances, craned their necks as the United States deputy marshals let in the 14 shackled, swarthy Sicilian prisoners," a newspaper proclaimed. "The buzz of whispered conversation between the array of legal talent that followed made it difficult for Judge Tayler to hear the words of Assistant U.S. Attorney Thomas H. Gary."

The newsmen called them swarthy, but in fact, the Sicilian prisoners were well groomed and impeccably dressed. Sam Lima had swapped his baggy trousers for a stylish suit. He wore no tie, and his collar was so white and starched around his thick neck it appeared to hold his head like a giant egg cup. Giuseppe Ignoffo, Sam Lima's brother-in-law, whom Oldfield had arrested in November 1909 after he continued to threaten John Amicon, had his handlebar mustache nicely waxed. Salvatore Rizzo groomed his giant mustache to run parallel on each side of his face to his sloping eyebrows, giving him a permanently surprised look. However, even with a shave and dressed to the nines, Sebastian Lima had the look of a bandit. His face was covered with stubble, his brow furrowed.

Severio Ventola, the old man from Columbus, was still somewhat rumpled but cleaned up to appear quite "harmless." Salvatore

Demma, also from Columbus, looked handsome and businesslike, with a dark suit and a striped silk tie. Augustino Marfisi, the saloon owner from Bellefontaine, looked every bit the Sicilian Mafioso: a bit wide around the middle with a black suit and silk tie, heavily lidded eyes with thick lashes, and a wide mustache. Antonio "Tony" Vicario, Marfisi's employee, was the only defendant not wearing a suit. Perhaps on the advice of his attorney, Vicario, who was not yet twenty years old, appeared fresh-faced and boyish in a casual shirt and trousers.

Cologero "Charlie" Vicario from Bellefontaine looked every bit the assassin that he was, dressed in a black silk shirt and black tie. In contrast, nervous Pittsburgh boss Orazio Runfola did not look threatening at all, with his loose curls and elegant suit. Pippino Galbo arrived in court in an expensive suit, looking like the quintessential gangster of a fiction novel. Of all the defendants, Salvatore Arrigo had made the biggest transformation since the time of his capture. His spiky gray beard was completely gone and he was cleanly shaven, his mouth forming a perfect straight line across his weathered face. Salvatore's son, Vincenzo Arrigo, appeared more casual than the others. At five foot ten inches tall, with fair skin, he looked more northern Italian than Sicilian. Saloon owner Frank Spadaro, captured minutes after a clean shave, had his big walrus mustache back as well as adding a few pounds from having food delivered to jail. His double chin now extended below his collar.

Judge Tayler was well aware that many criminal cases against Sicilian defendants ended in mistrials. The effort to prevent justice from being done took place either behind the scenes with jury tampering or when some mysterious person sat in the gallery during a witness's testimony. The stranger would make eye contact or wave a handkerchief at the person testifying, causing the witness to tremble, then clam up or change his testimony. To keep this from happening in his courtroom in this incredibly high-profile case, Tayler banned anyone of Italian descent from watching the trial. Marshals stood by turning away anyone with Mediterranean looks or an Italian accent. By 2:00 p.m., the jury was in place, and Tayler brought the room to order to begin the proceedings. One by one, Tayler asked each defendant how did he plead to the charges. Each Sicilian stood and resolutely stated, "Not guilty."[17]

As William Day expected, the lead defense attorney, John O'Leary, put in a motion to quash the new indictment. The thickly bound indictment sat on the judge's desk as well as the notes from the grand jury.[18] Oldfield and Day held their breath. Minutes ticked by.

"Motion denied."

Oldfield let out an audible sigh.

O'Leary asked to approach the bench. "Your honor, we would like to ask for a continuance. There is just not enough time to prepare for the defense with these conspiracy charges."

"Denied."

"Your honor, may we please ask for separate trials for each defendant? It would be much more appropriate . . ."

"Denied."

Oldfield was near euphoric and could barely contain himself. Day maintained his composure. They had a long way to go.

The jury was sworn in at 2:30 p.m. and the court adjourned for the day.

Oldfield went upstairs to his temporary office in the courthouse and got busy shoring up evidence. He would not stop trying to link the defendants to other crimes, believing it would help with the conspiracy charges. He fired off telegrams to police departments in San Francisco and Portland, and a letter to the editor of the *Picayune* in New Orleans. Frank hoped to get a picture of Antonio Lima, who he had recently learned had been arrested for murder there twenty years before.[19] Although Lima had escaped capture and might have very well been back in Sicily, Oldfield hoped he could get a conviction in absentia on conspiracy charges.

The next morning, on Wednesday, January 19, Judge Tayler called the court to order. Assistant U.S. Attorney Gary immediately began opening arguments for the "People of the United States." Gary, balding, with a bow tie and a good decade older than William Day, had years of courtroom experience. He was solid and to the point. He outlined the case methodically. Conspiracy charges against each of the defendants were ironclad, he said. The prosecution would prove its case with the evidence in letters from the U.S. mail.

Gary stepped toward the jury box and looked into the eyes of each juror as he spoke. The prosecution will exhibit a desk blotter seized in the house of Sam Lima, he said, that shows the name "John Amicon" and portions of the letter sent to extort money from Mr. Amicon. The United States will show that certain defendants came to Marion, Ohio, last March, where they were seen by Post Office inspectors in an all-night conference with Sam Lima. Gary told them a book was found in the Lima house containing the names of the defendants under the header Society of the Banana. He had letters from Salvatore Lima notifying the men that funds would be divided among them. He showed evidence that Sam Lima bought one thousand dollars' worth of money orders in a single day at the Marion post office.

The jurors were wide awake when the dashing John O'Leary made the opening statement for the defense. He represented Salvatore and Sebastian Lima, Giuseppe Ignoffo, and Salvatore Rizzo, all from Marion, and he would speak only for the four of them. Attorneys for the others would follow. O'Leary denied his defendants were part of a conspiracy. "It will be shown that they were engaged in legitimate business ventures," O'Leary opened. "The letters seized in the Lima home will be proven to have been written in furtherance of the fruit business and had no connection with Black Hand plots." Attorneys for the other defendants followed and made similar statements.

The room was electric as the prosecution called its first witness. "The People of the United States call Inspector John Frank Oldfield of the United States Post Office Inspection Service." The slight-of-build man in the black derby hat was the celebrity the entire gallery was waiting to see. Here was the Great Inspector Oldfield who had dazzled them with Black Hand stories for the last year in newspapers across the country. Oldfield walked confidently to the witness stand carrying a file folder. Once seated, he kept his hat on. For once, his hair was not perfectly in place. In fact, Oldfield looked exhausted. For the first time in his life, he'd been too busy to pay attention to his appearance. He had spent the time normally spent obsessing over his hygiene building ironclad testimony that the defense couldn't possibly penetrate.

If the newsmen were hoping for theatrics and wild tales from Oldfield, they were soon disappointed. Oldfield was methodical, calculated, and direct.[20] He read from his notes. He had every date, name, amount of money, and city written down. He tied the story together bit by bit, more like a deposition than an entertaining monologue. Still, the jury kept attentive. He told them that on the night of March 9, 1909, Lima and his coworkers made plans to extort $118,000 from forty-three Italians in Ohio, Pennsylvania, New York, and Indiana. Oldfield told the court that most of the recent Black Hand cases in Ohio had been planned by Sam Lima and his father, Antonio Lima, who was still at large, and Severio Ventola, a fruit salesman in Columbus.

That night, Frank slept only a few hours. He knew the defense was busy trying to find a crack in his testimony. He studied his notes and practiced his delivery over and over. The next day, Thursday, January 20, as he took the stand to finish testifying, he looked the worse for wear.[21] Mentally, though, he had never been more on top of his game. Under Day's careful guidance, Oldfield spent the entire morning identifying documents and weapons and detailing the steps of his investigation. From a large trunk he pulled shotguns, stilettos, and revolvers. He deftly identified exactly the house or business that each came from and connected the fourteen defendants with the conspiracy. When William Day asked if Oldfield could point to the persons in the courtroom responsible for the nefarious acts, Frank responded with a bit of flair.

"Absolutely," he said.

One by one, he put a face to the criminal acts for the jurors to see, dramatically pointing to each defendant and identifying each by name. Some of the Sicilians bristled, some appeared nonchalant. O'Leary, sitting next to a seething Sam Lima, tried to curtail Oldfield's testimony over and over with various objections. Judge Tayler denied almost all of them.

Having tamped down his usual theatrics, Oldfield wanted to finish with a bit of drama. He deliberately reached into his vest pocket, took out a small metal cap, and held it up for the audience to see.

"This tiny instrument of terror," Oldfield proclaimed, "is a fulminating cap used to set off a giant dynamite explosion. It was recovered from an iron box in the home of Mr. Salvatore Lima of Marion." Sam Lima looked as if he would explode.

John O'Leary took the floor and did his best to cross-examine Oldfield. For more than two hours he twisted Oldfield's story, trying to trip him up. The inspector was not rattled. One newspaper reporter commented on Oldfield's uncanny memory for names and dates and wrote that O'Leary's cross-examination was for naught.

The next witness was a heavily guarded surprise. Young Orazio Parabelli, the nineteen-year-old who'd been conscripted into The Black Hand and forcibly extracted by Francis Dimaio, was next up to testify. Dimaio had had the young man in hiding for the past week. Parabelli was obviously terrified, but very earnest and convincing. He told the court that he was approached many times by his countrymen, who insisted he join the Society of the Banana. If he didn't, they promised to kill him. Nine men inducted him into the Society.

Assistant U.S. Attorney Thomas Gary asked Parabelli, "Do you see any of those nine men in this courtroom?"

"Yes."

Parabelli pointed to Sam Lima and eight others, including Orazio Runfola and Pippino Galbo from Pennsylvania. Then he told the court that he recognized the other defendants as being members of the Society as well.

Friday, January 21, got even worse for the defense. The first witness for the prosecution was a young girl by the name of Francesca Amicon, the niece of John Amicon who lived with his family in Columbus. Francesca testified that on the morning of January 15, 1909, when starting for school, she found a package lying on the front doorstep. Picking it up, she found it contained a strange-looking object loosely wrapped in a copy of the *Pittsburgh Dispatch*. She carried it into Mrs. Amicon, who recognized it as dynamite. Frightened, they put it in a pan of water and carried it to the barn. Charles Amicon testified next. He told of seeing Antonio Lima, Vincenzo Arrigo, and Cologero Vicario in the vicinity of his store many times. He'd been tortured with threats of death to his family for several months in early 1909, in letters signed by The Black Hand. Ignazio Iannario of Marion said that after he was called to testify against the Limas, he began to receive letters threatening to kidnap his children. While he was on the stand, the Marion police were guarding his family.[22]

Not every witness was a guaranteed winner for the prosecution. One fruit vendor from Indianapolis testified in the afternoon.[23] The old man suffered from rheumatism and had to be helped into the witness stand. When Day asked him to identify Black Hand letters he had received, he said he couldn't read and seemed reluctant to say anything at all. The man's son testified afterward that he once gave Vincenzo Arrigo fifty dollars, but it was a gift, nothing more. Over the next several days, two dozen more victims testified. The jury almost became inured to the horrifying stories.[24]

On Friday court adjourned. There was no time for Oldfield to rest. He spent the weekend following up on dozens of queries he had out all over the country. He made phone calls and sent telegrams. In a spare few minutes, he likely sent a card home to Margaret Galena with a sweet phrase or two. He slept for only a few hours and lived off adrenaline. He was feeling a kind of frenetic optimism. Still, he knew things could flip on a dime once it was the defense attorneys' turn.

On January 24, Monday morning, the witness whom everyone was waiting for took the stand.[25] John Amicon had become something of a hero himself in the larger-than-life Black Hand caper. The press loved the story of the first-ever immigrant to turn on his criminal countrymen in federal court. He was considered brave beyond reproach. John Amicon, fruit mogul and tough guy extraordinaire, was the ultimate immigrant pursuing the American dream, afraid of *nothing*. The portly millionaire businessman was the key to breaking open The Black Hand Mafia.

From the witness stand, John Amicon identified Sam and Sebastian Lima, Severio Ventola, Joe Ignoffo, and Salvatore Arrigo as men he had seen around his shipping and receiving depots in Columbus each time the threatening letters came. Then he told a captivated courtroom about a conversation with Ventola.

"Severio Ventola asked me if I was suspicious that he was the one who wrote me the letters. I told him, 'If I thought you wrote them, I wouldn't have to go to court. I would shoot you right here on the sidewalk.'"[26] The gallery hooted and hollered with delight. Judge Tayler called the room to order.

William Day asked Amicon what it was like to be the target of extortionists for so many months. Amicon described to the jury walking home in the evening, wondering if his child would be missing, his house blown up, or if he'd make it home at all. It didn't matter, he said. "They tried all different kinds of schemes to make me pay." Still, he refused to give in. This was not what he came to America for.

Next up was the solid testimony of Inspector George Pate, who told of the defendants' arrests. "Pate was subject to a searing cross-examination by six of the attorneys for the defense," reported the *Marion Weekly Star*, "but his direct testimony was not shaken in any essential particular." Columbus postmaster Harry Krumm described the day that John Amicon came into the post office demanding help from the federal authorities. He identified a marked stamp that he'd given to the square-jawed Columbus man Salvatore Demma. The stamp ended up on a letter that was later sent to Dennison saloon owner Augustino Marfisi. The defense tried hard, but couldn't rattle Krumm in the slightest. Herman Holland, the Amicon Brothers' manager, took the stand and identified Orazio Runfola and Severio Ventola as the two men he'd seen loitering around the Amicon fruit yards.

In the afternoon, the prosecution finally produced direct evidence to the jury. A mail carrier from Marion named R. J. Pennell testified that he frequently handled Sam Lima's mail. Between the middle of March and June 8, 1909, when he was captured, Lima constantly sent letters to Augustino Marfisi in Dennison and Orazio Runfola in Pittsburgh. Pennell also identified Sam Lima's signature on several checks drawn on the Marion County Bank.[27] William George Pengelly, of Columbus, a handwriting expert hired by the government, testified that the various letters were written by the hand of four of the defendants: Sam Lima, Pippino Galbo, Cologero Vicario, and Giuseppe Ignoffo.[28] The accused glared at Pengelly, but the academic was unshaken. Certain markers run through the correspondence of the various accused, he said.

William Day said he was introducing more than one hundred letters, both correspondence between the defendants and threatening letters to victims. He also wanted to enter as evidence the Society of the Banana roster and ledger book, which named every defendant in the courtroom.

The defense attorneys huddled. If all of the letters and the Society roster and ledger were allowed to be entered as evidence, it would be the death knell for their clients' cases. The next morning, Tuesday, January 25, O'Leary and the others arrived with a prepared formal motion to quash the evidence and to dismiss the cases altogether.

Judge Tayler was not interested in the corporate attorneys' arguments anymore. "The evidence seems to show that an organization exists between the defendants, and that organization may be the Society of the Banana," he responded to O'Leary and the others.[29] "The examination of the mails proved the Society to be the backbone of the system for carrying out the schemes of the members. It is my opinion that there has been an unlawful conspiracy, but as to who should be held or dismissed is a matter for the jury to decide. Motion overruled."

Oldfield and Day were euphoric. The judge Oldfield had despised two weeks ago was now his best ally. Every last piece of evidence the prosecution introduced would be entered into the trial.

That same day, William Day was onstage like a Broadway actor in a starring role, his audience a mesmerized jury. He theatrically read all sixteen bylaws of the Society of the Banana, point by point. This proves, Day told the twelve jurors, "that there was an organization known as the Society of the Banana, with rules and regulation prescripting horrible penalties for disobedience of its mandates."[30] The crowd gasped at the barbarity. Day followed with mountains of documentary evidence. There were letters to prospective victims, receipts for money extorted, telegrams and other communications between the defendants. He said the conspirators used ambiguous words and code in the letters, such as "objects," "packages," "shipments," and "steaming the bananas."

Day then told the jury that Ignazio Camillo, of Cleveland, one of the intended Black Hand victims, was ill and unable to travel to the trial. Day identified one of the letters as having been turned in by Camillo to the Cleveland police. In the afternoon, Deputy U.S. Marshal Amos Owen testified to capturing Joe Ignoffo, and John D. Gist, an employee of the Athens post office, related several events connected with the arrest of the Limas in Marion.[31]

The prosecution rested. Once again, the defense called on Judge Tayler to dismiss the charges and end the proceedings. The judge would have none of it.[32] That freezing evening, bundled-up witnesses for the prosecution climbed on trains heading for all points home. Some had police or private guards. All were looking over their shoulders. All prayed to make it home alive. At the same time, witnesses for the defense arrived at Toledo's Central Union Terminal from Marion, Cincinnati, Dennison, and Columbus.

On Wednesday, January 26, it was the defense attorneys' turn to prove the fourteen Sicilians were actually upstanding citizens and not murderous extortionists. To do so, O'Leary and others brought fifty character witnesses and one expert witness. The one ringer was Dr. Henry D. Gould, a professor, author, and handwriting analyst from Cleveland.[33] In direct opposition to the United States' handwriting expert, Gould explained his "nerve tremor" theory, which he used to analyze handwriting. The letters in the government's possession were not written by the same person, he said. He gave a detailed explanation of the exactness of his methods, sounding very scientific and convincing.[34]

Then came the fan club. One by one, good Italian citizens and American businessmen stood up for the defendants. Fifteen-year-old Maria Cira of Bellefontaine testified to the good character of thirty-year-old Cologero "Charlie" Vicario, raving about what a kind and upstanding man he was.

"And who is Charlie Vicario to you, Miss Cira?" asked William Day on cross-examination.

"I am Charlie's sweetheart," the girl answered, beaming. Oldfield cringed.

Next, Maria Lima, Sam Lima's teenage stepdaughter, testified that the trunk in which detectives found the ledger book didn't belong to Sam Lima at all. It was the property of Francesco Lima, a former boarder at the Lima house who moved out around the time of the arrests.[35] So many of Marion's bankers and bank employees were summoned to Toledo to testify for the defense that day that nearly every bank in Marion closed.[36] The manager from City National Bank and several tellers testified that the letters in the prosecution's evidence did not match Sam Lima's or Sebastian Lima's handwriting at all—same for Joe Ignoffo and Salvatore Rizzo. Other locals came to testify about the Limas' great contribution to Marion. A doctor and a bank teller from Pittsburgh testified that Pippino Galbo was a businessman of high reputation.

Then the defendants themselves took the stand. All were skillfully guided by their expert attorneys. The ultrasmooth Salvatore Demma explained that his frequent visits to Columbus were not to stalk the Amicon brothers at all, as the prosecution suggested. His trips to the city were affairs of the heart, visits to his girl, whom he truly loved.[37] He had never signed any bylaws for a Mafia organization, he said, nor had he ever heard of the Society of the Banana.[38]

The devilishly handsome Pippino Galbo took the stand in the afternoon. About the unfinished Black Hand letter found in his house? He received it from an unknown gangster in New York, he said. He put the letter in his desk because he feared for his life if he informed the police.[39] Gary asked Galbo to explain the meaning of the phrase "steaming the bananas," which he had used in a letter to Salvatore Lima. Galbo calmly explained that the expression referred to an ocean steamer with a cargo of bananas. Galbo's brother Tomaso took the stand to corroborate his brother's testimony.[40]

Unlike some of the other defense attorneys, John O'Leary wanted his personal clients from Marion on the stand for as short a time as possible. He didn't want the jury to perceive his defendants had something to hide by their not testifying at all, but he also didn't want to open a can of worms that William Day could exploit on cross-examination. A likely third consideration for O'Leary was that Sam Lima obviously had a short fuse. Putting the society ringleader on the stand was risky. He might explode and threaten to murder every lawman in the room and take the jury down with them.

Oldfield and his colleagues left for dinner. It was dark and cold, but as they did every morning and evening, the lawmen and attorneys had to make their way through throngs of Sicilians and Italians protesting the trial and testifying to the innocence of the good businessmen.

On Thursday, January 27, the ninth day of the trial, the prosecution won a battle to introduce what was referred to as the "roster" of the Society of the Banana.[41] Because of Maria Lima's testimony that the trunk in which the book was found did not belong to her stepfather, Sam Lima, the defense attorneys were fighting to get it excluded. Judge Tayler again sided with the prosecution, and William Day theatrically produced the roster to the jury. The title of the list, translated into English, was "The Society of the Banana, November 3, 1908." The list of names below included all fourteen defendants. The names Sam Lima, Sebastian Lima, Antonio Lima, and Giuseppe Ignoffo all appeared separated by a bracket and were labeled "The Directorate." Day told the jury that the list was in the handwriting of Ignoffo.

Orazio Runfola took the stand. In very proficient English, he made a sweeping denial of the charges. His attorney had him give a long explanation of suspicious phrases written in letters between him and Sam Lima. They were all terms used in the fruit business, he said. He admitted that he was a member of the Pittsburgh Society of the Banana, a fruit merchant organization, but denied he was its president. "Then why did you sign the letters as the 'President'?" asked Assistant U.S. Attorney Thomas Gary on cross-examination. "I did it because I was ambitious to appear big before my people from the old country," Runfola responded demurely.[42] When Gary asked what Sam Lima meant when he wrote to Runfola commending him for "doing good work and making satisfactory collections," Runfola testified that he was a member of a religious beneficial society and had been collecting money among friends to replenish its fund, which was low. Several witnesses took the stand and swore that Runfola was in Pittsburgh on March 9 and couldn't possibly have been at the Society of the Banana meeting.[43]

Sam Lima's brother-in-law, Giuseppe "Joe" Ignoffo, and his diminutive henchman, Salvatore Rizzo, briefly took the stand and denied any knowledge of anything at all.[44] Sebastian Lima said that the numerous weapons found in Lima's shop were there when they bought the store, and were included in the sale along with all the stock. Finally, Sam Lima appeared in the witness box. He appeared very uncomfortable. Pretending to be an upstanding guy wasn't in his bag of tricks. O'Leary rushed through some questions about the letter to John Amicon, to which Lima grunted practiced denials. On cross-examination, Day read passages from letters written by Lima to other Society members that Judge Tayler had allowed as evidence. "What is the meaning of this phrase; 'When the machine is adjusted'?" Lima was calm and matter-of-fact. "That meant 'When times are better'—we use such expressions among ourselves." [45] Day could extract nothing.

On Friday, January 28, ten days after the trial began, creative and convincing closing arguments on both sides offered Oldfield no clear idea which side had swayed the jury. William Day said he was dropping the fifteenth count on the indictment, which accused the young Antonio Vicario of writing one of the threatening letters. The letter was printed, rather than handwritten, and therefore there was no way of comparing the script to Vicario's handwriting.

Oldfield was utterly relieved that it was finally over, although still desperately worried about the outcome. He had obsessed every day of the trial over the jurors' security. There were twelve American-born men on the jury to decide the fate of fourteen Sicilian immigrants, in a time when there was a lot of bigotry toward Italians in general. While Oldfield knew he had cultural bias on his side as well as plenty of evidence, it was impossible to know if any of the jury members had been bought or threatened.

Judge Tayler gave his instructions to the jury on Friday afternoon. "There is a tremendous mass of documentary evidence in this case," the judge said, belaboring the obvious to the jurors, who had sat through the exhausting trial. "I caution you to peruse the evidence minutely." Then he explained the conspiracy charge and what that meant to their task at hand. "If any of the accused are found to have even in a remote way aided in connection with the conspiracy, knew of it, or caused any of the threatening letters to be mailed, or if they knew that such letters were mailed by members of the Society of the Banana, of which the accused are members, they should be found equally guilty with the actual writers of the letters."

For the four men whose lives collided in the spring of 1909 in America's booming industrial heartland, all there was to do now was wait. Frank Oldfield went back to his office in the Toledo federal building. For the first time in a year, he didn't have anything to do on the Black Hand case. He called home to touch base with Margaret Galena and the boys, then fell asleep in his chair. John Amicon was already back in Columbus, working on plans for a new warehouse to replace his current aging headquarters.[46] He tried not to think of what would happen if Lima and his murderous tribe got loose again. He was still full of bravado publicly, but he was exhausted after a solid year of living in fear. In Pittsburgh, Pinkerton detective Francis Dimaio waited to hear the verdict by telephone from Oldfield. Dimaio was deep undercover in a new investigation, and the public barely knew of his involvement in the country's most sensational Mafia trial ever. In an uncomfortable cot in a frigid Toledo jail, Sam Lima imagined his future.

They didn't have to wait long.

The very next morning, on Saturday, January 29, 1910, the jury was ready to read their verdict. Everyone was called back to court. Oldfield ran up the courthouse steps and into the gallery. He took a deep breath. The jury foreman stood to read the decision. "We find all of the defendants guilty of the charges of conspiracy and using the United States mail in furtherance of the same."[47]

An enormous celebratory roar came from the galley, drowning

out expletives and threats spouted by the defendants. Frank Oldfield, for the first time, was silent. William Day moved immediately for a sentence on the verdict. The defense attorneys interposed a motion for a new trial. Oldfield braced himself, trying to read Tayler's face.

"For the cases of three defendants; Salvatore Rizzo of Marion, Augustino Marfisi of Bellefontaine, and Vincenzo Arrigo, of Cincinnati, the court will sustain the defense's motion. A new trial is granted to these three men. They are to be released immediately on their own recognizance." A collective gasp came from the audience as the newly freed Sicilians embraced each other and their attorneys. Oldfield must have felt his blood pressure go through the roof.[48] It was a hard hit, but he had to agree with the judge. The evidence was shaky against those three. None of them had been positively identified as directly writing or mailing any of the threat letters, only as being at the meeting on March 9 and listed in documents in Lima's collection. Frank sat on the edge of his seat, practically coming unglued waiting to hear the rest of the sentences.

Judge Tayler went on. "In the decision of sentencing, the proportion of each man's guilt and other circumstances will influence the length of the respective penalties. The sentences are as follows:

"Antonio Vicario, Dennison, two years in the Elmira, New York, reformatory.

"Cologero Vicario, Bellefontaine, two years in Leavenworth Penitentiary.

"Francesco Spadaro, Cincinnati, two years Leavenworth Penitentiary.

"Severio Ventola, Columbus, two years in Leavenworth Penitentiary.

"Salvatore Demma, Columbus, two years in Leavenworth Penitentiary.

"Salvatore Arrigo, Cincinnati, four years Leavenworth Penitentiary.

"Pippino Galbo, Meadville, four years in Leavenworth Penitentiary.

"Orazio Runfola, Pittsburgh, six years in Leavenworth Penitentiary.

"Sebastian Lima and Giuseppe Ignoffo, Marion, ten years each in Leavenworth Penitentiary."

In sentencing Sam Lima, Judge Tayler stared directly at the convicted director of the Society of the Banana: "You seem to have been the moving spirit in this nefarious business," he said.[49] "All of these suspicious circumstances point toward you. Salvatore Lima, *you* are sentenced to *sixteen* years in Leavenworth Penitentiary." The *Toledo Blade*'s sketch artist scribbled furiously, trying to capture Sam Lima's emotional state at that moment, but Lima showed nothing at all.

As the convicted men were led away, William Day, Frank Oldfield, and Thomas Gary celebrated. The men kept the press at bay for a few minutes to soak it all in. While there had been hundreds of Black Hand criminals arrested and convicted in New York, Chicago, and New Orleans for individual crimes over the last decade, the postal inspectors, led by John Frank Oldfield, were the first to successfully take down a widespread organized crime ring in federal court. "There has not been a sign of Black Hand operation in this section of the country since these men were arrested," Oldfield said to the mass of press at a pop-up press conference on the courthouse steps. This was another Oldfield stretch, since there were many copycat Black Hand groups. But one thing was for sure: The Society of the Banana was no more. A proud William Day echoed Oldfield's optimism. "We have broken the backbone of the Black Hand in this part of the country," he told reporters.[50]

"What do you have to say, Judge?" a newsman yelled to Tayler. For once, the shy judge appeared emotional. "The cases were the most sensational ever tried in the criminal wing of the United States court.

This is the first instance in which the government of the United States was able to secure a conviction on Black Hand charges, so cautious and cunning have been the methods used by the Mafia societies. This verdict sounds the death knell of Blackhandism in the United States."[51]

While William Day, Judge Tayler, and Frank Oldfield were happily grandstanding on the courthouse steps, Sam Lima and his fellow prisoners filed out of the building into the freezing cold, closely accompanied by federal marshals. The Sicilian men still looked elegant in their expensive suits and long wool coats. All wore dark fedoras that shielded their eyes from the flash powder bursts of the giant news cameras. Still, from under the brims, they appeared to be looking around, possibly for their confederates, whom they expected to make an attempt to free them.

Sam Lima, Sebastian Lima, Joe Ignoffo, and seven others piled into the horse-drawn bus that was waiting. Salvatore Arrigo, his rheumatism kicking in, moved slowly and had help getting on board. Only the young Tony Vicario was taken separately. He left in a small horse-drawn cab to the jail, from where he'd be shipped off to a New York maximum-security reformatory. Three marshals guarded the men in the bus. More deputies rode in a carriage behind them. United States Federal Marshal Hyman Davis was in charge.

Every day of the trial, a crowd of Italians had surrounded the courthouse protesting for the release of the "law-abiding businessmen," and now the courthouse steps were eerily quiet. Even with no sign of his associates, Sam Lima was likely confident that somewhere along the trip back to jail to wait for their transfer to prison, his men would launch an ambush and pave the way for an epic escape. He may even have known an exact plan, communicated to him by a visitor through his cell bars. He rode along unconcerned. His ego, even after his failed defense in court, told him that he was still more clever than

Uncle Sam. The bus was quiet with the silent thoughts of ten men mulling over their futures and deputies watching their every move. Then, suddenly, the bus changed course. The driver had taken the same route every day for two weeks from the jail to the courthouse and back. Lima and the others immediately knew that something was up.

Because of the death threats to Oldfield, William Day, and Judge Tayler during the trial, as well as the threats still going out to victims and trial witnesses, Oldfield knew there were many Black Hand cohorts still lurking around Toledo. Oldfield and Day didn't want to take any chances that Lima's friends could bounce the gang during a transfer to jail or at Union Depot boarding the train for Leavenworth. He tasked Oldfield and Marshal Davis, a former lawyer and a brilliant strategist, to come up with a plan.

During the final days of the trial, Davis made arrangements with the Lakeshore Railroad Company.[52] Instead of using the regular train service with stops and transfers, Davis contracted a private car to take the prisoners all the way to Kansas, nonstop. And instead of loading them up at the train station where their friends could be lying in wait, Davis had the Lakeshore manager park a single car and engine a half-mile north of the train depot. Then he made contact with every single railroad company from there to Kansas. When he gave the word, each switch along the tracks would be set in position so the car could pass right through.

Sam Lima and the others likely spent the rest of the ride with clenched jaws as the bus headed in a completely unknown direction. When the driver arrived at the switch in the middle of a pasture, it was obvious that there was no way the gang could escape the armed guards. There was nowhere to hide. Marshal Davis and eight of his deputies escorted the men quickly from the bus to the train car, keeping watch to prevent any chance of an ambush by the Society's colleagues.

The car that would transport the convicts was a dining car, and it was stocked with enough provisions to last until the end of the twenty-six-hour journey to Leavenworth. The state hired Patterson's Café, a restaurant near the courthouse, to provide meals for the prisoners. Mr. Patterson placed his manager, George Randall, in charge of the cooking, and Marshal Davis swore Randall in as a deputy. The wide-eyed restaurant manager suddenly had the double duty of looking after the prisoners' meals and keeping them from escaping or killing him or each other. When all the convicts were inside, Marshal Davis made a final visual check of each man to make sure each was who he was supposed to be. The men barely noticed Davis. Some were salivating over the smell of a pasta dinner that Randall had prepared. Others took out playing cards. One opened a bottle of wine and settled into the leather bench seat in the dining booth. Marshal Davis slid the door closed and put an iron bar through a metal ring on each door. Then he had one more thought. He called for a blowtorch from a railroad hand and directed the door be welded shut. He'd tell Oldfield about that final touch later on.

Back at Union Depot, a nearly emaciated and exhausted Frank Oldfield must have appeared curious to other passengers on the Toledo and Central Ohio train headed for Columbus and then to Athens. Perhaps some of them recognized the famous lawman from the newspapers, with his gaunt cheekbones and extra-tall derby hat. But what was really odd about the meticulously dressed man was that he had the porter load *seven* steamer trunks into the luggage car to carry with him.

There was really no solid protocol in the U.S. Post Office Inspection Service for keeping trial evidence. Oldfield couldn't bear to have what he had worked to collect for an entire year of his life hidden in some dusty archive or possibly tossed out. He was a collector at heart. So was Margaret Galena. She had lovingly archived every single mention of her husband she could find in the newspapers for the past ten years as well as hundreds of clippings sent to her by friends and other Post Office inspectors across the country. She would love to add all of his notes and letters to her well-organized collection of photos and documents. Oldfield also really wanted to keep the collection of weapons that he'd confiscated from Lima and his cohorts. He wanted to show them to his sons and to leave the collection in his will, perhaps for his grandsons one day.

Frank took a seat on the train bound for Columbus, flashed a star-shaped silver badge to the conductor, and closed his eyes.

CHAPTER 11

GOOD-BYES

It was a crisp November evening in Toledo when Judge Robert Tayler and his wife, Helen Vance, attended a charity ball for St. Luke's Hospital at Engineer's Hall on the corner of Main and Barker Streets. Handsome in his tuxedo, Judge Tayler enjoyed dinner with a table of other esteemed Toledo guests. Just before the program began, the judge took a spoonful of dessert. Seconds later, Tayler fell to the ground, seizing his stomach, foaming at the mouth, and struggling to breathe.

He was rushed by ambulance to Lakeside Hospital with his wife by his side. His personal physician and hospital doctors attended to him. At 11:00 p.m., the partially paralyzed judge lost consciousness. His family physician admitted to reporters that Tayler's condition was extremely critical. What caused his collapse? a reporter asked. The physicians were puzzled. Some guessed it was a cerebral hemorrhage because Tayler fell over in his seat at the banquet. One physician suggested acute indigestion or gastritis.[1] One suggested poisoning. Tayler's personal doctor refused to offer a diagnosis. "All I can say now is that Judge Tayler's condition is critical—very critical," he said.

Judge Robert Tayler never regained consciousness and died at two in the morning.[2] It was his fifty-eighth birthday. None of the doctors could ever prove what killed him, but rumor was that a Sicilian waiter served him a dessert of poisoned bananas and other fresh fruit after the catered dinner. Oldfield found out about the death in the newspaper. He was devastated. For all the good he believed he'd accomplished bringing Sam Lima and the Society of the Banana to justice, he knew he'd won only a small battle in a festering, widespread war. It was a war that would be waged for many years to come and fill many more graves with innocent victims along the way.

In December, Frank's father, Hamilton, came to Athens to spend the Christmas holiday. After losing his mother to heart failure in 1907, Frank kept a close watch on his father, checking in often with his siblings back in Ellicott City. What he learned concerned him greatly. After the death of his wife, Wilhelmina, Hamilton was never the same. The tall, elegant statesman seemed to wither a little more every day. Now, at seventy-one, Hamilton was not doing well at all. In the family photograph taken that Christmas of 1910, the four Oldfield boys stand surrounding their grandfather. Hamilton is thin, mostly bald, but still very handsome and polished in his suit and ever-present bow tie. Margaret Galena looks sternly at the camera. The boys look serious, as if they had been ordered by their father to stand perfectly still. As usual in posed photos, Frank looks awkwardly off camera as if in deep thought. It was a pose he often took to get laughs, but this time, he succeeded only in looking forlorn.

For the first time since taking the job as Post Office inspector in Ohio, Frank Oldfield was tired of the work. He was not interested in small-time burglaries, corrupt postmasters, or postal workers stealing this or that. Unless there was a really big case, Oldfield really didn't want to be bothered. The bad blood with his boss Abraham Holmes was still not resolved.

His boss in Cincinnati was a constant source of frustration. Holmes complained that Oldfield was too slow in solving his cases. He still disparaged Oldfield to the higher-ups in Washington. He continued to accuse Oldfield of mishandling funds and spending far too much on Italian detectives and translators whom Oldfield refused to name in his expense reports. It was a constant headache for Oldfield to defend himself. He didn't want to have to explain why he needed to protect his sources. It had gotten so bad that Oldfield had asked U.S. Attorney William Day to intervene:

Mr. A. R. Holmes, Inspector in Charge,
Cincinnati, Ohio.

Sir:

In the investigation of the Black-Hand Cases against Salvatore Lima, Sebastian Lima, Antonio Lima, Severio Ventola, Salvatore Rizzo, and other Sicilians in various sections of Ohio and Pennsylvania under arrest awaiting action of the United States grand jury at Toledo, Ohio, on the charge of using the mails to extort money from wealthy Sicilians, I directed Inspector Oldfield, who had charge of the investigation relative to securing evidence necessary to a successful prosecution of the case against the parties suspected. . . .

From January 20th, 1909, Inspector Oldfield has given his entire attention to this investigation and had expended a considerable sum of money in securing necessary evidence. It became necessary owing to the fact that these men spoke the Sicilian language to employ any Sicilian who could assist these inspectors. In employing these men it was found necessary to first assure them that they would not be called as witnesses in the prosecution of these cases, nor would their names

247

be used in any manner. The statement of expenditure presented by
Inspector Oldfield is in my opinion reasonable and just, and should
be passed and allowed by the Post Office Department.

Very respectfully,
William L. Day, United States Attorney[3]

The other issue was that there didn't seem to be a huge amount of appreciation for Oldfield in the service. In the chief Post Office inspector's annual report for 1909, there was only a small paragraph about the Ohio Black Hand arrests. There was no credit given to Oldfield for leading the investigation. However, that was not unusual.[4] In the 1910 official report, there wasn't a single mention of the trial and conviction that put the Post Office Inspection Service on the map for its enormous win against organized crime in America.[5] Oldfield didn't know if the chief inspector's cold shoulder was the result of Abraham Holmes's badmouthing him to the top brass or the fact that the agency liked its work to fly under the radar.

Mostly, though, Oldfield wanted to spend time with his father and his boys. He knew that his father's days were numbered. He couldn't see leaving his father right now to go back to Columbus, so he told his superiors that he would work from home.

Frank's absence both mentally and physically from the Columbus post office didn't sit well with Harry Krumm, who wrote to Oldfield complaining of his absence:

Jan 6, 1911,

My dear Barney [Krumm's nickname for Frank],

On the night of January 4th, or early morning of January 5th, the Post-Office at Grogan, Ohio, was burglarized and stamps and money to the amount of $170.78 was stolen. Mr. Cookson, your fellow Inspector in this district, after consulting his clue-book, very promptly arrested two men suspected of the job, and after a slight effort, succeeded in locating the missing stamps.

The two men arrested had a pawn ticket in their possession covering a ladies' gold filled watch, and subsequent inquiry developed the fact that two other watches were disposed of by one of these men the day before. This leads to the belief that perhaps the men in custody here may possibly know something about the Haydenville job, and if you will be kind enough to communicate with us and give a description of the articles missing through the Haydenville burglary, it may possibly be the means of identifying the watched disposed of in this city.

It is suggested, if you find it convenient, that you come up and look after this end of it, and by the way, I venture the opinion that you might learn something about thief-catching if you would stay around Columbus, Ohio, and see the operations of your competitors in the service. Have in mind some of your previous efforts and the long time it takes you to apprehend criminals, I am not underestimating your ability when I say that you certainly need a new clue-book after the results of yesterday.

Respectfully,
HW Krumm. Postmaster

p.s. Hope your father is better.

While Oldfield went ballistic on frontal assaults to his character, he never seemed to be bothered by Krumm's passive-aggressive attacks on his work ethic. Besides, Krumm was like a brother to Frank, and fraternal relationships were always fraught with conflict, in his experience. He ignored Krumm's bait to his ego. The only thing that was important at that moment was that Frank's father was ill and failing fast. Hamilton wasn't eating much and could barely get his food down. His skin looked gray, his face gaunt.

After a month in Athens mostly feeling terrible, Hamilton was desperate to go home to Ellicott City. Frank tried to persuade his father to stay. He wanted to take care of him, to be the son that Hamilton now needed him to be. He also knew how much Hamilton loved being in his Maryland hills. It was something that Frank understood very well because he felt the same. There was no place like Maryland and the beautiful mill town on the Patapsco River. Hamilton pushed, and Frank finally agreed to make the trip with him.

On January 11, during a bumpy ride on the B&O heading east, Hamilton's condition worsened. Frank made the decision to skip Ellicott City and go one more stop to Baltimore. Frank got two rooms at the Rennert, an elegant eight-story hotel that served as an opulent outpatient facility for wealthy patients receiving care at Johns Hopkins hospital. Frank made his father as comfortable as he could and called for the prominent Dr. William Thayer of the Hopkins staff. Thayer came quickly, but he was unable to offer Hamilton any relief. It was only a matter of days, Thayer said. Oldfield sent for Margaret Galena and the boys and his brothers and sisters in Ellicott City. On Saturday, January 14, John Frank was at his father's bedside as Hamilton slipped away.

Oldfield returned to Ellicott City, crestfallen. In all the years of his adult life, had he ever truly thanked his father for the gifts that he'd bestowed upon him, for the sacrifices Hamilton made for his family? He wondered if his father had forgiven him for his many indiscretions and embarrassments. All of the things that Oldfield never spoke of with his father consumed him. Was his father proud of the man he had become?

He soon had the answer. In his father's will, it was John Frank Oldfield, second son, the rebel, the black sheep, who was named executor; "to sell and convey any and all of my property to carry into the effect the provisions of my will." Frank's heart swelled. He was forty-four years old. He had no idea how much his father's acceptance of him meant until that moment. Somewhere and at some point in time, he had earned his father's trust.

Oldfield stayed in Ellicott City to deal with Hamilton's estate. The hard work he once despised at the mill and pump company now gave him solace and helped him heal. He and Clarence, now a high-level customs official in the port city of Baltimore, settled affairs for the rest of the family. Hamilton had a considerable fortune, and the H. Oldfield Pump business and sawmill were still thriving. Oldfield made sure all of his siblings were well taken care of and turned the companies over to his younger brother, Walter, and prayed that Ulysses S. Grant Oldfield, the youngest brother, would keep from squandering his family's fortune.

While he was not excited about getting back to work, a fascinating interstate crime lured him back to his office in February 1911. Early in the month, there was a robbery at the Erie Pennsylvania Cemetery. The mausoleum of the Scott family—which contained the body of the late railroad magnate and congressman William Scott—was broken into. The thieves attempted to steal the bodies of Scott and his wife and took jewelry and heirlooms from the crypts. Scott's daughter, Annie Strong, reached out to the Perkins Detective Agency in Pittsburgh, which had worked for her husband, the multimillionaire businessman Charles H. Strong, some two years before.[6]

The Strongs were very intelligent. When they began to receive extortion letters demanding payment for the return of their family treasures, they soon felt that things weren't adding up. Like nearly everyone in America, Mr. and Mrs. Strong followed the Black Hand trial closely and knew of Frank Oldfield's celebrated work. Since they were receiving threats through the mail, the couple reached out to their congressman, who asked Inspector Oldfield to address the case. Frank quickly discovered that it was actually the Perkins detectives who broke into the crypts and were now trying to extort money from the Strongs for the return of the heirlooms. After a ten-day trial, on July 29, 1911, the defendants were found guilty and sentenced to federal prison.[7]

The fifty-five-year-old Annie Strong was completely taken with Oldfield. The slight and sophisticated federal officer was at once charming and incredibly cunning. The Strongs, with their enormous wealth, were under constant threat, as were their daughter and granddaughter. They already employed multiple security crews. But when Annie Strong observed the way that Oldfield embarked on a case, the way he paid attention to detail and missed absolutely nothing, she convinced her husband to make Oldfield an offer he couldn't refuse. Over an elaborate dinner, Annie Strong asked Frank Oldfield to leave his Post Office employment to be the Strong family's director of security.

At first Oldfield couldn't even imagine it. He was one of the top lawmen for the United States government; he wasn't some private eye for hire. He gracefully declined the proposal, although he was incredibly fond of Mrs. Strong and found her proposition quite flattering. Soon afterward, the idea began to take hold of his thoughts. The Strongs were offering him ten times his civil servant salary. That was just a retainer. When he was not actively working on a case for them, he was free to pursue work with other wealthy clients. What he learned from collaborating with other private detectives was that not only was the money better, there was tremendous autonomy. If he took the Strongs' generous offer, he would never be under the thumb of another man, ever again.

From all the publicity his Post Office cases received, Oldfield knew his stock was high among America's millionaire class. Clients would stand in line for his services with checkbooks and cash in hand. It all played out perfectly in his imagination, so Inspector Oldfield did the unthinkable. Nearly two years after the trial of the century put away eleven Sicilian Mafiosi, and thirteen years after his father greased the political wheels so he could enter the Post Office Inspection Service, John Frank Oldfield wrote his letter of resignation. The *Baltimore Sun* reported: "Columbus, Ohio, November 15th, 1911. Post office inspector John Oldfield who has been with that department of the Government for the past 13 years, today announced that he had tendered his resignation in order to engage in private business. Mr. Oldfield took a leading part in the running down of the Black Hand gang headed by Salvatore Lima, of Marion, and was instrumental in sending the members to the federal penitentiary; he has also been identified with a number of the greatest cases of the department in the past 13 years."

Oldfield felt a pang of nostalgia for his old job and his cramped Columbus office, but he didn't let it get him down. Over the next several years, Frank earned so much money working for railroad CEOs, shipping and steel magnates, bankers and oil barons that he had little time to miss his days on the government clock. The tycoons of twentieth-century America were constant targets of bad guys who found endless ways to extort, blackmail, and kidnap aristocratic heirs. Oldfield got calls from Mathers, Vanderbilts, Carnegies, and Rockefellers who offered him contracts in the tens of thousands of dollars.

253

Frank was so well connected among lawmen and had such a deep reach into America's criminal underbelly that he could often resolve a problem with one threatening phone call.

During the 1911–12 presidential campaign season, President William Howard Taft held many campaign events in Ohio. During this 1911 event in Cincinnati, Ohio, Margaret Galena Oldfield and her niece, Nancy Noss (both in white dresses on right), attended and grabbed a picture with the president and a few other dignitaries.

The money coming in didn't change Frank's lifestyle much. Margaret Galena, however, was in heaven. She became the queen of Athens, Ohio. She rented grand halls and threw lavish parties. She bought her four school-age boys the finest clothes, sporting equipment, Thor-

254

oughbred horses, and purebred dogs. She hobnobbed with members of the president's cabinet, and called their wives daily to catch up on the latest gossip of the super wealthy and politically connected. The German baker's daughter shopped and shopped until her Athens house was so full of fine things there was little room to move.

And the money just kept coming. When the Strongs' granddaughter was kidnapped and held for ransom, Oldfield rescued the child unharmed in a matter of days and the press never got wind of the matter at all. The Strongs gave Oldfield an enormous bonus. Multiple letters of gratitude to Frank from Annie Strong bordered on reverence. If Margaret Galena was worried, she didn't show it. She simply tucked the notes away with stacks of letters of appreciation from other of her husband's fans.

After Frank Oldfield's retirement from the Post Office in 1911 and his entrance into private investigative practice, the Oldfield family began to take extended vacations during the summers. This 1914 photo is of the family and others on a motor tour of the park around Pikes Peak, Colorado, while staying at Cliff House. Frank is sitting next to the driver.

There was one downside to having an unlimited cash flow. In 1914, Frank had so much extra money on hand that when a former Ohioan from Nelsonville came from California looking for oil investors, Oldfield jumped right in with a ten-thousand-dollar investment. Oldfield had never been one for sketchy deals, and he'd spent his life highly suspicious of just about everything. Somehow, with no money worries at all, his balderdash meter had stopped working. The first California oil boom was in full swing. Everyone wanted in on the action. With Oldfield on board, many prominent people from central Ohio handed over thousands of dollars to invest in George Metcalf's Coalinga oil field in Fresno County, California. Months went by. There was no word how the oil field was faring, and there were no dividends to investors. Oldfield heard that Metcalf was blowing investors' money living a lavish lifestyle out in California, even acting as a venture capitalist for wild upstart inventors. He had raised over a million dollars with his scheme. All the while, not a single drop of oil came from Coalinga. Oldfield was furious. He was the number-one private detective in Ohio, if not the nation. Many important people had followed his lead to invest in a crooked deal, and now he was being humiliated. He had to do something.

With little evidence to offer an Ohio circuit court judge from Athens, who was Oldfield's friend, Oldfield secured an indictment for Metcalf on November 20, 1914. This was just a ruse. Oldfield knew that if Metcalf was brought to trial, the investors would never see their money again. He called his good friend H. T. Mulligan, the sheriff of Athens County, and the two left for Oakland, California. Oldfield and Mulligan quickly tracked down Metcalf, finding him on his morning walk. They then laid their story on thick.

"I know you're an honest man," Oldfield told the swindler. "But you see, there's this indictment signed by the governor of Ohio, and you're about to go to prison for a long time. The only way that you

Oldfield Collection

It continues to be a humorous tradition of Oldfield family men to take entertaining poses for the camera. This photo is of Frank Oldfield at one of his family homes in 1914.

can get out of going to prison is to come back to Ohio have a chat with your investors. Explain the situation out in the oil field and why they're not seeing any money. I'm sure you can get them to understand. Then, attorney Mulligan"—Frank lied about who Mulligan was—"will make sure the indictment goes away."

Metcalf did his best to appear unconcerned. "Not interested," he told Frank smugly. Metcalf knew how hard it would be for Ohio to extradite him from California. Oldfield wanted nothing more than to beat Metcalf to a bloody pulp. He kept calm.

"Well, there's also the issue of your son," Oldfield said. Metcalf's body went rigid, and Oldfield smelled fear. Oldfield knew that Metcalf's son was in his twenties, newly married, with a baby on the way.

"It seems that they're ready to indict him, too, in Columbus. Could mean a long time in prison for the both of you." In truth, Oldfield had nothing on Metcalf's son at all.

Sherriff Mulligan chimed in. "Listen, these Ohio folks are reasonable folks. You just need to come back with us and straighten this thing out."

Metcalf resigned himself. He called the Oakland bank where he worked as vice president and asked for leave.[8]

When the three men arrived in Columbus, Oldfield and Mulligan held Metcalf in a safe house and put the screws to the faux oilman. It worked like a charm. With Oldfield literally breathing down his neck, Metcalf grudgingly wrote out promissory notes to each Ohio investor. To Oldfield, Metcalf wrote two. One was for Frank's original investment of $10,251. The other was $10,000 to pay Oldfield and Mulligan for the inconvenience of having to track Metcalf down. Both notes held 4 percent interest and were payable in United States gold coin.[9]

The stress of dealing with the fraudulent oil deal took a toll on Oldfield's health and exacerbated a recurring stomach problem. He'd avoided seeing a specialist in Maryland, or telling Margaret Galena how bad he was feeling. But now things were so bad that he could barely keep food down. In early 1915, Frank went to see Dr. William Thayer, his father's doctor at Johns Hopkins in Baltimore. There, a team of surgeons, led by William Halsted, operated on Frank's stomach to remove tumors. Oldfield went back to Athens feeling better than he had in a long time. He told everyone he would be fine. There was nothing wrong with him at all.

To celebrate getting $20,000 out of Metcalf and the fact that he felt really good after the surgery, Oldfield decided to take the entire family and close friends on a six-month expedition across North America. Margaret Galena was thrilled. She packed trunks full of fancy clothes for all of the expected occasions. The caravan traveled by train, motorbus, steamship, and riverboat. They visited Chicago, St. Louis, and Dodge City. They watched geysers in Yellowstone expel the earth's intensity and marveled at ancient layers of history exposed in the Grand Canyon. The air and adventure invigorated Oldfield. In Tijuana, the three younger boys, wearing knickers with ties and jackets, rode burros for fun and posed in serapes and sombreros. In San Diego, Frank and the boys posed for a photo in a park, all of them covered in pigeons, wings a-flap. The Oldfields' traveling troupe finally landed in San Francisco for the 1915 Panama Pacific Exposition in December. They rode in a giant open motorbus around the Presidio's Bayfront, learning about the construction of the world's biggest engineering feat, the Panama Canal. Frank sat up front with the driver. It was by far the most fun they'd ever had as a family. It was the happiest Frank had ever been.

Toward the end of their expedition, the relief provided by Oldfield's stomach surgery began to wear off as they made their way back to Ohio. What Frank had told no one was the result of the medical tests at Johns Hopkins. The tumors were malignant. The doctor told Oldfield that the gastrectomy had removed the cancerous part of his stomach, but the tumors were likely to grow back. Into the winter of 1916, Oldfield faded as the mass in his stomach grew and shut down his body's mechanism for absorbing nutrients. What at first had not been a painful condition now caused him great distress. He had never had any extra weight on his small frame, and now his body withered. His skin turned gray.

This photo from the summer of 1915 is of the Oldfield family and friends on their cross-country tour culminating in their south-to-north visit to California and attendance at the Panama Pacific Exposition in San Diego. They regularly paid for the addition of close family friends on their tours. The names of family members are written on the photo.

Oldfield's mind stayed sharp into the spring. As the end neared, Frank gave instructions regarding his burial. He would like his brothers at the Elks Lodge to participate in the funeral rites. His four sons came to his bedside. Frank Junior was fully grown at eighteen. Like his mother, he was sturdy with a round, pleasant face. Hamilton was sixteen, wiry like his father, and becoming a man. The two youngest, Harry Edward, fourteen, and Fulton, twelve, were still boys, their eyes wide with unknowing. Frank sensed his sons' fear and anguish and wasn't quite sure what to do. Never having been openly emotive as a father, Frank did his best to give his boys solace. "When I die, they are going to bury me," he said, with as much sensitivity as he could muster. "It is important that you realize that you still have a life to live. Don't let my death disable you." Margaret Galena sent telegrams to her husband's good friends and siblings, asking them to come at once. Several arrived to say their good-byes, including George Pate, Frank's fellow inspector, to whom he'd stayed close after leaving the Post Office Department. Frank's brother Clarence came from Baltimore as quickly as he could, praying he would make it. He was ten minutes too late. On May 25, 1916, John Frank Oldfield passed away at 12:10 p.m. He was forty-nine years old.[10]

Margaret Galena and the Oldfield siblings laid John Frank to rest at Union Street Cemetery in Athens. At home, Margaret Galena then lovingly tended to the seven steamer trunks that contained her husband's memories.

What Margaret Galena found in those trunks was a life extraordinary and also ordinary. Like most people, Frank Oldfield was loved and he was despised. He was feared and he was revered. Margaret Galena secured the trunks and told the boys that they need not go anywhere near them. One trunk still contained most of the weapons that had been introduced in the trial as evidence. Margaret Galena was terrified of the guns, stilettos, and knives, some of which still had dried blood of their human victims. She told the family gardener to bury that trunk in the backyard. The other six trunks were to remain locked and protected at all costs. For the boys' own protection, she told them, there would be no discussion with their school friends or anyone in Athens about their father's remarkable history.

CHAPTER 12

OUTCOMES

F rank Oldfield and State's Attorney William Day rightly took credit for finishing off the Society of the Banana. The heroic courtroom showdown of lawmen versus mobsters left a once-proud consortium of criminals disjointed and scattered irrevocably across America. While there was no shortage of bad guys to fill the vacuum left in America's industrial heartland, Sam Lima's Black Hand monopoly expired with his gang's convictions in 1910.

Some Society members did better than others in the aftermath. A handful reinvented themselves and thrived. Others appear to have left the Mafia business behind. Some with family networks created new alliances. Others were never heard from again. One lived only weeks after his release from prison. Another went completely mad. While the convicted men found their freedom over the next decade, they would never reunite under the banner of the Banana. Instead, the "honorable" men of Ohio and Pennsylvania, of fruit crates, cobbler shops, and smoke-filled saloons, split and scattered as a result of their state-sponsored punishments, courtesy of Frank Oldfield and the United States Post Office Inspection Service.

There is little information about what happened to many of the men after the trial. Of the three who were released pending a new trial, only Augustino Marfisi, the Dennison saloon owner, appears to have been tried and convicted. In April 1914, Marfisi sold some land in Dennison for twenty-eight hundred dollars, perhaps to pay for attorney's fees. In June 1916, Marfisi's attorney lost his appeal in *August Marfisi* v. *the State of Ohio*.[1] After his release, Marfisi bought commercial real estate and became a landlord to illegal speakeasy operations during Prohibition.[2] He was arrested in 1924 for selling banned liquor and released on a two-hundred-dollar bond. Marfisi died in 1946 at the age of eighty. He left a sizable estate to his five daughters and put his son-in-law in charge of executing the will.

Salvatore Rizzo, the railroad section hand who worked for Sam and Sebastian Lima, remained free after the trial. In November 1912, Rizzo married Mariama Batagalia, a young woman from Sicily who had arrived in Marion nine months earlier.[3] They were attended by the bride's parents and a party of friends. The *Marion Star* reported that after the ceremony, the party proceeded to the home of the bride on Park Street for an Italian feast on a table decorated with flowers.

Vincenzo Arrigo, apparently wanting a clean start, took advantage of his freedom and moved to Chicago from Cincinnati. He bought property on the northeast corner of Addison and Perry Streets for twenty-three thousand dollars. He opened a produce shop and appears to have stayed out of trouble with the Chicago police. He and his wife, Girolima, raised three daughters and three sons. One son, Joseph, J. Arrigo, became the assistant district attorney for Illinois. In 1947 Girolima died. Vincenzo passed away the following year.[4] He was in his eighties.

The first convicted Black Hand criminal to be paroled was the young Antonio "Tony" Vicario, Augustino Marfisi's employee in Dennison. Barely twenty at the time, and with his brother, Cologero "Charlie" Vicario, and the rest of the Society of the Banana still locked up, Tony had no support network. He made his way to Erie County,

Ohio, and got a job in a rock quarry. He scored a room with four other men at the quarry camp.[5]

Soon after, Tony's nude body turned up, bloated, with multiple stab wounds in his back, his throat and abdomen slashed. Two days later, a fisherman found two other roommates, also murdered and mutilated.[6] According to one witness in the camp, the men were fighting and Vicario owed them money. Another said it was about a woman.[7] Rocco Lavechic, alias Rocco Klawetch, and Dominick Selvaggio were charged and convicted for the three murders and electrocuted in the annex of the Ohio Penitentiary during the latter part of November 1911.[8]

Cologero Vicario was released from Leavenworth on September 7, 1911, just days before his younger brother's murder. Along with him were Cincinnati saloon owner Francesco Spadaro and Columbus Blackhanders Salvatore Demma and Severio Ventola. All four men were paroled a few months shy of the end of their two-year sentences. After their release, all four virtually disappeared into society. Perhaps they changed their names or went into legitimate businesses. All kept their names out of the newspapers.

Salvatore Arrigo was released on February 27, 1913. The retired Society Godfather did not follow his son Vincenzo to Chicago. Instead, he remained in Cincinnati with his health deteriorating until he died in 1922. He was seventy-nine years old.

Pippino Galbo, released at the same time as Salvatore Arrigo, dusted off Leavenworth and quickly regained his dignified reputation in the Meadville, Pennsylvania, community. In 1914, Galbo built a large industrial building called "the Galbo Block" on Pine Street, where he opened the Pippino Galbo Wholesale Fruit and Produce House on the ground floor.[9] Galbo stayed out of trouble for a decade until

1935, when he was arrested by U.S. Treasury agents for passing counterfeit bills in Pennsylvania and New York. He was sixty-three years old. He got five years.[10] He did the time at the federal penitentiary in Lewisburg, Pennsylvania. Galbo died in 1966 at home in Meadville. He was ninety-four years old.

Orazio Runfola was released next; however, there is no exact date in his file from the Leavenworth archives. The Pittsburgh cigar maker appears to have stayed out of trouble, at least under his own name, for the rest of his life.

Family photo of Pietra Lima and her husband, Giuseppe Ignoffo, circa 1920s. Joe Ignoffo was a member of the Society of the Banana and was sentenced to the federal penitentiary at Fort Leavenworth, Kansas. Pietra Lima was the sister of Salvatore Lima, Director "Overseer" of the Society. Courtesy of Melanie Butera, DVM (descendant of Sebastian Lima).

For the criminal Lima clan, there appeared to be a much more solid infrastructure on the outside to facilitate a pathway back into organized crime. To Frank Oldfield's chagrin, he never caught up with Sam Lima's father, Antonio Lima. After the mass arrests, Antonio made his way back to Sicily, leaving relatives in the business all across the United States and Canada. One of his sons was running a mob operation in Toronto, another in Portland. His son Sam, of course, was temporarily out of commission in Leavenworth. Antonio Lima died in 1912 with his wife, Annunziata Cancilla, by his side, and likely a ton of U.S. currency in his mattress.

Antonio's two sons-in-law, Giuseppe Ignoffo and Sebastian Lima, were both released from Leavenworth in 1916. Ignoffo left first, in February, after his sentence was commuted by President Wilson.[11] He headed for Portland where his wife, Pietra (Sam Lima's sister), had a cousin named Antonio Lima. This Antonio Lima had a thriving legitimate business in olive oil and cheese, and an even more thriving business of extortion, drugs, illegal liquor, and prostitution.

Sebastian Lima fared far worse than the rest in prison. In the beginning, the warden took a liking to Sebastian, who he could tell was a family man who cared deeply about his wife. When Sebastian became highly distressed when he didn't hear from his wife for several weeks, the warden took it upon himself to write the chief of police in Johnstown, Pennsylvania, to see if he would inquire about Caterina Lima and their children. "He is a very well behaved prisoner," the Leavenworth warden wrote, "and seems to be quite intelligent, therefore I am anxious to help him, if possible, as he appears to be in such distress of mind about his family."[12] Sebastian became very ill with diphtheria around 1914 and was treated with quinine. He recovered physically, but mentally, he was never the same.

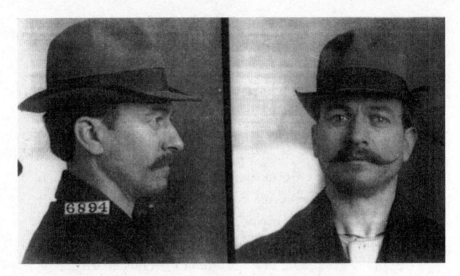

Sebastian Lima received ten years in federal prison for his activities as a member of the Society of the Banana. Lima's time in the federal penitentiary at Fort Leavenworth, Kansas, was fraught with physical and mental disease. This mug shot was taken upon Lima's uptake into the penitentiary. From the Fort Leavenworth inmate records at the U.S. National Archives.

Sebastian's prison file contains dozens of pages of written violations. *Talking loudly in his cell. He hangs his shirt at the front of bed and reads behind it, prays and talks in a voice that is much louder than is necessary. . . . This prisoner came up from boiler stove to get a shave and because he could not pick his barber he refused to be shaved and talked insolently to guard. . . . This man was very disorderly at drill on Sunday morning. . . . This prisoner loafed the best part of this P.M. quit work to rest actual count 18 different times. Not much time remained for work.*[13] Sebastian received harsh punishments. He was stripped naked, chained to iron bars, and left without food. He continued to decline, but the parole board never chose to grant him his freedom even though the warden wrote letters on his behalf. Sebastian was finally released on October 16, 1916, a broken man. He went back to Johnstown and moved in with his sixteen-year-old daughter Millie, who was now married to a thirty-three-year-old man named Sal Butera. Sebastian died of a heart attack in a mental hospital in 1924. His wife, Caterina, also died of a heart attack shortly thereafter.

Family photo of Sebastian Lima with his daughters Annie (left) and Mary (right) in Johnstown, Pennsylvania, after Sebastian had served his term in federal prison, circa 1920s. Courtesy Melanie Butera, DVM (descendant of Sebastian Lima).

For the last two years of his incarceration, Sam Lima was the sole Society member still locked up. It appears that it didn't bother him much. He made friends, got out of hard labor in the rock quarry to work in the prison hospital as a nurse, and received tons and tons of correspondence from his family, the Italian consulate, a doctor friend who lobbied for preferential treatment for him, and his mother, Annunziata Cancilia, back in Sicily.

By January 1917, Sam Lima had ingratiated himself with the prison doctor, A. F. Yoke, who wrote to Lima's doctor friend, Bendetto Tripi Rao, in Kansas City on January 30. "Your friend Lima was, much to my surprise, not given a parole at the time we expected but he is to go out January 29, 1918, as I am informed by the ruling of my superior. Lima is still one of the most trusted nurses in the hospital, where I am quite sure he will remain until such time as he is released. The more I see of the man, the more I am impressed with his sterling worth and effort to please and I am quite sure that when released, he will make a good citizen."[14]

Salvatore Lima received one of the longest sentences in federal prison for his activities as a leader of the Society of the Banana. Lima was sentenced to sixteen years hard labor at the federal penitentiary in Fort Leavenworth, Kansas. This mug shot was taken upon Lima's intake into the penitentiary. From the Fort Leavenworth inmate records at the U.S. National Archives.

In 1918, Sam Lima was paroled into the custody of his cousin, Antonio Lima, in Portland. His letter to the Leavenworth parole board promised he would be working for his cousin's business, A. Lima Wholesale Fruits & Produce, at 202 Washington Street. Salvatore and his family remained in Portland for a decade until his very enterprising nephew, Anthony J. Lima, invited Sam to come to San Francisco. Anthony, who was only twenty-three at the time, was quickly rising up the ranks in the Lanza family, San Francisco's main organized crime syndicate. Sam jumped at the chance to help his nephew infiltrate the longshoremen on Fisherman's Warf, strong-arm protection money from various labor unions, and bribe the political establishment in the city.

In 1937, Anthony became the boss of the San Francisco Mafia following the death of founder Francesco Lanza. Nephew and uncle lived large and worked extremely hard building an empire, small by New York standards, but just as brutal and just as calculating. Anthony ran the crime family for approximately sixteen years with his uncle, Sam Lima, by his side.[15] In 1953, when Anthony was tried and convicted of federal tax evasion, he owned car dealerships and several import operations. With his nephew in San Quentin, Sam Lima strengthened his grip on the unions and became a big-time donor to the corrupt San Francisco political machine. By all accounts, he loved every minute of it. Salvatore "Sam" Lima died on January 9, 1965. Eighty-seven cars snaked through San Francisco's narrow streets in the funeral procession, one for every year of his life. On Sam Lima's death certificate, his occupation is listed as *grower, grapes and olive oil industry*.

EPILOGUE

When Margaret Galena died in 1946, the six remaining steamer trunks full of my great-grandfather's tangible legacy went to my grandfather William Hamilton, Frank's favorite son. Hamilton was a gentleman, a well-liked postal clerk in the community, a member of the Elks Club, and known to be generous to his friends. Perhaps because of Frank's reputation in the Inspection Service, so tarnished by Abraham Holmes, Hamilton was repeatedly turned down by the Post Office to become an inspector like his well-known father. Hamilton stowed the steamer trunks away in the basement of his Athens home on Oak Street. A few years later, the Hocking River flooded its banks into the university town. The river rose into the first floor of Hamilton's home, poured down the stairs and into the basement. Maybe a Black-hander's ghost came with the floodwaters that night. Or maybe it was the spirit of Abraham Holmes. Maybe it was just another flood on a river that continued to redefine itself, unconcerned with the human drama on its banks. However it came, the water destroyed five of the six steamer trunks and all of their contents.

A devastated Hamilton carefully salvaged what he could from one trunk and put two boxes of his father's history in the attic, where they would stay until he died in 1953. The collection landed next with Hamilton's oldest son, my uncle Hammy. Eventually the boxes ended up with my father, Edward Fulton.

I lost my father in 1989. I was in my late twenties. He had never allowed me to study any of my great-grandfather's treasures. He almost never spoke of his grandfather. The mysterious boxes were forbidden for so long, I didn't give them much thought at the time. Thirteen years later, as my mother faded away, I broached the subject of the mysterious boxes again. I was forty years old. My mother's imminent passing left me aching for knowledge of where I came from. At first she brushed off the topic. Instead, we spent hours and days talking about and documenting details of her ancestors and my father's. She told me of the trip she took with my sister to Great-great-grandfather Oldfield's land in Pennsylvania and showed me all of the interesting things they learned. She made me write down the family recipes we all loved.

About two weeks before she died, my mother finally mentioned the boxes. To her, the fear of retaliation by The Black Hand was long past. Instead, a new worry festered in her mind. Throughout Ohio, there were prominent Sicilian-Americans who were her friends; some had been colleagues. They were donors to the Ohio Ballet and Cleveland Orchestra. They were people in top business and political positions and people with whom she'd sat on community boards and task forces. Some, she believed, had no idea that their forefathers may have been serious criminals. Some of her former colleagues or friends could be descendants of kidnappers, extortionists, or murderers. It could crush them. It could greatly embarrass them. She knew I wanted to write a book, or a screenplay, or donate the collection to the Smithsonian National Postal Museum. I was sure the institute would make it a centerpiece exhibit. She warned me to think long and hard. "If I were you," she said, "I'd just burn the whole lot of it and get on with your life."

However, I do think she may have known that destroying what was left of my great-grandfather's collection was something that I could never do, so she'd given me an out. "If you do write something, be accurate. Be true to the story of your great-grandfather. Be true to all the others, too."

It took me a few months after her death to pull the boxes out. Everything that was left of John Frank's life belonged to me. In addition to all the clippings and materials from the Black Hand case there were hints of other headline-grabbing investigations: a human ear delivered by mail to the CEO of a shipping company, a Hungarian archbishop shaken down for money by extortionists in Ohio, and even mention of French-Canadian women being imported into the United States through Buffalo, New York, as indentured labor.

I decided to take some time off before looking for a job in my new home of Annapolis, Maryland. Since my great-grandfather's death, none of the family members who had access ever took the time to investigate the collection. They had jobs and families and other things to do. Some, like my father, were given dire warnings like the one he passed along to my sister Allison and me: *imminent dangers inside.* Instead, the Oldfields who did speak of my great-grandfather relied on family lore. The stories traveled through the generations like the Hocking River—sometimes slowly meandering, hugging close to the outline of truth, other times brimming over the levees and taking on an entirely new appearance.

What I found was that there was no detailed history of Frank Oldfield in the U.S. Post Office archives, save for a personnel document detailing his many infractions. Purposely or not, the U.S. Post Office Department took a giant eraser to Frank Oldfield's life and his merits. Then the Hocking River did its best to wash away the remaining evidence. My family's code of silence finished the job. As I paged through each document in the collection, I felt an overwhelming sense of responsibility. It was my duty to make sure that Frank's story did not die with me. I was forty-one. Frank made it only to forty-nine.

In the stories I overheard as a boy, Frank was always the unadulterated hero. Much of that is absolutely true. Literally hundreds of documents and newspaper reports from the country's biggest and smallest dailies prove his cunning and brilliance in bringing criminals to justice. But Frank Oldfield, like all driven men, was complex. He enjoyed the power and autonomy his position gave him. He truly enjoyed the fame and grandstanding. But mostly, he enjoyed bringing the bad guys to justice, no matter what the cost.

In 2007, when I approached the Smithsonian National Postal Museum after being encouraged by two modern-day postal inspectors to whom I'd been introduced, I was shocked to learn that they'd never heard of Inspector Oldfield. Even though the museum was developing a significant collection and exhibit of other celebrated inspectors, no one knew of my great-grandfather. I carried to Washington some of the best documents and weapons and laid them carefully on a conference table, first at the Postal Inspection Service headquarters, then at the museum. The inspectors and curators were literally speechless. I was thrilled when they wanted to include my collection in their upcoming exhibition.

When I saw what they eventually put together at the exhibit, I was crushed. John Frank's name or likeness was nowhere to be found in the museum. Later, the curators and staff graciously allowed me to give two entertaining lectures and show my grandfather's extensive collection to the attendees. The opportunity was uplifting, but the unfortunate result was that Frank's legacy was buried once again. I can't say that it didn't hurt.

From the time I was a boy, I was a willing captive of my great-grandfather's ghost. Frank gripped me by the heart. Oldfield blood pumped through my veins and fueled my sense of adventure, my quest for justice. Once I learned that the world had truly forgotten him, Frank's memory took over my thoughts, shook me by the shoulders, and refused to give me any peace. I embarked on an extensive search to put all the pieces of his life together. Exhausted after months of nonstop research, I put Frank aside to deal with my own life. He returned again and again over the next fourteen years. One day, he convinced me it was time to finish our journey. *Inspector Oldfield and the Black Hand Society* is our journey's end.

—William Hamilton "Hammy" Oldfield

NOTE FROM VICTORIA BRUCE

From the moment I met William H. "Hammy" Oldfield and heard bits of his great-grandfather's story, I was obsessed. I'm not a historian, but I have an obsessive love of stories. When I learned he had hundreds of documents, letters, and photos chronicling a larger-than-life tale of Sicilian gangsters and American lawmen never before told, my mind was blown.

It took four more years after that initial meeting for the stars to align. In 2016, Hammy and I embarked on our writing adventure. He came to my house with heavy bins and white gloves and Bertillon cards and yellowed files. He came with daggers and photographs and the well-worn magnifying glass used by his great-grandfather. And he came with stories. A decade before, his mother's death had freed him to take his family's legacy public. Hammy logged hundreds of hours over many states and two continents. He met with dozens of experts and found family members of men sent to prison long ago. He told me he spent his childhood eavesdropping on adults whispering about his grandfather's heroic arrests. I wanted to know all of it. Hour after hour I listened. I examined piles of evidence, news clippings, and family stories. I understood what had paralyzed Hammy in his tracks. The obstacles to the project seemed insurmountable. I assured him it was not. Frank's ghost had already grabbed me and came alive through his great-grandson's stories.

Together we dove in. It was overwhelming, to say the least. The story of Inspector Oldfield was a puzzle equal to Frank's investigation of The Black Hand Society. To understand what went down so many years ago, we had to think like Frank. We had to strategize like Frank and his fellow investigators, digging deep into turn-of-the-twentieth-century American crime. We let Frank guide us. His notes, his quotations, the stories he told that were passed down through generations—all revealed a narrative both intimate and immense.

The telling of Frank's century-old story was greatly helped by the twenty-first-century digital age. With Newspapers.com, we found hundreds of sources that even Frank's wife, the amazing archivist Margaret Galena, had missed. We borrowed the tenor and humor of long-gone reporters who used spunky prose to build up the inspectors, condemn the criminals, and record the intricacies of a mesmerizing true-crime story. Many had their own creative ways of spelling the Italian names, which made our job a little harder and our research take a little longer. Ancestry.com was an excellent source to find birthplaces and death dates and names of siblings and children. In Findagrave .com we found crowd-sourced biographies written by descendants hungry for ties to their ancestors. Google Maps, Google Street View, Google Satellite, and Google Images led us across the Great Lakes, down to New Orleans, and to a nineteenth-century New York federal building where Frank punched out an assistant district attorney.

After cataloguing miles and miles with boots on the ground, in cyberspace, and through the dusty pages of crumbling notebooks, the backbone of *Inspector Oldfield and the Black Hand Society* began to emerge. In time, the book gained flesh and blood and life. Here John Frank Oldfield lives on.

NOTES

Chapter 1: The Printer

1 Lawrence C. Wroth, *A History of Printing in Colonial Maryland, 1686–1776* (Typothetae of Baltimore, 1922), 132.
2 Wroth, *A History of Printing in Colonial Maryland,* 6.
3 Ed Siskin, "US Postal History Before the United States Post Office Part II: Understanding Rates," *New Jersey Postal History Society*, 1972, 7.
4 "United States Postal Inspection Service," accessed July 23, 2017, https://postalinspectors.uspis.gov/aboutus/History.aspx.
5 "Benjamin Franklin Trips to England," Revolutionary War and Beyond, accessed December 17, 2017, http://www.revolutionary-war-and-beyond.com/benjamin-franklin-trips-to-england.html.
6 Ward L. Miner, *William Goddard, Newspaperman* (Durham, N.C.: Duke University Press, 1962), 15.
7 Lawrence C. Wroth, *The Colonial Printer* (Charlottesville, VA: Courier Corporation, 1964), 225.
8 Lawrence C. Wroth, *The First Press in Providence A Study in Social Development,* reprint edition (American Antiquarian Society, 1942), 352.
9 "The Providence Gazette and Country Journal," accessed May 21, 2017, http://chroniclingamerica.loc.gov/lccn/sn83025571/.
10 Wroth, *The First Press in Providence A Study in Social Development,* 365.
11 Wroth, *The Colonial Printer,* 140.
12 "Stamp Act | Great Britain [1765]," Encyclopedia Britannica, accessed December 27, 2017, https://www.britannica.com/event/Stamp-Act-Great-Britain-1765.
13 Wroth, *The Colonial Printer,* 141.

14 "Sons of Liberty—Dictionary Definition of Sons of Liberty,"
Encyclopedia.Com, accessed May 21, 2017, http://www.encyclopedia
.com/history/encyclopedias-almanacs-transcripts-and-maps/sons
-liberty-0.

15 Post Staff Report, "The Road That Paved the Way to Revolution," *New
York Post* (blog), July 4, 2010, http://nypost.com/2010/07/04/the-road
-that-paved-the-way-to-revolution/.

16 Post Staff Report.

17 William Goddard, *The Partnership: Or, The History of the Rise and
Progress of the Pennsylvania Chronicle, &c. Wherein the Conduct of
Joseph Galloway, Esq., Speaker of the Honourable House of Represen-
tatives of the Province of Pennsylvania, Mr. Thomas Wharton, Sen.,
and Their Man Benjamin Towne, My Late Partners, with My Own, Is
Properly Delineated, and Their Calumnies against Me Fully Refuted*
(Philadelphia: Printed by William Goddard, in Arch-street, between
Front and Second Streets, 1770), 5–12.

18 John J. Zimmerman, "Benjamin Franklin and The Pennsylvania Chronicle," *Pennsylvania Magazine of History and Biography* 81, no. 4 (September 30, 1957): 354.

19 Carl Bridenbaugh, "The Press and Book in Philadelphia," *Pennsylvania
Magazine of History and Biography*, 1941, 5–6, https://journals.psu.edu
/pmhb/issue/view/1931.

20 Bridenbaugh, 8.

21 "The Maryland Journal, and the Baltimore Advertiser," accessed December 27, 2017, https://chroniclingamerica.loc.gov/lccn/sn84020149/.

22 John J. Zimmerman, "Benjamin Franklin and the Pennsylvania Chronicle," in *Benjamin Franklin's Letters to the Press, 1758–1775* (Chapel
Hill: University of North Carolina Press, 1957), 352, https://journals
.psu.edu/pmhb/article/viewFile/41308/41029.

23 Ralph Frasca, *Benjamin Franklin's Printing Network: Disseminating
Virtue in Early America* (Columbia, MO: University of Missouri Press,
2006), 197.

24 "Franklin's Philadelphia: Benjamin Franklin's Post Office," accessed
August 27, 2017, http://www.ushistory.org/franklin/philadelphia
/postoffice.htm.

25 "William Goddard and the Constitutional Post," accessed August

24, 2017, https://postalmuseum.si.edu/exhibits/current/binding-the
-nation/starting-the-system/william-goddard-and-the-constitutional
-post.html.

26 Wroth, *The First Press in Providence A Study in Social Development*,
352.

27 Eric Jaffe, *The King's Best Highway: The Lost History of the Boston
Post Road, the Route That Made America* (New York: Scribner, 2010),
64.

28 "Benjamin Franklin (1706–1790), Postmaster General," accessed August
19, 2017, https://postalmuseum.si.edu/outofthemails/franklin.html.

29 "Anthony Todd," The British Postal Museum & Archive Blog, accessed
August 27, 2017, https://postalheritage.wordpress.com/tag/anthony
-todd/; "Benjamin Franklin (1706–1790), Postmaster General."

30 "Boston, March 17," *Virginia Gazette*, April 14, 1774, 1.

31 Alex L. ter Braake, *The Posted Letter in Colonial and Revolutionary
America* (American Philatelic Research Library, 1975), H-9.

32 Wroth, *A History of Printing in Colonial Maryland, 1686–1776*, 135.

33 Ward L. Miner, *William Goddard, Newspaperman.* (Durham, N.C.:
Duke University Press, 1962), 133.

34 Wroth, *A History of Printing in Colonial Maryland, 1686–1776*, 132.

35 Joseph M. Adelman, "'A Constitutional Conveyance of Intelligence,
Public and Private': The Post Office, the Business of Printing, and the
American Revolution," *Enterprise & Society* 11, no. 4 (2010): 740.

36 "Journals of the Continental Congress, Volume 2" (1775), 71, https://
memory.loc.gov/cgi-bin/ampage?collId=lljc&fileName=002/lljc002
.db&recNum=70&itemLink=r?ammem/hlaw:@field(DOCID+@lit
(jc00221))%230020071&linkText=1.

37 "Memorial of William Goddard to the Commissioners or Delegates
from the Several American States, Now Sitting in General Congress:
Having Completed the Duties Required of Him as Surveyor of the
Post-Office, He Solicits an Opportunity of Serving His Country in the
Army for One Year At Least," American Archives, accessed August
26, 2017, http://amarch.lib.niu.edu/islandora/object/niu-amarch
%3A95382.

38 "Journals of the Continental Congress, Volume 2" (1775), 71.

39 "Founders Online: Editorial Note on the Founding of the Post Office,

26 July 1775," accessed August 26, 2017, http://founders.archives.gov /documents/Franklin/01-22-02-0074.

40 "Memorial of William Goddard to the Commissioners or Delegates from the Several American States," accessed January 5, 2018, http:// amarch.lib.niu.edu/islandora/object/niu-amarch%3A95382.

41 Wroth, *A History of Printing in Colonial Maryland, 1686–1776*, 135.

42 "Mary Katherine Goddard's Declaration of Independence," The New York Public Library, accessed August 31, 2017, https://www.nypl.org /blog/2016/06/29/mary-katherine-goddard-declaration.

Chapter 2: Politics

1 "Howard Political Assault Cases," *Baltimore Sun*, July 23, 1895, 6.

2 "Brutal Murder of Daniel F. Shea in Ellicott City," *Baltimore Sun*, February 22, 1895, 6.

3 "Jacob Henson, MSA SC 3520-13743," Archives of Maryland (Biographical Series), August 7, 2015, http://msa.maryland.gov/megafile/msa /speccol/sc3500/sc3520/013700/013743/html/13743bio.html.

4 "Henson Convicted," *Baltimore Sun*, March 29, 1895, 2.

5 "Jacob Henson, MSA SC 3520-13743."

6 "Howard County," *Baltimore Sun*, September 5, 1895, 2.

7 "The Lynching of Jacob Henson, in Howard County," *Baltimore Sun*, May 29, 1895, 2.

8 "His Skull Fractured," *Baltimore Sun*, July 2, 1896, 6.

9 Heinrich Ewald Buchholz, *Governors of Maryland: From the Revolution to the Year 1908* (Williams & Wilkins company, 1908), 256.

10 "Howard County," *Baltimore Sun*, September 18, 1896, 8.

11 "Wandered From Home," *Baltimore Sun*, July 20, 1896, 2.

12 "Shot by a Sheriff," *News* [Frederick, Maryland], July 30, 1897, 3. http://www.newspapers.com/image/8938093/?terms=oldfield.

13 "Shot by a Sheriff."

14 "Oldfield Exonerated," *Baltimore Sun*, August 5, 1897, 8.

15 "A Sheriff's Fatal Shot," *Baltimore Sun*, August 2, 1897, 7.

16 "Oldfield Exonerated."

17 "Shot by a Sheriff."

18 "The Governor's Callers," *Baltimore Sun*, March 31, 1897, 10.

19 "First Degree Murder," *Baltimore Sun*, April 12, 1898, 10.

20 "Sentenced to Death," *Baltimore Sun*, April 14, 1898, 8.

21 "Governor Pardons Two," *Baltimore Sun*, August 30, 1912, 1.

Chapter 3: The Raven

1 James D. Horan and Howard Gardner, *The Pinkerton Story* (New York: G. P. Putnam's Sons, 1951).

2 Thomas Hunt, "The American Mafia—Who Was Who: Esposito, Giuseppe (1847– ?)," *The American Mafia—Who Was Who* (blog), accessed December 27, 2017, http://mob-who.blogspot.com/2011/04/esposito-giuseppe.html.

3 "History," *Pinkerton* (blog), May 13, 2016, https://www.pinkerton.com/about-us/history/.

4 "History."

5 Michael O'Brien, "Pinkerton's Detective Agency Special Crimes Unit" (Michael O'Brien, 2013), http://wrgmr.com/pinkertons.pdf.

6 James David Horan, *The Pinkertons: The Detective Dynasty That Made History* (New York: Crown Publishers, 1968), 423.

7 Horan, 423.

8 Horan, 421.

9 Horan, 420.

10 "David Hennessy," *Wikipedia*, August 30, 2017, https://en.wikipedia.org/w/index.php?title=David_Hennessy&oldid=798074707.

11 Bruce Macintyre, *The Mafia Unveiled*, 31.

12 Horan, 421.

13 Horan, 424.

14 Horan, 423.

15 Macintyre, *The Mafia Unveiled*, 32.

16 Horan, 423.

17 Horan, 426.

18 Hunt, "The American Mafia—Who Was Who: Esposito, Giuseppe (1847– ?)."

19 Hunt, "The American Mafia—Who Was Who: Esposito, Giuseppe (1847– ?)."

20 Migration, "Sicilian Lynchings in New Orleans," Know Louisiana, accessed September 12, 2017, http://www.knowlouisiana.org/entry/sicilian-lynchings-in-new-orleans.

NOTES

21 Hunt, "The American Mafia—Who Was Who."

22 Macintyre, *The Mafia Unveiled*, 33; Anne T. Romano, *Italian Americans in Law Enforcement* (Bloomington, IN: Xlibris Corporation, 2010), 30.

23 Horan, 427.

24 Horan, 428.

25 Horan, 428.

26 Horan, 434.

27 Horan, 432.

28 Horan and Gardner, *The Pinkerton Story*, 255.

29 Macintyre, *The Mafia Unveiled*, 33.

30 "Articles: When Will New Orleans Apologize for the Italian Lynchings?" *American Thinker*, accessed December 27, 2017. http://www.american thinker.com/articles/2017/08/when_will_new_orleans_apologize_for _the_italian_lynchings.html

31 "Shot to Death," *Rushville Republican*, March 19, 1891, 3.

32 Horan, 436–37.

33 "Lima's New Trial," *The Daily Picayune*, March 22, 1896, 12.

Chapter 4: Society of the Banana

1 Robert Watchcorn, "The Black Hand and the Immigrant," *The Outlook*, July 31, 1909, 794.

2 "Marion Steam Shovel Company—Ohio History Central," accessed December 28, 2017, http://www.ohiohistorycentral.org/w/Marion _Steam_Shovel_Company.

3 *Columbus City Directory* (G.J. Brand & Company, 1902), 326.

4 "Statement of Mrs. Mary Fasone," deposition, July 29, 1909.

5 Black Hand, "Black Hand Extortion Letter to Fasones," September 29, 1908.

6 Black Hand, "Black Hand Extortion Letter to Fasones 2," October 9, 1908.

7 "Statement of Mrs. Mary Fasone."

8 "Statement of Mrs. Mary Fasone."

9 Rino Coluccello, *Challenging the Mafia Mystique: Cosa Nostra from Legitimisation to Denunciation* (New York: Springer, 2016), 40.

10 Aldo Gelso, *Mafia: Capitalism & Democracy* (Bloomington, IN: Xlibris Corporation, 2007), 27.

11 "Omertà—The Mafia," accessed September 19, 2017, http://the-mafia
   .weebly.com/omerta.html.

12 "Senate Report No. 1333. In the Senate of the United States:, Ordered
   to Be Printed,: Mr. Chandler, from the Committee on Immigration,
   Submitted the Following Report (to Accompany S. 3786)" (Senate of
   the United States, February 22, 1893), 266.

13 Margaret Adams, "Mafia in New Orleans" (New Orleans: Tulane University, 1924), 12.

14 Watchcorn, "The Black Hand and the Immigrant," 794.

15 Adams, "Mafia in New Orleans," 12.

16 "Suspect Is Held Under Heavy Bond," unknown, from Oldfield Collection, 1909.

17 Stephan Talty, *The Black Hand: The Epic War Between a Brilliant
   Detective and the Deadliest Secret Society in American History* (Boston:
   Houghton Mifflin Harcourt, 2017).

18 "Running Down the Black Hand," *New York Times*, February 13,
   1910, 1.

19 "History," accessed December 17, 2017, https://www.secretservice.gov
   /about/history/events/; U.S. Marshals Service (USMS), "U.S. Marshals
   Service," accessed December 17, 2017, https://www.usmarshals.gov
   /history/timeline.html.

20 "How Federal Sleuths Land Black Handers," 1909. Source unknown.

21 "Sweeping Raid on Black Hand in Ohio," Associated Press to *Gazette
   Times*, June 1909, 1.

22 "Black Handers Found Guilty," *Marion Weekly Star*, February 5,
   1910, 4.

Chapter 5: The Inspector

1 "An Act Making Appropriations for the Post Office Department for the
  Fiscal Year Ending June 30, 1923, and for Other Purposes.," Pub. L.
  No. H.R. 9859 (1922).

2 C. E. Caine, "Special Agents and Post Office Inspectors," accessed
  September 22, 2017, http://narpi.org/SpecialAnnouncements/Special
  AgentsAndPostOfficeInspectors.pdf.

3 "Strange Story of a Watch," *Morning News* [Wilmington, DE], June 8,
  1901, 9.

NOTES

4 "Must Return to Tennessee—Oldfield," *Baltimore Sun*, August 10, 1899, 6.

5 "Howard Republicans—Delegates to Convention and Central Committee Elected," *Baltimore Sun*, August 15, 1899, 8.

6 "Day on Democrats," *Baltimore Sun*, April 24, 1900, 8.

7 "Big Graft for Clerks in Capitol," *Buffalo Enquirer*, June 25, 1903, 12.

8 United States Post Office Dept, *Investigation of the Post-Office Department: Letter from the Postmaster-General Transmitting So Much of the Report of the Fourth Assistant Postmaster-General on the Investigation of the Said Department as May Be Made Public Without Harm to the Public Interest. January 11, 1904* (U.S. Government Printing Office, 1904), 153.

9 "Federal Officers Fight," *New York Times*, May 16, 1903, 6.

10 "Fought with Inspectors," *Washington Post*, May 16, 1903.

11 "Federal Officers Fight."

12 "Office Scandal," *Elwood Free Press*, December 17, 1903, 10.

13 "Postal Warrants Are Out," *New York Times*, September 12, 1903, 2.

14 "Beavers Gets Two Years," *Washington Post*, February 14, 1906, 19.

15 "Postal Frauds Are Laid Bare," *New York Times*, November 30, 1903, 1.

16 "Ernest E. Baldwin's Denial 30," *Brooklyn Daily Eagle*, November 30, 1903, 6.

17 "Driggs Says Jail and Fine Have Cured Him," *Boston Post*, January 15, 1904, 2.

18 United States Post Office Dept., *Memorandum of the President and Report of Fourth Assistant Postmaster-General J. L. Bristow on the Investigation of Certain Divisions of the Post-Office Department* (U.S. Government Printing Office, 1903), 185.

19 "On This Day: September 19, 1903," accessed September 28, 2017, http://www.nytimes.com/learning/general/onthisday/harp/0919.html.

20 Gerald S. Greenberg, *Historical Encyclopedia of U.S. Independent Counsel Investigations* (Westport, CT: Greenwood Publishing Group, 2000), 29.

21 United States Post Office Dept., *Memorandum of the President and Report of Fourth Assistant Postmaster-General J. L. Bristow on the Investigation of Certain Divisions of the Post-Office Department*, 186.

22 "Postage Stamps Clue," *Cincinnati Enquirer*, August 31, 1923, 10.

23 "Politicians Fight Blows Exchanged," *News* [Frederick, Maryland], August 11, 1903, 4.

24 "Politicians Fight Blows Exchanged."

25 "Postal Hearing," *Lewiston Daily Sun*, March 22, 1904, 1.

26 "Ninth's Republicans Are at Dagger's Edge," *Atlanta Journal and Constitution*, October 30, 1904, 10.

27 "Ninth's Republicans Are at Dagger's Edge."

28 "Cut Off Their Respect," *Indianapolis News*, April 30, 1908, 8.

29 John Frank Oldfield, "Untitled Status Report of Black Hand Case Through March 30, 1909," April 4, 1909.

Chapter 6: The Immigrant

1 "The National Road—Back in Time—General Highway History—Highway History—Federal Highway Administration," accessed September 30, 2017, https://www.fhwa.dot.gov/infrastructure/back0103.cfm.

2 "Columbus Central Market House Photograph :: Ohio History Connection Selections," accessed September 29, 2017, http://www.ohiomemory.org/cdm/ref/collection/p267401coll32/id/1326.

3 "Central Market House :: Columbus Memory," accessed September 29, 2017, http://digital-collections.columbuslibrary.org/cdm/ref/collection/memory/id/52484.

4 Cindy Bent, "City of Arches," *Short North Gazette*, January 2003, http://www.shortnorth.com/CoverStoryJan03.html.

5 "History of the Banana," www.jimmccluskey.com, accessed December 17, 2017, http://www.jimmccluskey.com/history-of-the-banana/.

6 "Black Hand Gang Meets Nemesis in John Amicon," unknown from Oldfield Collection, 1909.

7 "Black Hand Gang Meets Nemesis in John Amicon."

8 J. H. Senner, "Immigration from Italy," *North American Review* 162, no. 475 (1896): 649.

9 Mailing Address: Ellis Island, National Museum of Immigration, Statue of Liberty National Monument, New York, NY, 10004. Phone: 363-3200; Contact Us, "Frequently Asked Questions - Ellis Island Part of Statue of Liberty National Monument (U.S. National Park Service)," accessed December 29, 2017, https://www.nps.gov/elis/faqs.htm.

10 "Why Did Italians Immigrate to the US Between 1880 & 1900?,"

Synonym, accessed September 30, 2017, http://classroom.synonym
.com/did-italians-immigrate-between-1880-1900-8321.html.

11 "Black Hand Gang Meets Nemesis in John Amicon."

12 "Black Hand Gang Meets Nemesis in John Amicon."

13 "Black Hand Gang Meets Nemesis in John Amicon."

14 "Black Hand Gang Meets Nemesis in John Amicon."

15 Black Hand, "Black Hand Threat Letter to John Amicon (Count Your-self)," January 20, 1909.

16 "Sleuth Exposes the Black Hand Methods," *Marion Star*, June 21, 1910, 5.

17 "Black Hand Threat Letter to John Amicon."

18 "Black Hand Gang Meets Nemesis in John Amicon."

19 "Black Hand Gang Meets Nemesis in John Amicon."

Chapter 7: Stakeout

1 "Running Down a Gang of Crooks," *Piqua Daily Call*, March 21, 1902, 1.

2 "Appointed Cashier of Columbus Post Office To Succeed Wallace, Who Committed Suicide," *Cincinnati Enquirer*, May 24, 1907, 12.

3 "Postoffice [*sic*] Cashier Resorted to Suicide When Caught Short In Accounts," *The Citizen*, May 23, 1907, 2.

4 United States and Post Office Department, "Annual Report of the Post-master General," *Annual Report of the Postmaster General*, 1909, 89.

5 United States and Post Office Department, "Annual Report of the Post-master General," *Annual Report of the Postmaster General*, 1909, 94.

6 United States and Post Office Department, "Annual Report of the Post-master General," *Annual Report of the Postmaster General*, 1909, 94.

7 United States and Post Office Department, "Annual Report of the Post-master General," *Annual Report of the Postmaster General*, 1909, 94.

8 "Sebastiano Lima Declaration of Intention" (Department of Commerce and Labour Bureau of Immigration and Naturalization, November 6, 1907).

9 "P.O. Inspector to Be Domiciled Here," *Chillicothe Gazette*, July 20, 1907, 1.

10 "Government Inspector Looking Over Coshocton Field," *Times Recorder* [Zanesville, Ohio], April 4, 1906, 3.

11 "Return to Danville," *Wichita Daily Eagle*, August 18, 1903, 6.

12 "Recovering From Injuries," *Indianapolis News*, February 8, 1904, 13.

13 "Police Brutality: A Prisoner Shamefully Mal. Treated by Officers. Kicked and Pounded in a Cell—Probably Fatally Injured," *Chicago Daily Tribune*, October 12, 1872.

14 "Bivens v. Six Unknown Fed. Narcotics Agents" (1971).

15 "A Successor to Burns. Another Buckeye Sleuth," June 1909. Source unknown.

16 "Running Down the Black Hand," *New York Times*, February 13, 1910, 1.

17 "Ex Parte Jackson 96 U.S. 727 (1878)," Justia Law, accessed September 22, 2017, https://supreme.justia.com/cases/federal/us/96/727/case.html.

18 John Frank Oldfield, "Untitled Status Report of Black Hand Case Through April 3, 1909."

19 Oldfield, "Untitled Status Report of Black Hand Case Through April 3, 1909."

20 United States Postal Inspection Service, and United States Post Office Department, *Photographs, Descriptions and Records of Persons Charged with Violation of the Postal Laws* (Washington, D.C.: [The Dept.], 1916), 338, http://archive.org/details/photographsdescr21916unit.

21 "Raids Made in This City," *Cincinnati Enquirer*, June 18, 1909, 14.

22 "More Black Hand Arrests," *The Sun* [New York], June 18, 1909, 1.

23 "August Marfisi," *New Philadelphia Daily Times*, April 25, 1946.

24 United States Postal Inspection Service, and United States Post Office Department, *Photographs, Descriptions and Records of Persons Charged with Violation of the Postal Laws*, 340.

25 "Search Results for Pippino Galbo," familysearch.org, accessed January 25, 2018, https://www.familysearch.org/search/record/results?count=20&query=%2Bgivenname%3Apippino~%20%2Bsurname%3Agalbo~.

26 "Pippino Galbo 1872–1966," Ancestry, accessed January 21, 2018, https://www.ancestry.com/genealogy/records/pippino-galbo_13677031.

Chapter 8: The Boss

1 Salvatore (Sam) Lima, "By Laws and Regulations of the Society of Bananas (Translated from the Original Italian)," March 9, 1909.

2 Lima.

3 John Frank Oldfield, "Untitled Status Report of Black Hand Case Through April 3, 1909."

4 "A Successor to Burns. Another Buckeye Sleuth," 1909.

5 "Federal Officials Uncover Blackmail," *Toledo Daily Blade*, June 9, 1909, 1.

6 "Letter from Orazio Runfola to Salvatore Lima," March 25, 1909.

7 Oldfield, "Untitled Status Report of Black Hand Case Through April 3, 1909."

8 Oldfield, "Untitled Status Report of Black Hand Case Through April 3, 1909."

9 Oldfield, "Untitled Status Report of Black Hand Case Through April 3, 1909."

10 Deposition of Charles Amicon by Frank Oldfield, May 1909.

11 Deposition of Charles Amicon by Frank Oldfield.

Chapter 9: The Takedown

1 *The Chicago Daily News Almanac and Year Book For . . .* (Chicago: Chicago Daily News, Incorporated, 1909), 127.

2 Elroy McKendree Avery, *Biography* (Lewis Publishing Company, 1918), 96.

3 The Cavalry of the Black Hand, "Extortion Letter to Fabio Sebastiano," April 1909.

4 Black Hand, "Black Hand Extortion Letter to DeCamilli," April 3, 1909.

5 The Firm of Black Hand, "Extortion Letter to Gatto," April 3, 1909.

6 William S. Niederkorn, "New York Police Detective Shot Dead in Sicily," *New York Times*, March 14, 2009.

7 "Killing of Black Hand Victim Fell to Man Who Drew The Marked Card," *Topeka Daily Capital*, June 9, 1909, 1.

8 Oldfield, "Untitled Status Report of Black Hand Case Through March 30, 1909."

9 John Frank Oldfield, "Black Hand Investigation Timeline," December 3, 1909.

10 "Federal Officials Uncover Blackmail," *Toledo Daily Blade*, 1909, 1.

11 "Sweeping Raid on Black Hand in Ohio," Associated Press to *Gazette Times*, June 1909, 1.

12 "A Successor to Burns. Another Buckeye Sleuth," 1909.

13 "Punishment for Black-Hand Mailers Inadequate," 1909. Source unknown.

14 "Ohio Black Hand Beats the Mafia," *Daily Arkansas Gazette*, June 10, 1909, 1.

15 "Ohio Black Hand Beats the Mafia," *Daily Arkansas Gazette*, June 10, 1909, 1.

16 "'Black Hand' Run to Earth," *The Leader* [Cleveland], June 8, 1909.

17 John Frank Oldfield, "Black Hand Investigation Timeline."

18 John Frank Oldfield, "Black Hand Investigation Timeline."

19 "Ohio Black Hand Beats the Mafia," *Daily Arkansas Gazette*, June 10 1909, 1.

20 "More Evidence Is Secured Against Suspected Black Hand," *Marion Daily Mirror*, June 9, 1909, 8.

21 "Arrests of Black Hands Continues," *Coshocton Daily Times*, June 10, 1909, 1.

22 "Will Break Up Black Hand Gang Operating In Central States," *Akron Beacon Journal*, June 12, 1909, 1.

23 "Raids Made in This City," *Cincinnati Enquirer*, June, 18 1909, 14.

24 "Six Arrests Threaten in Black Hand Case," *Pittsburgh Daily Post*, June 22, 1909, 4.

25 John Frank Oldfield, "Black Hand Investigation Timeline."

26 "Black Hand Against Black Hand," *Pittsburgh Daily Post*, June 22, 1909, 4.

27 "Untitled Article on Antonio Lima, Oldfield Collection," 1909.

28 "Due to a Girl's Love," *Mansfield News-Journal*, July 17, 1909, 2.

29 "Black Hand's Chief Caught in Lone Cabin," 1909.

30 "Arrigo Found in Lonely Cabin," *Cincinnati Enquirer*, July 24, 1909, 2.

31 John Frank Oldfield, "Black Hand Investigation Timeline."

32 "Arrigo Found in Lonely Cabin."

33 "Prisoner Kept His Nerve," *Zanesville Times Recorder*, June 11, 1909, 1.

Chapter 10: The Trial

1 "Letter from O. C. Riches to J. F. Oldfield (Portland)," June 30, 1909.

2 E. C. Clement, "Inspector E. C. Clement to Inspector J. F. Oldfield," August 12, 1909.

3 "Letter from E. C. Clement to J. F. Oldfield," August 29, 1909.

4 E. A. Hempstead, "Meadville Postmaster E. A. Hempstead to Assistant Attorney General," December 16, 1909.

NOTES

5   "Ten Years in Prison for Mrs. Chadwick," *New Philadelphia Daily Times*, March 28, 1905, 1.

6   "Tayler, Robert Walker—Biographical Information," accessed December 28, 2017, http://bioguide.congress.gov/scripts/biodisplay.pl?index=T000061.

7   Vinton Randall Shepard and Rowland Shepard, *A Weekly Journal Published in the Interest of the Legal Profession in the State of Ohio* (Ohio Law Reporter Company, 1911), 439.

8   *The Corporation Bulletin* (United States Corporation Company, 1911), 16.

9   "Condemned to Death by the Black Hand," *Cleveland Leader*, January 9, 1910, 1.

10 "Guard Witnesses in Black Hand Trials," *Marion Weekly Star*, January 8, 1910, 6.

11 "Black Hand Trials Are Begun Today," *Marion Star*, January 10, 1910, 5.

12 "Black Hand Trials Are Begun Today."

13 "Black Hand Trials Are Begun Today."

14 "Sleuth Exposes the Black Hand Methods," *Marion Star*, June 21, 1910, 5.

15 "Separate Trials Are Denied by the Court," *Marion Star*, January 18, 1910, 7.

16 Roberta Sue Alexander, *A Place of Recourse: A History of the U.S. District Court for the Southern District of Ohio, 1803–2003* (Athens, OH: Ohio University Press, 2005), 82.

17 "Separate Trials Are Denied by the Court," *Marion Star*, January 18, 1910, 7.

18 "Separate Trials Are Denied by the Court."

19 "Letter from J. F. Oldfield to Colonel R. R. Munro," January 26, 1910.

20 "The Testimony Taken in Black Hand Trials," *Marion Star*, January 20, 1910, 4.

21 "Sleuth Exposes the Black Hand Methods," 5.

22 "Threatened by Black Hand," *Marion Star*, January 19, 1910, 1.

23 "Black Hand Finds Two Victims Here," *Indianapolis Star*, December 13, 1909, 1.

24 "Threatened by the Black Hand," *Marion Star*, January 19, 1910, 1,

25 "Black Hand Letters," *Marion Star*, January 25, 1910, 6.

26 "Black Handers Found Guilty," *Marion Weekly Star*, February 5, 1910, 4.

27 "Black Hand Letters and Their Authors," *Marion Weekly Star*, January 29, 1910, 7.

28 "Rules of the Society of the Banana," *Marion Daily Mirror*, January 26, 1910, 3.

29 "The Black Hand Rule of Terror Is Exposed," *Marion Star*, January 26, 1910, 5.

30 "Rules of the Society of the Banana."

31 "Rules of the Society of the Banana."

32 "Rules of the Society of the Banana."

33 "Black Hand Letters and Their Authors," 8.

34 "Black Hand Trial Develops Clashes," *Marion Star*, January 27, 1910, 7.

35 "Black Hand Trial Will Soon Be Over," *Marion Star*, January 28, 1910, 5.

36 "Businessmen Called to Toledo," *Marion Daily Mirror*, January 26, 1910, 8.

37 "Black Hand Trial Will Soon Be Over."

38 "Rules of the Society of the Banana," *Marion Daily Mirror*, January 26, 1910, 3.

39 "Black Hand Trial Will Soon Be Over."

40 "Explanations Made by Black Hand Conspirators in Their Defense," *Cincinnati Enquirer*, January 27, 1910, 2.

41 "Black Hand Trial Will Soon Be Over."

42 "Black Hand Trial Will Soon Be Over."

43 "Evidence Is Complete in Black Hand Trial," *Pittsburgh Daily Post*, January 28, 1910, 4.

44 "Jury Must Decide Who Wrote Letters," *Mansfield News-Journal*, January 27, 1910, 2.

45 "Black Hand Trial Will Soon Be Over."

46 "Will Erect Business Block," *Marion Daily Mirror*, May 6, 1912, 8.

47 "Black Hand Trial Will Soon Be Over."

48 "14 Black Handers Going to Prison," *Allentown Democrat*, January 31, 1910, 8.

49 "Justice Is Swift in Black Hand Case," *New York Times*, January 30, 1910, 5.

50 "Thinks Power of Black Hand Gone," *Perrysburg Journal*, February 4, 1910, 3.

51 "Knell of 'Black Handism,'" *Cincinnati Enquirer*, January 30, 1910, 1.
52 "Knell of 'Black Handism.'"

Chapter 11: Good-byes

1   "Federal Judge Stricken," *Cincinnati Enquirer*, November 26, 1910, 1.
2   "Judge Tayler Dies at an Early Hour," *Elyria Republican*, December 1, 1910, 2.
3   William L. Day, United States Attorney, "William L. Day Letter to Mr. A. R. Holmes, Inspector in Charge," July 19, 1910.
4   United States and Post Office Department, "Annual Report of the Postmaster General," 1909, 95.
5   United States and Post Office Department, "Annual Report of the Postmaster General," *Annual Report of the Postmaster General*, 1910.
6   "Charles H. Strong—Erie County, PA," accessed November 8, 2017, http://www.onlinebiographies.info/pa/erie/strong-ch.htm.
7   "Scott Mausoleum Burglary & Extortion," *Scott Mausoleum Burglary & Extortion* (blog), n.d., https://historyandmemorabilia.blogspot.com /2014/01/scott-mausoleum-burglary-extortion.html.
8   "California Oil Promoters Taken to Ohio to Stand Trial," *Fergus County Democrat*, December 10, 1914, 12.
9   "Promissory Note from George Metcalf to J. F. Oldfield," n.d.
10 "Famous Postal Detective Dies at Home Here," May 25, 1916.

Chapter 12: Outcomes

1   "Dennison Man Must Go to Pen; Hi Court Ends Session Today," *New Philadelphia Daily Times*, June 16, 1916, 1.
2   "Booze Joint Discontinued," *New Philadelphia Daily Times*, August 29, 1922, 1.
3   "Marriage Celebrated At Catholic Church," *Marion Star*, November 20, 1912, 4.
4   "Vincenzo Arrigo," *Chicago Tribune*, May 9, 1949, 33.
5   "County Officers Seek Murders," *Sandusky Star-Journal*, September 26, 1911, 5.
6   "Lake Casts Up Two More Crime Victims," *Sandusky Star-Journal*, September 28, 1911, 1.

7   "County Officers Seek Murders," *Sandusky Star-Journal*, September 26, 1911, 5.

8   "Lake Casts Up Two More Crime Victims."

9   "Evening Echos," *Evening Republican* [Meadville, PA] September 10, 1914, 8.

10 "Eight Bogus Money Passers Sentenced," *Pittsburgh Press*, October 20, 1935, 3.

11 "Sentence Commuted: Giuseppe Ignoffo," *Cincinnati Enquirer*, February 25, 1916, 6.

12 "Letter from Leavenworth Warden to Chief of Police, Johnstown, Pa.," November 11, 1911.

13 Various guards at Leavenworth Penitentiary, "Violations, Sebastian Lima," 1913 1911.

14 "Letter from Dr. A. F Yoke, M.D. to Cav. Dottore Benedetto Tripi Rao," January 30, 1917.

15 "Anthony J. Lima," Mafia Wiki, accessed January 24, 2018, http://mafia.wikia.com/wiki/Anthony_J._Lima.

BIBLIOGRAPHY

"14 Black Handers Going to Prison 31 Jan 1910." *Allentown Democrat*, January 31, 1910.

"A Brief History of the Cosa Nostra—a.k.a. the Mafia—in Sicily, Sicily." Accessed January 26, 2018. http://www.reidsitaly.com/destinations /sicily/mafia.html.

"A Sheriff's Fatal Shot." *Baltimore Sun*, August 2, 1897.

"A Successor to Burns. Another Buckeye Sleuth," June 1909.

Adams, Margaret. "Mafia in New Orleans." New Orleans: Tulane University, 1924.

Adelman, Joseph M. "'A Constitutional Conveyance of Intelligence, Public and Private': The Post Office, the Business of Printing, and the American Revolution." *Enterprise & Society* 11, no. 4 (2010): 711–54. https://doi .org/10.2307/23701246.

Alexander, Roberta Sue. *A Place of Recourse: A History of the U.S. District Court for the Southern District of Ohio, 1803–2003*. Athens, OH: Ohio University Press, 2005.

An Act Making appropriations for the Post Office Department for the Fiscal Year Ending June 30, 1923, and for other purposes., Pub. L. No. H.R. 9859 (1922). https://www.loc.gov/law/help/statutes-at-large/67th -congress/Session%202/c67s2ch227.pdf.

"Appointed Cashier of Columbus Post Office To Succeed Wallace, Who Committed Suicide." *Cincinnati Enquirer*, May 24, 1907.

"Arrests of Black Hands Continues." *Coshocton Daily Times*, June 10, 1909.

"Arrigo Found in Lonely Cabin." *Cincinnati Enquirer*, July 24, 1909, p. 2.

"Articles: When Will New Orleans Apologize for the Italian Lynchings?'" Accessed December 27, 2017. http://www.americanthinker.com/articles

/2017/08/when_will_new_orleans_apologize_for_the_italian_lynchings
.html.

"August Marfisi." *New Philadelphia Daily Times*. April 25, 1946.

Avery, Elroy McKendree. *Biography*. Lewis Publishing Company, 1918.

"Beavers Gets Two Years." *Washington Post*, February 14, 1906.

"Benjamin Franklin (1706–1790), Postmaster General." Accessed August 19,
2017. https://postalmuseum.si.edu/outofthemails/franklin.html.

"Benjamin Franklin Trips to England." Revolutionary War and Beyond.
Accessed December 17, 2017. http://www.revolutionary-war-and-beyond
.com/benjamin-franklin-trips-to-england.html.

Bent, Cindy. "City of Arches." *Short North Gazette*, January 2003. http://
www.shortnorth.com/CoverStoryJan03.html.

"Big Graft for Clerks in Capitol." *Buffalo Enquirer*, June 25, 1903.

Bivens v. Six Unknown Fed. Narcotics Agents (1971). https://www.lectlaw
.com/files/cas80.htm.

Black Hand. "Black Hand Extortion Letter to DeCamilli," April 3, 1909.

———. "Black Hand Extortion Letter to Fasones," September 29, 1908.

———. "Black Hand Extortion Letter to Fasones 2," October 9, 1908.

———. "Black Hand Threat Letter to John Amicon," 1909.

———. "Black Hand Threat Letter to John Amicon (Count Yourself),"
January 20, 1909.

"Black Hand Against Black Hand." *Pittsburgh Daily Post*, June 22, 1909.

"Black Handers Found Guilty." *Marion Weekly Star,* February 5, 1910.

"Black Hand Finds Two Victims Here." *Indianapolis Star,* December 13,
1909.

"Black Hand Gang Meets Nemesis in John Amicon." Unknown from Oldfield Collection, 1909.

"Black Hand Letters and Their Authors." *Marion Weekly Star*, January
29, 1910.

"Black Hand Letters." *Marion Star*, January 25, 1910.

"The Black Hand Rule of Terror Is Exposed." *Marion Star,* January 26,
1910.

"'Black Hand' Run to Earth." *Leader,* June 8, 1909.

"Black Hand's Chief Caught in Lone Cabin," 1909.

"Black Hand Trial Develops Clashes." *Marion Star*, January 27, 1910.

"Black Hand Trial Will Soon Be Over." *Marion Star,* January 28, 1910.

"Black Hand Trials Are Begun Today." *Marion Star*, January 10, 1910.

"Boston, March 17." *Virginia Gazette*, April 14, 1774.

Braake, Alex L. ter. *The Posted Letter in Colonial and Revolutionary America.* American Philatelic Research Library, 1975.

Bridenbaugh, Carl. "The Press and Book in Philadelphia." *Pennsylvania Magazine of History and Biography*, 1941. https://journals.psu.edu /pmhb/issue/view/1931.

"Brutal Murder of Daniel F. Shea in Ellicott City." *Baltimore Sun*, February 22, 1895.

Buchholz, Heinrich Ewald. *Governors of Maryland: From the Revolution to the Year 1908.* Williams & Wilkins Company, 1908.

"Businessmen Called to Toledo." *Marion Daily Mirror*, January 26, 1910.

Caine, C. E. "Special Agents and Post Office Inspectors." Accessed September 22, 2017. http://narpi.org/SpecialAnnouncements/SpecialAgentsAnd PostOfficeInspectors.pdf.

"California Oil Promoters Taken to Ohio to Stand Trial." *Fergus County Democrat*, December 10, 1914.

The Cavalry of the Black Hand. "Extortion Letter to Fabio Sebastiano," April 1909.

"Central Market House: Columbus Memory." Accessed September 29, 2017. http://digital-collections.columbuslibrary.org/cdm/ref/collection /memory/id/52484.

"Charles H. Strong—Erie County, PA." Accessed November 8, 2017. http:// www.onlinebiographies.info/pa/erie/strong-ch.htm.

The Chicago Daily News Almanac and Year Book For . . . Chicago Daily News, Incorporated, 1909.

Clement, E. C. "Inspector E. C. Clement to Inspector J. F. Oldfield," August 12, 1909.

Coluccello, Rino. *Challenging the Mafia Mystique: Cosa Nostra from Legitimisation to Denunciation.* New York: Springer, 2016.

"Columbus Central Market House Photograph: Ohio History Connection Selections." Accessed September 29, 2017. http://www.ohiomemory.org /cdm/ref/collection/p267401coll32/id/1326.

Columbus City Directory. G.J. Brand & Company, 1902.

"Condemned to Death by the Black Hand." *Cleveland Leader*, January 9, 1910.

The Corporation Bulletin . . . . United States Corporation Company, 1911.

"Cut Off Their Respect." *Indianapolis News*, April 30, 1908.

BIBLIOGRAPHY

"David Hennessy." Wikipedia, August 30, 2017. https://en.wikipedia.org/w
/index.php?title=David_Hennessy&oldid=798074707.

"Day on Democrats." *Baltimore Sun*, April 24, 1900.

Day, William L. United States Attorney. "William L. Day Letter to Mr. A. R.
Holmes, Inspector in Charge," July 19, 1910.

"Dennison Man Must Go to Pen; Hi Court Ends Session Today," *New
Philadelphia Daily Times*, June 16, 1916.

Deposition of Charles Amicon by Frank Oldfield, May 1906.

"Driggs Says Jail and Fine Have Cured Him." *Boston Post*, January 15, 1904.

"Due to a Girl's Love." *News-Journal*, July 17, 1909.

Ellis Island. Mailing Address: National Museum of Immigration, Statue of
Liberty National Monument, New York, NY, 10004. Phone: 363-3200;
Contact Us. "Frequently Asked Questions—Ellis Island Part of Statue
of Liberty National Monument (U.S. National Park Service)." Accessed
December 29, 2017. https://www.nps.gov/elis/faqs.htm.

"Ernest E. Baldwin's Denial 30." *Brooklyn Daily Eagle*, November 30, 1903.

"Evidence Is Complete in Black Hand Trial." *Pittsburgh Daily Post*, January
28, 1910.

"Ex Parte Jackson 96 U.S. 727 (1878)." Justia Law. Accessed September
22, 2017. https://supreme.justia.com/cases/federal/us/96/727/case.html.

"Explanations Made by Black Hand Conspirators in Their Defense." *Cincinnati Enquirer*, January 27, 1910.

"Famous Postal Detective Dies At Home Here." May 25, 1916. Source unknown.

"Federal Judge Stricken." *Cincinnati Enquirer*, November 26, 1910.

"Federal Officers Fight." *New York Times*, May 16, 1903.

"Federal Officials Uncover Blackmail." *Toledo Daily Blade*, June 9, 1909.

The Firm of Black Hand. "Extortion Letter from to Gatto," April 3, 1909.

"First Degree Murder." *Baltimore Sun*, April 12, 1898.

"Fought with Inspectors." *Washington Post*, May 16, 1903.

"Founders Online: Editorial Note on the Founding of the Post Office, 26
July 1775." Accessed August 26, 2017. http://founders.archives.gov
/documents/Franklin/01-22-02-0074.

"Franklin's Philadelphia: Benjamin Franklin's Post Office." Accessed August
27, 2017. http://www.ushistory.org/franklin/philadelphia/postoffice.htm.

Frasca, Ralph. *Benjamin Franklin's Printing Network: Disseminating Virtue
in Early America*. Columbia, MO: University of Missouri Press, 2006.

BIBLIOGRAPHY

Gelso, Aldo. *Mafia: Capitalism & Democracy*. Bloomington, IN: Xlibris Corporation, 2007.

Goddard, William. *The Partnership: Or, The History of the Rise and Progress of the Pennsylvania Chronicle, &c. Wherein the Conduct of Joseph Galloway, Esq., Speaker of the Honourable House of Representatives of the Province of Pennsylvania, Mr. Thomas Wharton, Sen., and Their Man Benjamin Towne, My Late Partners, with My Own, Is Properly Delineated, and Their Calumnies against Me Fully Refuted*. Philadelphia: Printed by William Goddard, in Arch-street, between Front and Second Streets, 1770.

"Government Inspector Looking Over Coshocton Field 04 April 1906." *Times Recorder* [Zanesville, Ohio], April 4, 1906.

"Governor Pardons Two." *Baltimore Sun*, August 30, 1912.

"The Governor's Callers." *Baltimore Sun*, March 31, 1897.

Greenberg, Gerald S. *Historical Encyclopedia of U.S. Independent Counsel Investigations*. Westport, CT: Greenwood Publishing Group, 2000.

"Guard Witnesses in Black Hand Trials." *Marion Weekly Star*, January 8, 1910.

Hempstead, E. A. "Meadville Postmaster E. A. Hempstead to Assistant Attorney General," December 16, 1909.

"Henson Convicted." *Baltimore Sun*, March 29, 1895.

"His Skull Fractured." *Baltimore Sun*, July 2, 1896.

"History." *Pinkerton* (blog), May 13, 2016. https://www.pinkerton.com/about-us/history/.

"History." Accessed December 17, 2017. https://www.secretservice.gov/about/history/events/.

"History of the Banana—www.jimmccluskey.com." Accessed December 17, 2017. http://www.jimmccluskey.com/history-of-the-banana/.

Horan, James David. *The Pinkertons: The Detective Dynasty That Made History*. New York: Crown Publishers, 1968.

Horan, James David, and Howard Gardner. *The Pinkerton Story*. New York: G. P. Putnam's Sons, 1951.

"How Federal Sleuths Land Black Handers," 1909. Source unknown.

"Howard County." *Baltimore Sun*, September 5, 1895.

"Howard County." *Baltimore Sun*, September 18, 1896.

"Howard Political Assault Cases." *Baltimore Sun*, July 23, 1895.

"Howard Republicans—Delegates to Convention and Central Committee Elected." *Baltimore Sun*, August 15, 1899.

Hunt, Thomas. "The American Mafia—Who Was Who: Esposito, Giuseppe (1847– ?)." *The American Mafia—Who Was Who* (blog), n.d. http://mob-who.blogspot.com/2011/04/esposito-giuseppe.html.

"Jacob Henson , MSA SC 3520-13743." Archives of Maryland (Biographical Series), August 7, 2015. http://msa.maryland.gov/megafile/msa/speccol/sc3500/sc3520/013700/013743/html/13743bio.html.

Jaffe, Eric. *The King's Best Highway: The Lost History of the Boston Post Road, the Route That Made America*. New York: Scribner, 2010.

Journals of the Continental Congress, Volume 2 (1775).

"Judge Tayler Dies at an Early Hour." *Elyria Republican*, December 1, 1910.

"Jury Must Decide Who Wrote Letters." *Mansfield News-Journal*, January 27, 1910.

"Justice Is Swift in Black Hand Case." *New York Times*, January 30, 1910.

"Killing of Black Hand Victim Fell to Man Who Drew The Marked Card." *Topeka Daily Capital*, June 9, 1909.

"Knell of 'Black Handism.'" *Cincinnati Enquirer*, January 30, 1910.

"Letter from E. C. Clement to J. F. Oldfield," August 29, 1909.

"Letter from J. F. Oldfield to Colonel R. R. Munro," January 26, 1910.

"Letter from O. C. Riches to J. F. Oldfield (Portland)," June 30, 1909.

"Letter from Orazio Runfola to Salvatore Lima," March 25, 1909.

Lima, Salvatore (Sam). "By Laws and Regulations of the Society of Bananas (Translated from the Original Italian)," March 9, 1909.

"Lima's New Trial." *The Daily Picayune*, March 22, 1896.

"The Lynching of Jacob Henson, in Howard County." *Baltimore Sun*, May 29, 1895.

Macintyre, Bruce. *The Mafia Unveiled*. Accessed September 12, 2017. http://studylib.net/doc/8049182/book-one-%E2%80%94-the-rise.

"Marion Steam Shovel Company—Ohio History Central." Accessed December 28, 2017. http://www.ohiohistorycentral.org/w/Marion_Steam_Shovel_Company.

"Mary Katherine Goddard's Declaration of Independence | The New York Public Library." Accessed August 31, 2017. https://www.nypl.org/blog/2016/06/29/mary-katherine-goddard-declaration.

"Memorial of William Goddard to the Commissioners or Delegates from the Several American States, Now Sitting in General Congress: Having

Completed the Duties Required of Him as Surveyor of the Post-Office, He Solicits an Opportunity of Serving His Country in the Army for One Year at Least. American Archives." Accessed August 26, 2017. http://amarch.lib.niu.edu/islandora/object/niu-amarch%3A95382.

Migration. "Sicilian Lynchings in New Orleans." Know Louisiana. Accessed September 12, 2017. http://www.knowlouisiana.org/entry/sicilian-lynchings-in-new-orleans.

Miner, Ward L. *William Goddard, Newspaperman.* Durham, N.C.: Duke University Press, 1962.

"More Black Hand Arrests" *The Sun* [New York], June 18, 1909. https://en.wikipedia.org/wiki/The_Sun_(New_York_City)]

"More Evidence Is Secured Against Suspected Black Hand." *Marion Daily Mirror*, June 9, 1909.

"Must Return to Tennessee—Oldfield." *Baltimore Sun*, August 10, 1899.

"The National Road—Back in Time—General Highway History—Highway History—Federal Highway Administration." Accessed September 30, 2017, https://www.fhwa.dot.gov/infrastructure/back0103.cfm.

Niederkorn, William S. "New York Police Detective Shot Dead in Sicily." *New York Times*, March 14, 2009. https://timestraveler.blogs.nytimes.com/2009/03/14/new-york-police-detective-shot-dead-in-sicily/.

"Ninth's Republicans Are at Dagger's Edge." *Atlanta Journal and Constitution*, October 30,

O'Brien, Michael. "Pinkerton's Detective Agency Special Crimes Unit." Michael O'Brien, 2013. http://wrgmr.com/pinkertons.pdf.

"Office Scandal." *Elwood Free Press*, December 17, 1903.

"Ohio Black Hand Beats the Mafia." *Daily Arkansas Gazette.* June 10, 1909.

"Oldfield Exonerated." *Baltimore Sun*, August 5, 1897.

Oldfield, John Frank. "Black Hand Investigation Timeline," December 3, 1909.

———. "Untitled Status Report of Black Hand Case Through March 30, 1909," April 4, 1909.

"Omertà—The Mafia." Accessed September 19, 2017. http://the-mafia.weebly.com/omerta.html.

"On This Day: September 19, 1903." Accessed September 28, 2017. http://www.nytimes.com/learning/general/onthisday/harp/0919.html.

"Pippino Galbo 1872–1966—Ancestry." Accessed January 21, 2018. https://www.ancestry.com/genealogy/records/pippino-galbo_13677031.

"P.O. Inspector To Be Domiciled Here." *Chillicothe Gazette,* July 20, 1907.

"Police Brutality: A Prisoner Shamefully Mal. Treated by Officers. Kicked and Pounded in a Cell—Probably Fatally Injured." *Chicago Daily Tribune*, October 12, 1872.

"Politicians Fight Blows Exchanged." *News* [Frederick, Maryland], August 11, 1903.

"Postage Stamps Clue." *Cincinnati Enquirer*, August 31, 1923.

"Postal Frauds Are Laid Bare." *New York Times,* November 30, 1903.

"Postal Hearing," *Lewiston Daily Sun*, March 22, 1904.

"Postal Warrants Are Out." *New York Times*, September 12, 1903.

"Postoffice [*sic*] Cashier Resorted to Suicide When Caught Short In Accounts." *The Citizen*, May 23, 1907.

Post Staff Report. "The Road That Paved the Way to Revolution." *New York Post* (blog), July 4, 2010.

"Prisoner Kept His Nerve." *Times Recorder*, June 11, 1909.

"Promissory Note from George Metcalf to J. F. Oldfield," n.d.

"The Providence Gazette and Country Journal." May 21, 2017.

"Punishment for Black-Hand Mailers Inadequate," 1909. Source unknown.

"Raids Made in This City." *Cincinnati Enquirer*, June 18, 1909.

"Recovering From Injuries Hosford." *Indianapolis News,* February 8, 1904.

"Return to Danville." *Wichita Daily Eagle*, August 18, 1903.

Romano, Anne T. *Italian Americans in Law Enforcement*. Bloomington, IN: Xlibris Corporation, 2010.

"Rules of the Society of the Banana." *Marion Daily Mirror,* January 26, 1910.

"Running Down a Gang of Crooks." *Piqua Daily Call*, March 21, 1902.

"Running Down the Black Hand." *New York Times*, February 13, 1910.

"Scott Mausoleum Burglary & Extortion." *Scott Mausoleum Burglary & Extortion* (blog), n.d. https://historyandmemorabilia.blogspot.com/2014/01/scott-mausoleum-burglary-extortion.html.

"Search Results for Pippino Galbo—FamilySearch.Org." Accessed January 25, 2018. https://www.familysearch.org/search/record/results?count=20&query=%2Bgivenname%3Apippino~%20%2Bsurname%3Agalbo~.

"Sebastiano Lima Declaration of Intention." Department of Commerce and Labour Bureau of Immigration and Naturalization, November 6, 1907.

"Senate Report No. 1333. 52nd Congress 2nd Session." Senate of the United States, February 22, 1893. http://hdl.handle.net/2027/pur1.32754082218821.

Senner, J. H. "Immigration from Italy." *North American Review* 162, no. 475 (1896): 649–57.

"Sentenced to Death." *Baltimore Sun*, April 14, 1898.

"Separate Trials Are Denied by the Court." *Marion Star*, January 18, 1910.

Service (USMS), U.S. Marshals. "U.S. Marshals Service." Accessed December 17, 2017. https://www.usmarshals.gov/history/timeline.html.

Shepard, Vinton Randall, and Rowland Shepard. *The Ohio Law Reporter: A Weekly Journal Published in the Interest of the Legal Profession in the State of Ohio*. Ohio Law Reporter Company, 1911.

"Shot by a Sheriff." *News* [Frederick, Maryland], July 30, 1897.

"Shot to Death." *Rushville Republican*, March 19, 1891.

Siskin, Ed. "US Postal History Before the United States Post Office Part II: Understanding Rates." *New Jersey Postal History Society*, 1972, 7.

"Six Arrests Threaten in Black Hand Case." *Pittsburgh Daily Post*, June 22, 1909.

"Sleuth Exposes the Black Hand Methods." *Marion Star*, June 21, 1910.

"Sons of Liberty—Dictionary Definition of Sons of Liberty | Encyclopedia .Com: FREE Online Dictionary." Accessed May 21, 2017. http://www .encyclopedia.com/history/encyclopedias-almanacs-transcripts-and -maps/sons-liberty-0.

"Stamp Act | Great Britain [1765]." Encyclopedia Britannica. Accessed December 27, 2017. https://www.britannica.com/event/Stamp-Act -Great-Britain-1765.

"Statement of Mrs. Mary Fasone." Deposition, July 29, 1909.

"Strange Story of a Watch." *Morning News* [Wilmington, DE], June 8, 1901.

"Suspect Is Held Under Heavy Bond." Unknown from Oldfield Collection, 1909.

"Sweeping Raid on Black Hand in Ohio." Associated Press to *Gazette Times* [Pittsburgh], June 1909.

Talty, Stephan. *The Black Hand: The Epic War Between a Brilliant Detective and the Deadliest Secret Society in American History*. Boston: Houghton Mifflin Harcourt, 2017.

"TAYLER, Robert Walker—Biographical Information." Accessed December 28, 2017. http://bioguide.congress.gov/scripts/biodisplay.pl ?index=T000061.

"Ten Years in Prison for Mrs. Chadwick." *Daily Times* [New Philadelphia, Ohio], March 28, 1905.

"The Testimony Taken in Black Hand Trials." *Marion Star*, January 20, 1910.

"Thinks Power of Black Hand Gone." *Perrysburg Journal*, February 4, 1910.

"Threatened by Black Hand." *Marion Star*, January 19, 1910.

Todd, Anthony. "The British Postal Museum & Archive Blog." Accessed August 27, 2017. https://postalheritage.wordpress.com/tag/anthony-todd/.

United States, and Post Office Department. "Annual Report of the Postmaster General." *Annual Report of the Postmaster General*, 1909.

———. "Annual Report of the Postmaster General." *Annual Report of the Postmaster General*, 1910.

"United States Postal Inspection Service." Accessed July 23, 2017. https://postalinspectors.uspis.gov/aboutus/History.aspx.

United States Postal Inspection Service, and United States Post Office Department. *Photographs, Descriptions and Records of Persons Charged with Violation of the Postal Laws*. Washington, D.C.: [The Dept.], 1916. http://archive.org/details/photographsdescr21916unit.

United States Post Office Department. *Investigation of the Post-Office Department: Letter from the Postmaster-General Transmitting So Much of the Report of the Fourth Assistant Postmaster-General on the Investigation of the Said Department as May Be Made Public Without Harm to the Public Interest. January 11, 1904.—Referred to the Committee on the Post-Office and Post Roads and Ordered to Be Printed*. U.S. Government Printing Office, 1904.

———. *Memorandum of the President and Report of Fourth Assistant Postmaster-General J. L. Bristow on the Investigation of Certain Divisions of the Post-Office Department*. U.S. Government Printing Office, 1903.

"Untitled Article on Antonio Lima, Oldfield Collection," 1909.

"Wandered From Home." *Baltimore Sun*, July 20, 1896.

Watchcorn, Robert. "The Black Hand and the Immigrant." *The Outlook*, July 31, 1909.

"Why Did Italians Immigrate to the US Between 1880 & 1900? | Synonym." Accessed September 30, 2017. http://classroom.synonym.com/did-italians-immigrate-between-1880-1900-8321.html.

"Will Break Up Black Hand Gang Operating In Central States." *Akron Beacon Journal*, June 12, 1909.

"Will Erect Business Block." *Marion Daily Mirror*, May 6, 1912.

BIBLIOGRAPHY

"William Goddard and the Constitutional Post." Accessed August 24, 2017. https://postalmuseum.si.edu/exhibits/current/binding-the-nation/starting-the-system/william-goddard-and-the-constitutional-post.html.

Wroth, Lawrence C. *The Colonial Printer*. Courier Corporation, 1964.

———. *The First Press in Providence A Study in Social Development*. Reprint edition. American Antiquarian Society, 1942.

Wroth, Lawrence Counselman. *A History of Printing in Colonial Maryland, 1686–1776*. Typothetae of Baltimore, 1922.

Zimmerman, John J. "Benjamin Franklin and the Pennsylvania Chronicle." In *Benjamin Franklin's Letters to the Press, 1758–1775*. Chapel Hill: University of North Carolina Press, 1957. https://journals.psu.edu/pmhb/article/viewFile/41308/41029.

———. "Benjamin Franklin and The Pennsylvania Chronicle." *Pennsylvania Magazine of History and Biography* 81, no. 4 (September 30, 1957): 351–64.

ACKNOWLEDGMENTS

William Hamilton "Hammy" Oldfield

Over more than a century, innumerable lives have touched our story, some remembered, many forgotten. We have strived to remember those who have helped us to bring our story to life in the modern era and those who have preserved and shared their memories and archival materials. We could go on and on, as so many have assisted us and guided us along our path. We graciously thank all those who have given their hearts and minds to help this story come to light and ask for the forgiveness of any we may not have mentioned by name.

This Century

Victoria Bruce has been the key to revealing the narrative of our family secrets. She has decoded immense amounts of archival materials and research and deciphered the truth from hearsay hidden within the accumulations. She has my deepest love and gratitude, most specifically because she expressed an innate curiosity and had the fortitude to make sure John Frank's story was not locked away in drawers of forgotten history. Peter McGuigan, Claire Harris, and the team at Foundry + Media, thank you for believing in this story. Matthew Benjamin, our editor at Touchstone/Simon & Schuster, showed great competence, creativity, and a love of history that made this book so much better and Frank's story so much richer. Thanks also to the team at Touchstone/Simon & Schuster art, publicity, marketing, and editorial, who all were part of guiding this special book to market.

Allison Lee Oldfield Sacker, M.D., has been my engine over the past sixteen years. Her love of family history, power of will, generosity, and constant pursuit kept me going through countless hours and years of research. My parents, Edward Fulton and Terry, will always have our limitless love and thanks. Their passion for family and history was granted to us. They generously gave permission for our secret to finally be revealed after their passing. Thanks, Mom and Dad. William Hamilton "Hammy" Oldfield, Jr. (deceased), with his ability to spin a great yarn and desire to expose the story to the world, is a deeply missed and never forgotten asset. Without "Uncle Ham," our family would never have preserved the archival materials of John Frank. Sharon Sue Oldfield-Richardson continues to keep our family stories alive and exciting. Thomas Wendell Oldfield (deceased) was one of our favorite caretakers of family lore. Thanks, Aunt Sharon and Uncle Tommy.

Postal Inspector-in-Charge Daniel Mihalko (retired) and Postal Inspector Tripp Brinkley helped to initiate the excitement about the story more than fourteen years ago. Their unofficial duties as historians within the Postal Inspection Service have continually provided us with unlimited assistance in whatever we required to bring the story to life. Very special thanks go to Nancy Pope, Historian/Curator, and K. Allison Wickens, former Director of Education, and the dedicated staff at the Smithsonian National Postal Museum. Their support, assistance, and constant internal lobbying to recognize Frank Oldfield, regardless of some of his controversies, deserves immense praise. Glen Hopkins, with his experience in the world of museums and monuments, and his patient ear to my constant pleadings, personally introduced us to his friend Nancy Pope at the Smithsonian. Al Hafner and the staff at

ACKNOWLEDGMENTS

the Howard County, Maryland, Historical Society, and the staff at the Maryland State Archives continue to provide any and all assistance we require. Al knows how to tell a great story and knows more about the history of Howard County than anyone else ever will. Melanie Butera, a descendant of Sebastian Lima, has been extremely generous in providing detailed historical information to us. Bobbie J. Hooper, Marion County, Ohio, Historical Society Administrative Assistant, who found the very post office where Sam and Sebastian unknowingly purchased marked stamps; Greer Heinzen, who copied all of the Black Hand trial transcripts from the National Archives in Chicago; Bruce Macintyre, who shared an unpublished but terrific draft of his book on Francis Dimaio; and Jack Blum and Nevin Young, both of Annapolis, two super great attorney friends who answered every question about obscure relic laws and ancient court cases; Paul Drexler, a crime historian in San Francisco; and Gregory Schmidt from the National Archives in Kansas City helped us wrap up the stories of the Society of the Banana members.

The Oldfield and Iacone families deserve our deepest gratitude. They have always been helpful, offering their memories and providing an endless supply of stories, love, support, and excitement. Barbara Bruce, Victoria's mother, spent hours looking over drafts, as did Kathleen Scarlet, a story wizard and great college friend of Victoria's who has never stopped helping with homework. Much love and thanks to you all.

Last Century

Descendants and peers of John Frank Oldfield require a most special thank you. It is especially important to note that they passed the secret tales of John Frank's exploits from generation to generation; keeping the story alive in our wondering minds. Family members from John Frank and Margaret Galena to their sons, John Frank, William Hamilton, Harry Edward, and Robert Fulton, were the first to pass on the

ACKNOWLEDGMENTS

secrets. John Frank's peers, including his close friend at the Athens, Ohio, Post Office, John Gist, United States Attorney William Day, fellow Post Office inspectors and their families, and William Hamilton and his son William Hamilton "Hammy" Junior then preserved the archival materials, eventually passing them on to our father, Edward Fulton, and mother, Terry. This collection of original and official investigative case materials from John Frank's career encompassing the years 1899 to 1916 was invaluable. It is unmatched in its comprehensive nature in the almost 250-year history of the United States Department of the Post Office Inspection Service.

Finally, thanks must continue to go to those we have not named from the United States Postal Inspection Service, current and retired, those at the Smithsonian National Postal Museum, and the dedicated staff at the National Archives. Their help and offers of help never seem to end.

Victoria Bruce

I second Hammy's heartfelt thanks for all of those above. In addition, I would be remiss not to express how incredibly grateful I am and how fortunate I feel to have been given the confidence of Hammy and his sister Allison. These two siblings, thick as thieves, had so much passion for getting this story right, it's really an honor that they believed I could help make it happen. Of course, this book, like all of my work, is a product of living in a tribe in which creativity is celebrated by those closest to me: Mom, Barbara Bruce, Dad, Joe Bruce, my brother Tim and sister-in-law Colette, my adopted sisters Dawn and Karin, who support all of my work all hours of the day and night, and the two who bookend me with so much love, Alex and Evelyn. Thank you all for encouraging me to continue to grow and explore.

INDEX

ABOUT THE AUTHORS

William Oldfield is an archivist and historical lecturer. He is currently engaged in entrepreneurial pursuits in the areas of environmental and sustainable operations. He grew up in Akron, Ohio, and currently lives in Annapolis, Maryland.

Victoria Bruce is the author of *No Apparent Danger*, *Hostage Nation*, and *Sellout*. She is the recipient of the Alfred I. duPont–Columbia University Award for excellence in broadcast journalism for her film, *The Kidnapping of Ingrid Betancourt*. She lives in Anne Arundel County, Maryland.